# The Healing Consciousness

## A Doctor's Journey to Healing

*Beth Baughman DuPree, M.D.*

*[handwritten inscription: Christie Thirupadiruasty we grow spiritually - Stay present in the moment. GB all about the journey! Love + Light Beth]*

**Praise for** *The Healing Consciousness:*
*A Doctor's Journey to Healing*

"*The Healing Consciousness* is enthusiastically recommended
reading for those with an interest in alternative medicine, the healing arts, holistic health, personal spiritual
development, emotional self-improvement, and adaptive
strategies to dealing with stress, illness, and the inevitable
hardships that all of us will encounter from time to
time. No personal improvement reading list or community library self-help reference collections should fail to
include Dr. Beth DuPree's *The Healing Consciousness.*"

*SMALL PRESS BOOK WATCH:*
July 2006
James A. Cox, Editor-in-Chief

"In *The Healing Consciousness*, you meet your perfect healer:
loving mother, sister, spouse, friend and skilled surgeon
who is aware of her angelic and divine connections.
Written in a style true to her personality (warm, passionate, wise, authentic and loving), Beth DuPree's intimate
and powerful story of her stunning transformation
empowers you, while touching your heart and soul. A
must-read for all patients as well as healers."

Susan Barbara Apollon
Author of *Touched by the Extraordinary*

"Your words and heart have inspired me . . . hearing how
your heart was asking to be heard, awakened something
inside of me."

Susan DeLorenzo

"I truly appreciate each day and I look for those who will
inspire me positively. You, Beth, are one of those people
. . . I respect that you remain true to yourself and your
convictions. *The Healing Consciousness* is a testimony to
that."

Desiree Benn

"I have read your book with great enthusiasm! I was unable to put it down and am amazed at how many times our paths have crossed . . . I am going to read it again and reach into my heart to those who have impacted my soul."

Connie Kleiman

"Bless Dr. DuPree who gave us a key to unlock our hearts, to care and share—for those in need—the love from above."

Unknown

"You captured so many things I've experienced, not only as a cancer survivor, but as a spiritual being navigating this world. Your insight into trusting your path to the universe is like no physician I've ever encountered."

Patricia Maley, LCSW

"Thank you for writing *The Healing Consciousness* . . . I felt it had been written for me. The timing was perfect (no surprise) and it has inspired a resurgence in my efforts and commitment to becoming more spiritually connected . . . I appreciate your openness in your book and respect how you are honoring your true essence."

Cynthia N. Paciulli, MD, FACS

In *The Healing Consciousness*, Dr. Beth DuPree shares with us her personal journey of self-discovery and spiritual transformation. Like a dynamic duo, she utilizes the mind and body of a highly skilled physician, coupling her remarkable talents with a boundless love and selfless desire to heal the body and the soul. Her words act as a powerful beacon, sharing her bold vision of a new physician-patient relationship, and lighting the way toward a paradigm shift of consciousness for a new generation of healers.

Robert Sasson, M.D.
Author of *Visions of Thought:*
*A Collection of Inspirational Imagery and Poetry*

"You have been and always will be my INSPIRATION!
Thank you for all of the love and faith you have given
me. I have become a better man."

Jim Gentile RN

"In reading your book I have felt a greater sense of purpose
which, in turn, has refreshed my spirit and introduced a
new positive energy that is palpable in my classroom."

Carrie Ann Kreber

"Your book has inspired me and has given my life new
direction."

Charissa Bermingham, RN

"Your words woven throughout this magnificent tapestry of
your manuscript touched me on a cellular level. You saved
my life and performed my surgeries with tenacity, convic-
tion, and great care. *The Healing Consciousness* is remarkably
powerful in its courage, honesty and generosity."

Josi, breast cancer survivor

"Thank you for the wonderful gift of your book. My
daughter died when she was two years old only two
years ago and she sends me dragonflies . . . thank you
whole heartedly for sending me magic."

Laura Fuller, Creator of "The Chakra Window"

"Your book has helped me tremendously. Love, friendship, spiritual healing—living in the moment, a positive
attitude—not putting aside all the things I want to do, is
not so important."

Bernice Schager

"Thank you so much for *The Healing Consciousness*. I found
richness, humanity, and an openness in your words and
I am grateful…"

Marie Jackson

"I felt you had healed me even before you performed my surgery. You had touched me deeply from our first meeting, with your professional confidence, your loving manner, and through the open wisdom of your book."
Sharon Harrison, Artist, breast cancer survivor.

Published by WovenWord Press
811 Mapleton Ave.
Boulder, CO 80304
www.wovenword.com

Cover and book art © 2006 by Frank Champine
Cover design © 2008 by Dominic J. Venticinque
Book design © 2008 by Vicki McVey
Author photo © 2006 by Dr. Robert Sasson

Hard cover ISBN 13  9780981576626
Soft cover ISBN 13  9780981576633

1. Medical/healing  2.Complimentary-holistic medicine
3. Breast disease/cancer

For many years, my childhood friends and I took credit for
Beth becoming the success she is today. While I still like to
fool myself that we helped shape her character, the truth is,
Beth is, and has always been, her own person. From a very
young age she knew what she wanted from life and she
grabbed it, holding on tight. In the process, Beth has become
one of the most compassionate and dedicated people I've ever
known.

She is intelligent and well-studied. She has made gold-star
breast cancer care her crusade. She makes time for any and
all who need her, as friend or doctor, often as both. She has
devoted her heart and soul to the pursuit of spiritual healing,
for herself, her patients, friends and family.

She is my friend,

Lee Ellen

~

*This book is dedicated to all of my patients and friends, who through their
disease process have been my teachers. I have immeasurable gratitude to
those teachers who now guide me in spirit.*

**Bart B. Baughman**

*Dawn Buck*

*Christine Duess*

*Kerry Inners*

*Sean Kilkenny*

*Tina McCaffrey*

*Chris McGill*

*Christina S. O'Donnell M.D.*

*Don Rogge*

*Brad Schroeder*

*Rosemarie Vassalluzzo*

*Matthew Walsh*

*May The Healing Consciousness facilitate your spiritual awakening on your
personal voyage of enlightenment.*

# Acknowledgements

Without my soul connections to my patients, friends and family this story would not exist. I am forever humbled by the trust and confidence that my patients have in me each and every day as I do my healing work as a surgeon. I thank everyone who has played a role in making me who I am.

Marie Duess—Thank you for typing and editing this manuscript, but most of all thanks for your love and support in all aspects of my life. Thank you for believing in my vision.Calryn Aston—my editor who I have known for lifetimes but have yet to meet. Thank you for sharing my journey, yes I'm still smiling!

Mary, Sally, Ann, Sue, and Amy—My sisters, I treasure your love, support, and energy.
Amy, Sue and Ann—Thank you for the weekend editing sessions.

Irv and Helena—I LOVE YOU! You are the best. That's why I chose you to be my parents.

To my husband Joe and my beautiful sons Tom and Dean—I love you and I thank you for understanding my need to write this book that took me away from you while I was writing.

Kelly Kolodney—Thank you for introducing me to the beautiful energy of Raphael. You are truly an angel on earth. I pray that my words do justice to her messages.

Graham and Judy Russell—Thank you for believing in my vision. I will be forever indebted to both of you for your gift of the audio recording of my book.

# Chapter Titles

# FOREWORD

Sometime during the mid-1980s when I was the Chairman of the Department of Psychiatry at the Mount Sinai Medical Center in Miami Beach, I awakened about six in the morning from a dream where I was giving a lecture, in this instance to a vast audience of psychiatrists. Upon awakening I wrote down the dream and later included it in my first book, *Many Lives, Many Masters.*

"In the rush toward the medicalization of psychiatry, it is important that we do not abandon the traditional, albeit sometimes vague, teachings of our profession. We are the ones who still talk to our patients, patiently and with compassion. We still take the time to do this. We promote the conceptual understanding of illness, healing with understanding and the induced discovery of self-knowledge, rather than just with laser beams. We still use hope to heal.

"In this day and age, other branches of medicine are finding these traditional approaches to healing much too inefficient, time-consuming, and unsubstantiated. They prefer technology to talk, computer-generated blood chemistries to the personal physician-patient chemistry, which heals the patient and provides satisfaction to the doctor. Idealistic, ethical, personally gratifying approaches to medicine lose ground to economic, efficient, insulating, and satisfaction-destroying approaches. As a result, our colleagues feel increasingly isolated and depressed. The patients feel rushed and empty, uncared for.

"We should avoid being seduced by high technology. Rather, we should be the role models for our colleagues. We should demonstrate how patience, understanding, and compassion help both patient and physician. Taking more time to talk, to teach, to awaken hope and the expectation of recovery—these half-forgotten qualities of the physician as healer—these we must always use ourselves and be an example to our fellow physicians.

"High technology is wonderful in research and to promote the understanding of human illness and disease. It can be an invaluable clinical tool, but it can never replace those inherently personal characteristics and methods of the true physician...."

Decades later, in eastern Pennsylvania, a surgeon embodies and manifests my decades-old dream of what the ideal physician should be. Dr. Beth DuPree has mastered modern surgical knowledge and techniques. She is a highly skilled and dedicated surgeon. She has also mastered the art of healing the whole patient, of understanding the mind-body-spirit connection in order to heal the root of the illness as well as its physical manifestations. She uses the scalpel and she uses her heart, wielding both with a skill and a power so rarely found in physicians today.

I admire Beth's courage. As a fellow physician, I know the strength she needed to make the profound changes in her clinical practice and in her life is considerable. Yet she conquered the obstacles and achieved her dream. Again, how rare.

This book, *The Healing Consciousness: A Doctor's Journey to Healing*, is a joy. I particularly love the case histories because they illustrate and illuminate the beauty of Beth's heart and the power of her compassion to forever change the lives of her patients and their families. Every doctor Beth touches, whether in person or through her book, will be enriched. Every patient will have more understanding and more hope.

Brian L. Weiss, M.D.
Miami, Florida
January, 2008

# Introduction

The air is crisp and damp. The screen door slams shut behind me. Somehow the same coffee I have been drinking every morning for years tastes better. The stillness and serenity are deafening. The only sounds I hear are those created by cicadas and birds. This has become my morning song and I begin to breathe in unison with nature. The lush green grass is covered with dew and my feet are drenched but the wet feels invigorating. The stroll to the garden is peaceful. As I approach the pond, the bullfrog awakens to bellow good morning.

I was missing this link for some time, not realizing that I needed to be connected to Mother Earth and to nature in order to nurture my soul. Somehow I was guided to this land, a piece of timeless history that could rejuvenate my spirit after a long day's work. I have been gifted as a caregiver, yet failed to give care to a most important person in my life—me. If I am not well and cared for, I will be unable to care for others, and I'll be useless as I try to guide my patients to wellness and healing.

We now live on a farm we call home. My children, Tom and Dean, have adjusted to the move and my husband Joe is seeing the benefits of it for our whole family. When I came upon this property, my family and friends thought I was certifiable for even considering a move from our comfortable modern home to an antique dwelling. How could we possibly find the time to restore this property when we are already busy? The buildings are all in need of repair. They have been standing for nearly three hundred years and will probably keep standing until we get around to repairing all of the disorders and squeaking complaints they have. We are all playing a role in the restoration of our new home.

The perennial garden needs love and attention, as does the entire property. I choose not to focus on the list of things that are broken and need repair; instead I choose to focus on what is right and healing and perfect about this place. As I do with my patients, I see the wellness in the land and the buildings. We will tend to the "disease" of the property just as I do with my patients, healing one person at a time, always focusing on what is healthy about each individual.

My heart warms as I drive down the tree-lined driveway and find my husband sitting with our two sons fishing at the edge of our neighbor's pond. What would have been a weekend adventure is now an after school bonus. It is a different way of life than we have known as a family. We are working together on projects and seeing the magnificent changes that we can manifest with our own hands. I am in awe of the beauty that has been preserved on this amazing piece of land in historic Bucks County and I find myself continually asking, "How did I arrive at this destination?"

Although I consider myself a spontaneous individual, I do take the time to make rational logical decisions. As a surgeon, that is considered mandatory. I have lived a rather planned life, knowing where I was headed all the time. In the past I would set my sight on a goal or a destination, and make it happen. This is no different than most other driven individuals in the world. I had a great college experience. It was a time to mature, become educated and heal the loss of my only brother. After college I was accepted to medical school, where I met and married my husband Joe as I prepared for my future as a surgeon. I then matched into a great surgical residency program that taught me the skills I needed to be a general surgeon.

I only had a four-month window in which I could deliver a child and still complete the program on time. I was able to make that work, too. I found a beautiful area in which to practice surgery and raise a family. For many years it seemed as though I was always working toward an undisclosed destination. I was working at a frenetic pace and was nearly spinning out of control, trying to be everything to everyone who needed me.

*It took my beautiful children, friends, and my amazing patients to teach me that it is truly the journey in life that is so magnificent.*

Once I was able to slow down the constant chatter in my head, I could actually enjoy that which was right

3

in front of me. As a result I have become a better mother, a better wife, a better friend and, as a physician, a better healer. In order to appreciate the life that I was living, I needed to change in so many ways, yet preserve and nurture those aspects of myself that really make my heart sing.

*Change is one of the only constants in our lives.* It can also be one of the most difficult things to accept, particularly when something unexpected comes upon us. Even when we are given time to prepare for change, the actual change can be very difficult to accept. Witnessing the effects our move to a farm had on my young sons—changing schools and having to make new friends—gave me a better perspective on this process. I was the one who really wanted to make this change in our lifestyle. Although they were afraid of the change, they began to trust my intuition and judgment.

This process also happens with my patients. When someone is diagnosed with a disease that is beyond their control, they must learn to adapt. As I have seen my children blossom in their new environment and grow to love the changes in their lives, I know that the changes I have made in the way I choose to treat my patients also have been the correct ones. Breast cancer, like any disease, brings about change that is seldom anticipated and never desired. My goal as a doctor and healer is to ease my patient's passage through this process of change.

Creating a new and better existence may not seem to go along with a diagnosis of cancer, yet the level of adversity cancer brings allows for tremendous growth in positive ways. Helping to eliminate the fear that surrounds the disease is often the most daunting task. Not only do patients manifest this fear, but also the spouse, parents, caregivers, and children involved. Fear has the ability to paralyze even the strongest human beings. Alleviating the fear is often more challenging than treating the physical cancer. Adversity can be the greatest teacher the universe can throw at us. If we are unable or unwilling to be open to change, we will miss the opportunity to grow and to experience the wonders of truly *living*. I have never been afraid of change, but now I welcome it as yet another opportunity to grow spiritually.

As physicians, the role we play in our patients' process of dealing with and recovering from disease is greater than many of us realize. Somewhere along the way there has been a "disconnect" in the relationship between doctors and patients. I have been working diligently on myself to reconnect with that healing art we call medicine. I have had some amazing teachers along my path and continue to be open to what the universe has in store for me. I have no fear, just loving intention as I do what I do. Others may not understand my methods, but the results I see in my patients tell me that I am truly on the correct path.

Western medicine (surgery, chemotherapy and radiation), is in my right hand as I treat women and men with breast disease. Modern technology has given us the ability to eradicate cancer from the body in some cases. Eastern healing modalities (Reiki, yoga, massage, meditation, guided imagery, diet, and wellness) are in my left hand. They complete the mind, body, spirit connection. Both hands work in concert to orchestrate the healing process.

If we rely solely on what the West has to offer and use two right hands in our approach to treat disease, there is dis-coordination. They do not join together naturally and we may cure a patient's disease yet leave them an empty shell. If we rely solely on Eastern modalities, often referred to as "alternative," and discount the wonderful gifts Western medicine has to offer, we may miss an opportunity to cure the physical body of its disease. As a team, the right and left hand can do much to create and manifest healing and wellness. The marriage of Eastern and Western medicine can lead to magnificent results. They enhance or complement one another. Therefore, I choose to refer to Eastern healing modalities as *complementary* as opposed to *alternative*, as they are a complement to Western medicine not a replacement for it.

I am privileged to experience the healing process on a daily basis. I tell my patients that the Universe has many ways in which to communicate with us. When I give a patient a diagnosis of cancer, it seems to them that the Universe has chosen to scream. As human beings, we tend to react to a scream differently than we react to a whisper. Facing a life-threatening illness, my patients make changes in their day-to-day lives they may have otherwise put off to a later date. They quickly learn to honor themselves and distance themselves from situations and people who do not enhance their wellbeing. Many of us are guilty of tolerating situations in our lives that are unhealthy for us.

When I have the great fortune to give a benign diagnosis (that the results are not cancer), I remind my patients that the Universe has just given them a whisper, and they should evaluate things in their lives they would have changed had I told them they had cancer. Every woman or man who experiences a breast biopsy has a time when they think, "What will I do differently if I have cancer?"

I have chosen to listen to the whispers in my life. When we begin to listen to the whispers in our lives, there will be no need for screaming. I hope patients, doctors, and all human beings might begin to awaken to their greatest gifts and find true happiness and love in every aspect of their lives through embracing The Healing Consciousness.

The Healing Consciousness is awareness, found deep within ourselves, where we embrace the eternal nature of our souls and release all fear of death. Embracing this awareness, we are free to experience the present moment fully. Illness and disease teach us to embrace the moment and live the journey to the fullest for no one is guaranteed tomorrow.

## Chapter 1

# East Meets West

How quickly I had forgotten the tremendous gift I have to impart upon my patients. As a physician, I needed to be a healer first and work toward cure when I can. The art of healing has been lost by the technologically advanced society we have embraced. Historically, masculine energy developed medical technology, with all its wonders. This technology focuses on cure as the ultimate goal. Feminine energy focuses on the mind, body, and spirit connection, embracing a concept of healing that includes more than curing disease.

I pride myself on staying current with the latest technological advancements in breast cancer care. I offer my patients the best that science has to offer both surgically and medically to treat their bodies when they have disease—the dis-*ease*—we call cancer. By dis-*ease*, I mean the lack of *ease* in function; a departure from mental, physical, and spiritual wellbeing, which often manifests in the processes we define as a disease of the body. Curing the disease of the physical body and its symptoms will not guarantee healing of the dis-*ease* within the individual.

But I no longer treat my patients with surgery, chemotherapy, and radiation alone, concentrating solely on the physical body. My patients need more—and deserve more—than the standard treatment and care traditional Western medicine has offered them.

Once the body has been treated for cancer, the healing process is just beginning. Adopting a holistic approach to breast cancer care has made a tremendous difference in my patients' lives and also in my satisfaction as a physician and "healer." Holism embraces the concept that a person is an interconnected being and all of the elements of that being must be treated equally to address the complexity of the whole.

It is unacceptable for me to treat only the physical disease without regard for the emotional and spiritual wellbeing of the individual. Holism is the basis for mind, body, spirit medicine. I understand I cannot cure disease in everyone with cancer. That does not make me a failure as a physician. It makes me a spiritual being having a very earthly experience. As a "healer," I find I can empower my patients to heal through their own dis-*ease* process. It is the need to promote healing in all aspects of life that has prompted me to share my personal journey.

When I began my career in medicine, my goals were very different than they are today. I give a great deal of credit to the physicians who trained me as a surgeon. They gave me the opportunity to develop exceptional surgical skills that I use every day to perform state-of-the-art surgery on my patients. However, although I have always considered myself to be a compassionate and caring individual, it has been through my increased awareness of my spiritual growth over the past seven years that I have truly come to understand the gift of healing that we, as physicians, have to share with our patients.

I have learned to make changes in my life by hearing the wake-up calls or screams that others have experienced. Their screams in essence have become the whispers of my life. It is also through the disease process, and the deaths of some of my patients and friends, that I have learned that the most precious gift of all is the gift of healing. I now understand that human interaction and connection are the most important things a physician can share with a patient. *The only thing we have eternally is the energy between two individuals.*

Long after the physical body is gone, the love and connection we have with another human being remains. It is the emotional and spiritual bond that transcends the physical world in which we live. This connection is why the loss of a loved one is so painful. When modern medicine cannot cure melanoma, colon cancer, breast cancer, or Lou Gehrig's disease (ALS), when it strikes a fellow physician, it is time to look beyond traditional medicine to find a new understanding of what is really needed in order to "heal."

As physicians, we often attach ourselves to outcomes and feel responsible for everything that happens to our patients. As a society, we often blame physicians for outcomes that are far beyond the responsibility of the physician. A paternalistic aspect in medicine creates circumstances in which patients allow physicians to make decisions about their care without taking any responsibility for their own healthcare treatments. They hold physicians completely responsible for any adverse outcomes, even those that are a result of the disease process itself. It is this mindset that contributes to the current malpractice crisis.

If the physician and the patient are not partners in the treatment of disease, the possibility of blame exists when the outcome is not as expected. Physicians need to be held accountable and practice medicine to the highest standards humanly possible. But we have created a healthcare system that demands physicians practice defensive medicine. Many physicians create a wall that separates them emotionally from patients in an attempt to protect themselves from litigation. If they feel they are constantly defending their actions, they may miss the opportunity to participate in their patients' healing process. As a result, the art of medicine being a "healing profession" has gone by the wayside.

Treating cancer in my patients has taught me to be *truly present in the moment.* Making a connection with another human being is the ultimate gift medicine gives to both the patient and the physician. We must stop the constant chatter in our minds long enough to become present and connect with another human being. This allows us to access *the healing consciousness.* If we utilize this higher consciousness while working with patients to attain holistic healing, we are using our healing consciousness—a powerful and positive energy—in its purest form. I have awakened to my healing consciousness and would like others to experience this awakening as well.

### There Really Are No Coincidences in Life.

My spiritual growth as a physician and an individual has been, and continues to be, a wonderful journey. I have learned valuable life lessons from the multitude of "synchronicities" in my life—those seemingly coincidental and even psychic occurrences—that have guided me on this path toward self-awareness.

Synchronicities are events that appear to have no apparent relationship to one another but are truly connected, often leading to increased awareness, or a novel way of looking at a situation. They are opportunities for tremendous growth and introspection. If viewed as incidental occurrences, these lessons, and the opportunities they offer, may not be apparent.

By writing this book and sharing my experiences with you, I hope to awaken you to your own higher healing consciousness. When you understand—or as I like to say, *get it*—you, too, will begin to appreciate the gifts the synchronicities in your life have to offer you. You will never look at occurrences as coincidental again.

None of us are guaranteed tomorrow. That is why we must always cherish the present.

*Yesterday is history*
*Tomorrow is a mystery …*
*Today is a gift. That is why it's called the present.*
Source unknown

13

## Chapter 2
# The Wake-Up Call

What is a spiritual awakening and when did mine begin? I define spiritual awakening as increased awareness of events in my life that have a deeper meaning than meets the eye; and a process of integrating this deeper awareness of the universe into my daily life.

My awakening began with the acceptance of the eternal nature of my soul. This was not an acceptance that came upon me overnight. It took many experiences and events to lead me to this understanding. As I reflect upon my past, I can recall many times that I had just a glimmer of this understanding. My spiritual awakening likely began at birth, but it wasn't until 1997 that I can honestly say I was able to hear the messages my life was sending me. The synchronicities that unfolded around me contained lessons that would catapult me into my spiritual awakening. Once I started to listen, the things I was able to see and hear were almost inconceivable to the scientist that I am. It took the diagnosis of brain cancer in a dear friend, Lauren, and her quest for healing to really jump-start my process. I always tell my patients that the messages in life can come in two forms, a gentle tap on the shoulder or a two-by-four across the head.

For years I had many gentle taps on the shoulder but I wasn't paying attention. Lauren's diagnosis was the universe's way of smacking me on the head with a two-by-four.

## My Second Wake-Up Call

In August of 1997, Joe and I had just returned from a spontaneous trip to Wyoming. We were visiting my sister, Susan and her husband, Bruce who had traveled to the States from their home in Australia. The night we returned from this trip we received a late night phone call from John, my girlfriend, Lauren's husband. Lauren, a radiologist who was thirty-eight weeks pregnant, had just had a seizure in their bathroom. Without warning, their lives were about to change in ways that would also affect the lives of many who loved them.

The ambulance was on its way to their home when John called, not knowing where else to turn. As divine timing is perfect, Amy Harvey, Lauren's obstetrician, who is also a dear friend of mine, was living with us that summer. Amy and I dressed quickly and met the ambulance in the emergency room at St. Mary Medical Center. As we drove to the emergency room, our minds were filled with all the possible causes for a seizure: preeclamptic hypertensive crisis, embolic stroke, amniotic fluid embolism, and worst of all, a brain tumor.

Over the course of the next twenty-four hours, Lauren Loverde, who had been the picture of health and experiencing an uneventful pregnancy, was diagnosed with a very aggressive brain tumor called an anaplastic oligoastrocytoma.

Because Lauren was now considered a high-risk obstetrical patient, she was transferred to the University of Pennsylvania where she gave birth to her beautiful daughter, Francesca. Lauren then embarked on treatment for her disease that included everything medical science could offer—surgery, chemotherapy, and varying prognoses given by many different physicians. The bottom line was that no one really knew what the future held for this new mother.

It was a time of great disbelief and shock. For me, it was a time when I questioned my medical knowledge and abilities. I was appalled by the insensitivity I witnessed in my fellow physicians as Lauren's disease process unfolded. While I searched for answers in clinical trials, radiation treatments and surgical solutions, Lauren found her answers in prayer. She began to practice a form of Japanese Energy Healing called Reiki.

Usui Reiki is an ancient tradition passed down for thousands of years from master to master. Dr. Mikao Usui, born in Japan in 1865, grew up knowing, understanding and practicing various "energy/spiritual" disciplines to support his spiritual and physical wellbeing. He developed a practice of channeling Universal Energy—Ki.

This practice, (Usui Reiki Royoho Gakkai) has been taught and passed down for generations. The techniques are passed via a direct lineage that can be traced back to Usui himself. Reiki essentially utilizes universal energy to help support and heal the recipient. The practitioner acts as a conduit of this energy. Some have referred to Reiki as focused prayer or intention. It requires formal training and attunements which are taught by a master practitioner teacher.

I didn't quite know what to think about this so-called "energy healing" at the time. The scientist and surgeon in me were quite skeptical. I didn't understand the basis for Reiki. I was much more comfortable with the surgery, chemotherapy, and radiation I offered patients to treat their cancers. When one of Lauren's doctors gave her an eighteen month prognosis (an estimate on her life expectancy), I decided to be open and supportive to therapies that could complement her surgery, chemo and radiation. I was deathly afraid of losing my friend who had barely begun to experience motherhood. The thought of her dying and leaving John to raise Francesca hit too close to home. I could only imagine how Joe would cope raising our boys, if I were to die young. I can't say I believed in Reiki at that time; yet, if it promoted Lauren's healing process I would be there to support her. I also felt as though Western medicine might let her down.

Lauren and John gave me two books for Christmas that year which would change the way I looked at my entire existence and my career as a physician. They were *Many Lives Many Masters* by Brian L. Weiss, M.D., and *Healing Hands of Light* by Barbara Ann Brennan. Due to my hectic schedule, it would take me nearly another year before I actually picked up these books and read them. They opened my eyes to something I had been unaware of before: reincarnation.

At that time I did not believe nor disbelieve in reincarnation, I just hadn't given it much thought. I had been raised a Christian in the Lutheran Church. Heaven and hell were, as far as I knew, the alternatives for a soul after death. My traditional religious education did not include any teaching or discussion about reincarnation. I often wonder how many opportunities I've missed that would have allowed me to awaken to the idea of reincarnation and my inner self earlier. I wasn't paying attention to divinely timed occurrences. But I now know that they have been guiding me throughout my entire life.

My early childhood memories are akin to a Norman Rockwell painting; at least this is what comes to mind. My hometown of York, Pennsylvania, is a typical, small industrial burg best known for Harley Davidson motorcycles, barbells, and peppermint patties. As the youngest of seven children, I was blessed to be raised by loving parents and could not imagine growing up in a more nurturing environment. My father is a cement contractor and a retired police officer. My mother was a stay-at-home mom whose main purpose in life was nurturing her offspring. Having six older siblings, I learned valuable lessons through their successes and failures. Ask any one of my five sisters and they will tell you my childhood was charmed. My upbringing allowed me to develop a very strong sense of self and a belief in my ability to accomplish any goal.

My brother Bart was the oldest child and only son. His birth was followed by the estrogen chain gang: Mary, Sally, Ann, Susan, Amy and me. Seven children in ten years was a tremendous physical and emotional strain on my mother. When she had a miscarriage after my arrival, my parents and her doctor decided there would be no more pregnancies. Bart's hopes for a younger brother were thwarted and so I became the surrogate younger brother.

I was your basic tomboy and tried to participate with Bart in all the activities a younger brother would be invited to attend. Bart's passion was flying, and every waking moment he could he spent at the York Airport. The York Airport also doubled as a drag strip, so I went to my first drag race at the ripe old age of eight. I rode on the back of my father's motorcycle and went flying with Dad and Bart all of the time. I received an ample dose of male energy in my early years.

Bart's love of flying was evident as early as I can remember. I still recall the manila folders he used as signs to hitchhike back and forth to York Airport before he had a driver's license. He and his friend George, better known as Flick, were "line boys," making money filling gas tanks, taxiing and washing airplanes. They would trade any chores for flying experience, often hitching rides to Peoria, Illinois, with the corporate pilots from Caterpillar. Bart and Flick were truly at home when they were in the air. Bart soloed at sixteen and continued to live at the airport as much as possible.

During his junior year of high school he became very ill. At the age of seventeen, Bart was diagnosed with Crohn's disease, or as they called it in 1970s, terminal ileitis. Even as a seven year old, I didn't like the word terminal in my brother's disease, but I know now it was referring to the terminal or distal end of the small intestine. At the time I didn't realize how sick he really was.

Today, as a physician, I know the true magnitude of his illness. Our family dynamic shifted as we all became care-givers for our eldest sibling. I can remember my mother's fear and anxiety surrounding Bart's illness. It is difficult for a parent to watch a child suffer and be unable to help him. It was at that time, when I was in second grade, I told my mother I was going to be a doctor and nothing would stop me. I suppose, subconsciously, I thought if I became a physician I could make Bart better.

Bart missed several weeks of high school while in the hospital. I was too young to be allowed to see him when he was hospitalized. I felt isolated and left out of the loop. This was the beginning of his medical night-mare. He had flare ups off and on through college. But with Crohn's there is no cure; it is a chronic disease that waxes and wanes. He never did regain total health, but coped with his illness the best he could.

Bart attended college at Penn State University, York campus. He met yet another friend who shared his pas-sion for flying. Mark* became his best friend from his Penn State experience. Bart, Mark and Flick were always at our house being nourished by my mother's cooking when they were not bumming flying time at York Airport. Mom was already cooking for nine, so two extra mouths were no big deal.

Bart's illness was put into perspective when Flick was nearly killed in a car accident at the age of twenty-one. He wrapped his car around a pole and it burst into flames. He sustained over eighty-five percent third degree burns and was lucky to have survived the ordeal. Suddenly Bart's illness seemed less devastating as he watched his friend fight for his life. Flick's recovery was long and involved. Bart stuck with him all the way, often

21

visiting the burn unit daily. Flick's healing took years physically, emotionally and spiritually. We all learned about the strength of the human spirit as he fought to be whole again.

Bart left college after two years to follow his passion as a pilot in the Air National Guard. His illness was kept at bay initially and he was able to train in jets. I think this was one of the happiest times in his life. Bart's time in jets was cut short when he contracted hepatitis from a blood transfusion. He had received blood to replenish his blood volume after an episode of bleeding from ulcerative colitis, a new bowel disorder that affected him. This time his illness took away his dream of flying in the Air National Guard. Bart received an honorable discharge from the military because of his disease. This was a devastating blow. The only thing that could have been worse for him would have been to lose his medical waiver. Without a medical certificate you cannot fly as pilot in command in any aircraft.

Bart returned to York and went into business with my father as a cement contractor. He continued to fly professionally as often as he could. As an instructor, he took great pride teaching others to safely share his passion. He married Beth, the daughter of an airport owner, and purchased a home right across from her father's airport. Now there were two Beth Baughmans.

Bart was so enthusiastic about flying, that he had a difficult time accepting the reality that his little sister, me—a sixteen-year-old girl (aka, the closest thing he had to a brother), was interested in sports, school, and boys. Flying wasn't even on my top ten list at the time. He wanted desperately for me to share his passion and learn how to fly. I was young, busy with high school life, and felt no sense of urgency. I figured he would always be there to teach me to fly when I was ready. My father had gotten his pilot's license at the same time as Bart. Dad had to work really hard at being a great pilot. Bart, on the other hand, was a natural. He was at home in the air. Bart and Dad's dream was to own a private airstrip. They talked about the day *when* it would happen, not *if* it would happen. Dad believed, and instilled in us, that there are no limitations in life other than those you place upon yourself.

## The First Wake-Up Call

September 30, 1978 was the day that would change my life forever. It was my sister Susan's twenty-first birthday. Mom planned a family get together and all of the siblings who lived in town attended. Sue's celebration was the usual: Mom's great food, German chocolate cake, and the company of loved ones. Bart and his wife had had a disagreement and he came alone. When Bart arrived he shared the events of his day. He had been instructing a young doctor in a small single-engine airplane. When they were taking off, the engine quit. No altitude and no engine are a recipe for disaster. Any pilot knows that loosing an engine on take off is one of the most difficult emergencies in flying. Without altitude, it is nearly impossible to maneuver an airplane safely to the ground. Bart grabbed the controls from the student pilot and was able, by some act of God, to crank the plane around and land, saving both his life and the life of the student pilot.

When he told us the story he joked that his number was up but he had bargained with God to get him on the ground. He said Mom would kill him if he missed Sue's twenty-first birthday. We laughed it off and were

23

~

glad that he was with us.

I modeled the Homecoming dress I had bought that day for the entire family. I thought it was perfect. Bart's final words to me that evening were, "Great dress, too bad you don't have any tits to put in it." I was a skinny, athletic teenager and, as usual, he knew how to push my buttons. I can't remember if I stuck my tongue out at him or something worse in response to his sarcasm.

I changed my clothes and left for the evening. My friends and I were heading out to the Parkton Inn in Maryland where the drinking age was eighteen. Pennsylvania's drinking age was twenty-one. We were still underage, no matter how you look at it. We were at least intelligent enough to have a designated driver. That evening when we arrived in Maryland, something just wasn't right with me and I decided to be the designated driver. As we were heading home, we heard about a traffic fatality north of York earlier in the evening. A twenty-seven year old male had been killed and the name of the individual was being withheld pending notification of the family. We sat in the car talking about how horrible it would be to find out by listening to the radio that your loved one had died. We changed channels on the radio and Billy Joel's "Only the Good Die Young" came on.

I pulled up to my house at 11:45 P.M. and all of the lights were on in the house. I surveyed the cars parked around the house and every sister's car was parked outside. I knew something was terribly wrong. When I walked in the door, I saw my brother-in-law Dan. He was crying. I don't remember who actually told me that it was Bart who had been killed, but I took off and ran out of the house. I ran to the playground where I had felt safe and secure as a child, yet there was no feeling secure that evening. When I found out that Bart had been killed by a drunk driver, I also felt guilt associated with my activities that evening.

The next week was a blur. The memorial service, the friends and family that had descended upon the house were all gone after the first week. I was the only sibling living at home with Mom and Dad. I tried to help my parents deal with the loss of their only son at the same time that I tried to deal with the loss of my brother. Initially, my dad could barely work through all of the pain. Since he shared both work and pleasure with Bart, he felt a void that nothing could fill. My dad wanted revenge. The man who killed my brother was underage and legally drunk. There was an empty bottle of Southern Comfort in his car and his blood alcohol was twice the legal limit. Dad wanted him to pay for the death of his only son. My mother, on the other hand, tried to deal with the loss by turning toward her faith. I didn't know what to feel or how to grieve.

No one taught me how to grieve. It is difficult to deal with death any way you look at it, but the sudden loss of someone you love is really difficult. It lacks the closure you can sometimes experience when you have an opportunity to say good-bye. I learned at the tender age of seventeen that we are not immortal and that all we are guaranteed is the moment. What I lacked at the time was the understanding that our souls are eternal. So my wake-up call came without the answers I needed to make sense of this loss.

My recollection of my senior year of high school is pitiful. I can't imagine how I graduated, let alone with honors. I was on autopilot and just went through the motions. I experienced so much pain, and to mask it I filled my days and nights with activities to stay busy. I allotted no time in my life to heal the loss of Bart.

Our family did the best we could do under the circumstances. Mom focused on Bart's chronic illness and felt that if his disease progressed as expected, that he would have ended up losing his medical waiver and would be unable to fly. If Bart couldn't fly then he would have been dead inside. I believe his chronic illness and the future it would have presented helped Mom to heal from his untimely death.

My dad didn't see it that way. Another human being made a choice to drink too much and get behind the wheel of a car and now his son was dead. After a year of seeing the effect of Bart's death on my parents, I was having trouble being in the middle of my mother's deepening faith and the desire for retribution from my dad.

My faith certainly had been challenged and I wasn't sure if there was a God. This doubt arose in a girl who had been an acolyte, choir member, president of the church youth group, and for years had taught Sunday school to kindergartners. I had never been given a reason to question my faith. What purpose could all of my family's pain serve? It made no sense to me at all. How can this be part of a master plan? I needed answers and I went in search of them.

## Chapter 3

# *Fear Paralyzes Knowledge Empowers*

Ten months after Bart's death, I started college at the University of Pittsburgh. I was young, confused, and looking for an escape from my grief. I was relieved to not be in the middle of my parent's grieving process. I knew I wanted a career in medicine. I was also dreaming of travel and wanted desperately to go to Hawaii.

Through the study abroad program I was able to go to
The University of Hawaii for my sophomore year. I was
in search of something.

Before I left for Hawaii I declared my major in the
History and Philosophy of Science, allowing me to spend
hours upon hours with atheists and agnostics, trying to
find answers to the questions I had about life and religion. My choice of major and my plans to study abroad
were criticized. I was chastised by my pre-med advisor
that both would look bad on my transcript, but I had to
take the risk. If I didn't know who I was or where I
wanted to go in life, my transcript appearance would be
the least of my worries.

My neighbor at UH, a medical student, had a
younger brother who had just obtained his flight
instructor's rating. Since the opportunity presented itself,
and I had always promised Bart that I would get around
to flying when I got older, I got my pilot's license while
in Hawaii. This allowed me to begin to heal the loss of
Bart. His death was the saddest, most difficult experience
in my life, and although I told myself and others that I
wanted to learn to fly just for fun before heading to
medical school, I know now that I needed that experience to connect with my brother's spirit. During my
flight training, I often felt his presence and had a sense
of being protected by him.

Attaining my license also helped my father to heal,
as well. While I was in Hawaii, Dad found land to build
his dream, the airstrip he and Bart had planned together.
I was so proud to take my dad flying for the first time
when I returned from Hawaii. I know he was proud of
me, too. It was really important to him that I became a
pilot before I became a doctor, if I intended to be both.

He needed to know that I would learn to fly without ego and treat flying with the respect it deserved. I knew that medicine was in my future and learning to fly jumped up on my list of things to do when he bought the land for his airstrip. I wanted him to be able to share his dream with one of his children. Sharing this dream brought healing to both of us.

After college, I headed to Hahnemann University in Philadelphia for medical school.

My interest in surgery began when my niece was born with a cleft lip. I was in the sixth grade when Jennifer was born, and it was then I learned a valuable lesson about beauty and healing. She was a beautiful baby, despite the huge gap in her upper lip. Her essence—that is, her soul energy—made her beautiful. You could see her inner beauty through her eyes even as a newborn infant.

She could not have her first reconstructive surgery until she was old enough to tolerate the anesthesia at three months of age. Her plastic surgeon, Dr. Robert Davis at York Hospital, was not only a skilled and gifted surgeon, but also a healer. It was our family's experience with Dr. Davis, and how he chose to treat, not only Jen, but also her parents, that gave me insight into who he was as a physician.

Robert Davis was not your typical paternalistic physician. He took the time to educate and empower his patients to make decisions. He did not make decisions for them. He imparted knowledge and then used his wisdom to guide decisions. He took time to really bond with my sister Mary and her husband Dan. They were so young to be dealing with a child born with a birth defect. I vividly remember going to Jen's appointments with Mary, then twenty, listening intently to what he had to say. The positive experiences I had with him solidified my desire to specialize in surgery. It became more than a curiosity; it was my focus as I continued to embrace the reality of being a physician.

During medical school training, I had several opportunities to work closely with Dr. Davis. I rotated on his service during a summer externship from medical school, and he became my role model, my mentor of sorts. My experiences with this doctor, for whom I have great respect, began to awaken the "healer" that resides within my soul. When a physician can teach the art of surgery and instill in students and residents the art of healing, then he is truly doing justice to the field of medicine. Many plastic surgeons I have worked with in my career were so absorbed by the physical beauty they were attempting to create, that they missed the internal beauty in their patients.

It wasn't until later in my training that I completely appreciated the lessons and gifts that Robert Davis gave to me. He took the time to connect with each patient on a personal level. He did not build a wall to protect himself from the outside world—on the contrary—he broke down barriers. Dr. Davis took great pride in training the surgeons of the future. As a first year medical student, he taught me how to suture a laceration on a farmer's nose. I remember vividly placing the individual sutures that would restore that gentleman's face to normal. I was honored that Dr. Davis trusted me enough to let me do this. I also know now that it was his tremendous confidence in his skills that made him a great teacher. By trusting me and allowing me to suture at such an early point in my training, he instilled in me a sense of self confidence that guided me to a career in surgery. When I finished the rotation, I decided I wanted to become a plastic surgeon to be able to restore a child's face from a birth defect or reconstruct a woman's breast after cancer. I had found my focus and I will always cherish the lessons I learned from Robert Davis.

After my first year of medical school, there were no more summer vacations; we went year round until graduation. During my third year of medical school, I met my husband Joe in the operating room at Hahnemann. I was assisting the surgeon and he was operating the laser. Joe was the Director of Surgical Research for the Department of Surgery at the time. He was in charge of my research project and was at first hesitant about getting involved with a student. We dated secretly for my entire senior year until we married the month before my graduation.

After our first date, I knew Joe was the man I would marry. We had different personalities but the balance between his yin and my yang just seemed to work. Eleven months later, in May of 1987, we eloped while on vacation with friends. One month after that I began my five-year surgical residency at Albert Einstein Medical Center in Philadelphia. Surgical residency is an experience unlike any other. When I trained there were no safeguards in place to limit the number of hours you worked per week. I am thankful that younger surgeons currently in training are being safeguarded. I had many experiences during training that, although I was not paying attention at the time, I would now consider part of my spiritual journey.

I remember a patient I treated in my fourth year of training. He had been diagnosed with pancreatic cancer. He needed to have a Greenfield filter placed in his vena

31

cava. (It is a device designed to catch a clot from the leg before it can travel to the lung and cause a potentially life threatening situation). I ran into his family in the hall-way while he was in the radiology department and they were concerned as he had been there for some time. I told them I would check on him. When I arrived in the department, I could hear the patient sobbing, scared, and anxious. The radiologist had been attempting, for over fifty minutes, to place a needle in the vein in the patient's neck to obtain access to his venous system. I donned a lead apron, in order to be shielded from the radiation, and asked the frustrated radiologist if he want-ed me to attempt to access the vein. I asked the patient to relax and trust me as I began the procedure. I was able to get the vein on my first try. The procedure was finished without difficulty. The patient was so thankful for my intervention that, prior to his discharge, he had his family purchase a Waterford Crystal Clock as a gift for me. The note read:

> *Dear Beth,*
>
> *This clock represents, in a very small way, the "time and life" you gave me. Very best wishes for a healthy happy future. A million thanks for your skill and compassion! I will never forget you!!*
>
> *S. K. (and my family)*

I took the clock home and placed it on my book-shelf in the living room. One evening, just six weeks later, the clock stopped at 7:30 P.M. I was surprised, as it had a brand new battery. When I went to work the next day, I found out that S.K. had passed away at seven thirty P.M. the night before; just when my clock stopped. I remember sharing the experience with fellow residents and they laughed it off. I knew there was a greater meaning, I just wasn't wise enough to know who to share it with!

In June of 1992, I began practicing general surgery at St. Mary Medical Center in Langhorne, Pennsylvania. My first few years were so hectic that I really didn't take time to slow down and process all of the things that were occurring in my life. I continued to have exceptional experiences with patients, and innumerable spiritual encounters. I was becoming more willing to share them with friends, patients and colleagues. As I began to share my journey, others would open up about their experiences.

My practice continued to grow and define itself. In the five years from 1992 to 1997, I enjoyed great success and acclaim as a surgeon. Ironically, it wasn't until 1997 that I began to understand the expression, "Physician, heal thyself." This started the journey that would bring together the physician and the healer that I am; that I know all physicians could be. After Lauren's diagnosis and treatment, I would never look at disease the same way again. It had hit too close to home. I was making changes in my life for the right reasons.

33

*Decisions*

In December of 1998, we went to my parents to celebrate Christmas. I was surprised to find a family friend staying with my parents for the holiday. Robert* is the son of my brother's closest college friend, Mark. Bart and Mark had not only been friends in college, they were also kindred spirits in flying. Mark went on to have a flight career in the Navy as a navigations officer. Mark and his wife had three children; the first, Robert, was born in 1979.

Robert was living in my parents' basement apartment while attending Penn State. When I met him and
looked into his eyes, there was a familiarity that was
unmistakable, yet I could not explain why. He just
seemed to fit in with our family. Robert had become
extremely close to my parents. At the time I believed this
attachment was a result of his being young, in college,
and perhaps a little rebellious against his own parents, as
often happens between teenagers and their parents during college years. But there was definitely an unexplain-
able connection between Robert and my family that
everyone felt, though none of us mentioned it at the
time.

My family's relationship with Robert rang bells for
me after reading *Many Lives Many Masters* right after the
Christmas holiday that year. Brian Weiss's story changed
the way I viewed the relationship between life and
death. A classic account of past life regression and reincarnation, it is a true story of a prominent psychiatrist,
his young patient, Catherine, and the past-life therapy
that changed both of their lives. It is a life-affirming book
that suddenly made everything about death so clear and
so right. For the first time in my life, I felt as though reincarnation was not a theory or religious belief, but a reality. I could see my brother's spirit when I gazed into
Robert's eyes. It was a huge awakening, and a sense of
calm came over me as though a heavy weight had been
lifted from my shoulders. I was able to feel peace instead
of sadness when I thought of Bart. This feeling came
some twenty years after his death.

The true nature of our soul, our spirit, became more
obvious to me after reading the book. I had always
known the core of our being is the soul, and now I finally

understood that death is not the end, it is a transition of spirit from one form to another. *I felt that I was remembering what I had somehow forgotten.*

I was excited to learn more about reincarnation and regression, and I bought copies of the book for my family, friends, and colleagues. I felt compelled to share the book with people I cared about. I think it was the way Brian shared his own story that touched me so deeply. His journey of enlightenment touched my soul and made my thirst for spiritual knowledge unquenchable. I needed to know more.

I could not wait to read Brian's subsequent books: *Through Time into Healing* and *Only Love is Real*. I was consumed by a need to continue on my path toward this new level of awareness. By this time, *I got it.* My friends *got it.* My family *got it.* We were all well on our way to navigating our individual paths of enlightenment. I got the true sense of what my soul actually is.

We are all spiritual beings that incarnate into human form to experience life and journey. While on earth we are in school learning lessons and having experiences for our souls to embrace as part of our essence. Our essence is what is constant through many lifetimes. Now that I got it, I wanted to make changes to honor that which I knew to be truthful and fulfilling, including changes in my professional life. I had been in practice for six years with another physician who is an excellent surgeon, but we were on diverging paths. Mine was one of combining Western medicine with the spirituality of Eastern medicine, while his was based purely on Western doctrine.

As I look back on the fall of 1998, a year into Lauren's healing process, I remember an event that occurred while I was driving my children home from

35

school. Tommy pleaded with me to stop and play at the park for awhile. Dean, who was only two years old at the time, didn't have an opinion either way, and since it was beautiful weather, I agreed to take them. The sky was blue and the wind was blowing gently when we arrived. Tommy played on the sliding board as I chased Dean around the jungle gym.

Twenty minutes later the weather shifted unexpectedly and a storm blew in from nowhere. I was hurrying the kids back to the car when Tommy found a book sitting on top of a post in the play area. This precocious seven-year-old was concerned that the book would get soaked in the rain and insisted upon taking it. "There's no one else in the park, Mom," he argued. "It will be ruined if we don't take it with us."

That was how Deepak Chopra's *Seven Laws of Spiritual Success* made its way into my life. I read the book and felt it had been left in the park as a message from the universe. Right inside the front cover was the message I needed at the time:

> *You are what your deep, driving desire is.*
> *As your desire is, so is your will.*
> *As your will is, so is your deed.*
> *As your deed is, so is your destiny.*

Brihadaranyaka Upanishad IV. 4.5

The universe had provided me with a guide to manifest my own destiny. I knew I had a unique purpose in this lifetime and all I needed to do was open my eyes and heart to find answers. (By the way, the book is inscribed: *To Paul with best wishes from Raj 10-2-98.* I will gladly return it to Paul if he reads this and wants it back.)

I had heard that divine timing is perfect and I was becoming a believer. The timing of the message from the book could not have been more perfectly planned. I knew I needed to be empowered to make a change in my professional life. I knew I would have to manifest my own destiny. I wanted to give more to my patients than I had been giving and I required much more from medicine than I had been receiving. Operating on people and helping to repair their physical bodies was just scratching the surface. I was light years away from being the *healer* I wanted to be. I wanted to live, breathe, sleep and promote healing in every aspect of my life, both personal and professional.

Once again, this quest to facilitate healing in all aspects of my life began with my friend Lauren's illness. Lauren had a rough road ahead of her in her healing process. She was given a prognosis that the tumor could recur within eighteen months and was potentially fatal. This prognosis was based on standard Western medical treatment and outcomes. But Lauren would not be deterred from her desire to find both healing from her dis-*ease* and a cure for her *disease*. She and John weathered the storms; through every complication and adversity they continued to grow and awaken. She taught me so much about how to heal. It wasn't about the disease we call cancer; it was about healing her dis-*ease* by making changes in her personal life to honor her spirit. Lauren chose to leave her partnership in a radiology group, and she and John bought land, built their dream home, and followed their passion of becoming full-time alpaca farmers.

Today, it has been nine years since Lauren's diagnosis, and she is the picture of health and the embodiment

37

of healing. She has made so many changes in her life for the right reasons. She inspires me daily to remember what is truly important in my life.

The more I awakened, the more difficult it was for me to remain in my surgical partnership. I was learning to be honest with myself, and started to listen to my inner voice. I was coming home from work complaining to my husband all too frequently about certain aspects of my practice that I knew were dishonoring me and keeping me from developing into the healer I wanted to become. Recognized in our community for my surgical skills, I was now also becoming known for embracing holistic and complementary healing therapies. But I felt I needed to downplay my desire to include complementary therapies and embrace the holistic approach to healing because my partner didn't share my passion. If I were to spend more time connecting with my patients, it would require expanding the practice and adding more partners. I realized that the only change that would ever make a difference would be to begin my own practice. I needed to define my own path and create a surgical practice that incorporated holistic healing. The decision to start a solo practice came after many months of soul-searching and heartfelt discussions with Joe. In order for my practice to be successful, I needed someone I trusted completely to manage the business. Joe was my only choice. This decision would have a significant impact on the growth and development of our two children.

Ever since Dean's birth, the boys had the benefit of having their father at home full time. I was working very long hours as a general surgeon, supporting the family, and I didn't want my children to have to give up the wonderful gift my husband had given to all of us as a stay-at-home parent. I came to the realization that following my passion and being true to myself would be the most important lesson for them to learn. Working together, we began the planning process for setting up a new practice.

Over the course of the next few years, I became more aware of frequent synchronicities occurring in my life, both professionally and personally. I believe this was the way the universe had chosen to remind me of my spiritual self. Had I denied a divine presence in my life up to this point? Yes, I had, and for me there was no more denial. Even now, the magnitude and profound nature of these experiences continue to give me goose bumps.

## Chapter 4

# *Present in the Moment*

In the summer of 1999, while making a Shiva call (bereavement visit) at my secretary Cheryl's house, I was reintroduced to her daughter-in-law, Alison. It was the afternoon following Cheryl's father's funeral and several people were around the kitchen table discussing life and afterlife issues. I mentioned that I had read the book by Brian Weiss, and Alison was so excited she jumped up and down and began to share her own story of spiritual awakening.

She was amazed that her mother-in-law's employer, a surgeon, was a believer in past life regression and therefore reincarnation. I suppose she thought reincarnation was not embraced by either the medical community or Christianity. She was pleasantly surprised that we shared a common bond. Alison then informed me that a one-day seminar with Brian Weiss was to be held in Fort Lauderdale in October of that year. I immediately decided I was going to meet her there and experience past life regression with Brian Weiss. It was the perfect opportunity for my friends and me to get away for a long weekend and to see what this Brian Weiss fellow was really like.

I had given *Many Lives Many Masters* to anyone and everyone I knew who I thought would read it and take it to heart. I had a core group of girlfriends who, like me, were eager to experience regression. So we packed our bags and headed for Fort Lauderdale for a weekend of regression therapy and spiritual growth.

My sister, Amy, had recently gone through a divorce and was very interested in finding out about her past lives. She wanted some insight into relationships she had with people in her current lifetime. My girlfriend, Amy Harvey, an obstetrician by profession, jumped at the opportunity to be a part of this experience. Our fourth partner in crime for the weekend was Dina*. She is also a surgeon and a long-time friend from medical school.

It was a charmed weekend. We arrived on Friday evening at a beautiful resort in Fort Lauderdale, and our adventure began with an amazing experience at a restaurant called China Grill in South Beach Miami.

When we arrived at the restaurant, we knew by the ambience that we were in the right place. Time stood still there. The lighting created a surreal atmosphere. The waiters were exceedingly handsome and polite. The food had a distinctive aroma. We deliberately took our time perusing the menu while each of us savored a glass of wine. We were having a charmed evening.

A gentleman and his two female companions at the table next to ours were being served an exquisite dish called Shanghai Lobster. It is one of China Grill's signature dishes. As the waiters carried it past our table, we couldn't help but notice how incredible it looked. We decided that it should be at the top of our list of dinner selections. While we continued to look at our menus, the woman at the next table who was eating the Shanghai lobster began to turn blue—she was choking. Amy (the doctor, not my sister) and I jumped up to rush to her rescue. The waiter also witnessed all this and pulled the woman out of her chair to administer the Heimlich Maneuver. She regurgitated the food, which hit her plate. We asked the woman if she could speak, knowing that if there was food still caught in her trachea she'd be unable to say anything. In response she hissed, "I can't talk, I'm choking to death!"

We couldn't help but notice that during this near death experience, the gentleman sitting with her never stopped eating. He didn't miss a bite of his lobster and crispy spinach. This man was so absorbed with his meal he hadn't even noticed his date was choking. The other woman was amazed by the whole scene. The waiter cleared off the table, brought another plate of food, and the threesome continued on with their meal as though nothing had happened.

If this food was so good that a man could continue eating his dinner while his date was choking, that was good enough recommendation for us. And, indeed, the lobster and spinach *were* extraordinary. But then everything about that evening was extraordinary,

43

and we all noticed it. The color, texture, taste, and aroma of the food—as well as the company—were beyond description.

Were we already experiencing something different? Were we more centered and balanced—open and living in the moment—experiencing what was going on around us more fully than we ever had before? Had we missed details of previous eating experiences because we had been failing to be in the moment? By simply embarking on this weekend of enlightenment were we more attuned into the energy of the universe? I began to wonder how many precious moments of my life I had skimmed over while I plowed through my day to day world working toward a goal. I began to see I focused so intently on where I was headed, I forgot to be present in the moment. Reality was setting in; I couldn't go back and recover lost moments, but I could make a conscious decision to be present from that moment forward.

The next day we relaxed in preparation for the regression seminar on Sunday. We scheduled individual spa treatments for the late morning and lounged around the pool in the afternoon. We saw a sign in the spa that advertised past life Tarot card readings. None of us had experienced Tarot readings before, but we decided we were there for the journey and would follow our hearts. The woman who was scheduled to do the readings came highly recommended by the spa staff. Her name was Wendy, and she was apparently something of a local celebrity as she wrote a column in the local newspaper. We decided that if we were meant to have readings, Wendy would have time available for all of us to participate, so we signed up. When we returned from the pool, there was a message in our room that we were all in with Wendy.

That weekend my companions and I were learning how to live in the moment in a most incredible way. We weren't thinking about what responsibilities faced us at work in the week to come. We didn't dredge up the past and waste time lamenting things that were behind us. We didn't worry about what time we needed to leave the hotel to make our return flights home. We didn't stress about not being home with our children. We simply enjoyed the present company, the delicious food, and thoroughly enjoyed the experiences that were right in front of us in the moment.

On Sunday morning we reported for our past-life Tarot readings. My sister went first. She had a very insightful reading and was happy with the experience. Amy received confirmation that she was to pursue her passion of writing a novel. She also was informed that a soul mate from a previous life—our brother, Bart—had returned to this world. We both felt that this was a reference to Bart's friend Mark's son, Robert.

I was the third person to receive a reading. Wendy somehow knew I was the seventh of seven children and that I had another sibling, who would have been younger than I, but that child had not been born. (My mother had indeed had a late third trimester miscarriage after my birth, and my parents decided not to have any more children on the advice of her doctor.) She also informed me that my brother was no longer in spirit, but had quickly reincarnated back to this planet, "to play." She told me that I had already made contact with him and his return was a gift. This message confirmed for me, in a profound way, the eternal nature of our soul and that death is but a transition to another dimension.

Wendy wanted to know if I had any questions. Still agonizing over the idea of leaving my practice, I asked if it was the right thing to do. She told me I needed to give my current practice a chance to work out. (*It was good advice, and I took it. I have never felt guilt that I made a hasty decision.*)

Then Wendy looked into my past lives. She stated that I was not to know who I was in recent past lives. She told me it is my energy, my essence, which I carried over from that lifetime to this one, that allows people to open up to me and feel instant trust. This is also the reason why so many people are drawn to my energy; it is familiar to them. She also told me that I had been world famous, and that I would be world famous again in this lifetime. (Neither of us could know what was about to transpire in my professional career. Ten days after this trip, I performed the first mastectomy to be broadcast live around the world via the internet.)

During our stay at the resort, I repeatedly ran into Brian Weiss in the elevator. We were staying in the same building and must have been on the same cosmic time schedule. I assured him I was not a stalker, and that our meetings were just coincidence. He reminded me that there really are no coincidences. By the end of the weekend he recognized me and knew me by name. At that point in my life, I never could have imagined we would become friends; I had placed him on a pedestal. I now know he is the gentlest, most unassuming, grounded soul I have ever known.

The conference itself was great. Alison and I shared some amazing experiences with energy exercises. We each held an item in our hands that belonged to the other person, and we were able to use the energy in that object to recount an event in one another's lives. I felt the energy in her locket and accurately described an event which she shared with her cousin, who had passed over several years earlier. She was able to accurately recount an event involving my brother. She gave me a detailed description of a four-foot stuffed giraffe Bart had given to my niece, Jen, when she was born. Alison and I were clearly connected that weekend.

Amy, Dina, Amy, and Alison all regressed successfully to past life experiences. These experiences were very profound and reduced all of them to tears. I fell asleep during the regression exercises. (This is a habit left over from residency. I fall asleep whenever I am totally relaxed.) I really didn't feel left out since I had had some amazing meditations. I was able to see the vivid colors of indigo and violet. I felt I was floating out of my body and soaring with the colors. (And the answer is: no, I have never taken LSD!)

My sister Amy had a lot of healing to do involving the loss of our brother, Bart. For almost all of the nineteen years Amy and Bart spent together on this earth, their relationship was tumultuous. They could never really see eye-to-eye because they were very much alike. Stubbornness runs in our family and Amy and Bart had cornered the market on it. Because of the sudden nature of his death, there was no opportunity for any healing and closure in Amy and Bart's relationship. It was a lesson we all learned too late. We now understand that no one is guaranteed a tomorrow to make up for what is said or done today.

During one of the sessions that weekend, we were participating in a healing meditation and Brian directed

47

us to visualize a garden. Amy and I both had the exact same visualization. Bart walked up to me and handed me a box. Amy had the same experience. In her box was a perfect white feather. It represented peace and light. She was also given the knowledge that her son, Owen, had been a gift Bart had planned for her healing. In my box was a knife. My first thought was, "how appropriate, a knife for a surgeon." However, I soon realized that it was a special knife meant to help me cut through whatever was preventing me from finding the true healer that lives within me.

We were emotionally drained after that session. The past life memories were intense experiences for the others, yet they also felt they were very healing. We laughed and cried and had an enormous craving for fresh air. We were recounting the experiences of the day when the greatest gift of all came floating down in front of my sister. It was a beautiful white feather, a gift from the universe, representing peace between Amy and my brother, and perhaps a light to guide her path.

I returned from Florida with a new sense of calm and wellbeing. My sense of spirituality had deepened and I felt a real, almost palpable connection to those around me, personally and professionally. I knew that remaining focused in the moment would help me to maintain the sense of calm I felt at the conference. I also realized that it would help enhance my connection to my patients. I needed to lead by example. As my journey continued, I began to awaken every day to new realizations about life. I started to recognize the synchronicities and beautiful experiences each day holds out to me.

In late October I was named one of three recipients of an American Red Cross Spectrum Award. I would receive the Clara Barton Humanitarian Award for my work in breast cancer care and education in our community. It was a tremendous honor for a thirty-eight-year-old surgeon to be recognized with two other distinguished women of Bucks County. To maintain the equilibrium in my practice, I felt a need to downplay my enthusiasm regarding any recognition I was receiving.

As I mentioned before, two weeks after the Fort Lauderdale conference, I was privileged to perform a surgery that was broadcast on the internet to educate and empower women about the choices they have when diagnosed with breast cancer. Dr. Rob Skalicky is a plastic surgeon who reconstructs my patients' breasts after breast cancer surgery. Rob and I had been approached the year before as part of Breast Cancer Awareness month to perform the live surgery. America's Health Network had wanted us to perform a mastectomy and TRAM (Trans Rectus Myocutaneous Flap, a form of breast reconstruction) for the world to watch. We did not have an appropriate patient at that time, so we suggested the surgery be performed at another institution. When we declined, we assumed they found another group of physicians to perform the procedures.

A year later, they approached us again, asking us to take part in this first-time event. It was no coincidence that Patty Derman, the perfect patient for this broadcast, appeared back in my office in August of 1999. Patty is a nurse in a local Emergency Room who had been referred to me by her friends who were nurses at St. Mary Medical Center. She had been my patient two years earlier when she was diagnosed with Ductal Carcinoma Insitu (DCIS), a non-invasive form of breast cancer. At the time, she sought a second opinion at Thomas Jefferson University in Philadelphia. Patty had made the choice to have bilateral mastectomies and TRAM reconstruction and was already scheduled for surgery. However, she had some personal issues which delayed that surgery. She later came to my practice for further follow-up.

When she was first diagnosed, Patty was making a decision about surgery based purely on fear. Decisions based on fear often come with a very hefty price. She took a step backward and looked at her situation more clearly. Once she was able to overcome her fears, she chose clinical observation for her DCIS. This was a totally acceptable alternative given the size and grade of her DCIS. She decided to take the anti cancer drug, Tamoxifen as a preventative measure.

It took a second atypical (pre-cancerous) biopsy in the summer of 1999 to make her reevaluate her risk. Patty became empowered at this point to choose mas-tectomies and implants for her own peace of mind. She was very athletic and decided against the TRAM feeling it would restrict her outdoor activities.

During my residency, it always perplexed me why any woman would choose to remove her breasts when she didn't have to. I was conditioned by my training to wonder what sort of physician would recommend—let alone perform—such unnecessary surgery. What narrow-minded thinking I possessed at that time. I didn't realize that for some women to find healing, and to make peace with what they are facing, they need to be proac-tive and eliminate the fear that plagues them. It is para-lyzing for some people to feel as though they are carry-ing around a genetic time bomb, and that level of dis-*ease* (unease) can steal precious moments from their daily lives. Now I understand that when there is a history of cancer in a woman's family, or a woman tests positive for the cancer gene, she needs to decide for herself what it will take for her to be comfortable enough to live every day without fear. Feeling empowered to decide on a course of action makes a huge difference in these women's lives.

I have learned through treating women with breast cancer that I cannot judge patients' decisions about their course of treatment unless I have journeyed on their path. There is a certain amount of surrender necessary for a physician to come to this understanding and this has been a difficult lesson for me to learn. It is a daily struggle for me to learn to surrender to things I cannot control.

Not everyone can find healing in prophylactic surgery, but in Patty's case this was the procedure she wanted in order to feel more confident about her future. Prophylactic surgery, by definition, is surgery that is not necessary to treat a current disease but to prevent a disease from occurring. It does not remove all risk of breast cancer but decreases the risk substantially.

I was in Florida when Patty decided to go public about the impending surgery in hopes of raising more awareness about breast cancer and treatment options. She believed that if there was a face and a name associated with breast cancer surgery, people would be more inclined to pay attention and hear the message. She was correct. By agreeing to allow her surgery to be broadcast on the internet, Patty attracted the attention of the media. By the time I returned home, it was a media free-for-all.

It was a bit overwhelming to be hounded by the media. Rob and I kept the focus on Patty and the incredible thing she was about to do to educate other women. This was before reality TV, and we were on the hot seat. The hospital initially questioned how it would reflect upon them as a Catholic institution. I reminded them that we were focused on the educational aspect and how empowering this could be for all women. If a woman feared the loss of her breasts, this surgery and reconstruction could help her to see that it is not mutilating but restorative.

The tarot card reader's prediction came true. One and a half million people around the world logged on to watch the surgery live. I was amazed at the level of media coverage the procedure received. St. Mary was just a community medical center in bucolic Bucks County, yet the event received national attention. It was a human-interest story, but a controversial one, primarily because the surgery was prophylactic. People were very vocal either in support of Patty's decision or against it.

Critics, who didn't understand why Patty made the decision she did, were vociferous in their arguments against such a drastic operation for such minimal disease. But the truth is, none of these detractors had traveled the path with Patty and her family members who had been affected by breast cancer, and neither had they walked in her footsteps when she was first diagnosed and then experienced another atypical biopsy. They could not understand the anxiety surrounding Patty's annual mammograms or the fear she experienced every time microcalcifications required a biopsy.

Microcalcifications are small specs of calcium visible on a mammogram. Not all microcalcifications are cancer, but certain types require a biopsy to determine what caused them.

Patty is an amazingly strong woman who taught me

so much about her spirit through this journey. I will be forever indebted to her. Her courage showed the world, and all the women who followed her story, that one can gain personal power in making knowledgeable decisions. Patty's decision came from wisdom, not from fear. It had taken her nearly two years to reach that place, and it required her to search her soul and find answers to difficult questions.

The surgery itself was scheduled for Wednesday morning, October 20, at eleven A.M. The time was chosen so that viewers on the West coast could watch the surgery. The film crew had been in the hospital the week before to plan the logistics of the surgery, which would be performed in Operating Room D, as it had the best access for satellite transmission. I was unbelievably calm about the impending surgery. I had maintained the sense of calm and wellbeing I found at the Brian Weiss conference. I felt in my heart that the surgery would be so powerful for so many and I felt honored to be a part of it.

The Friday before the surgery, when I was performing a surgery in that same room, a pressurized saline bottle broke free from the plastic tubing and shot saline across the room directly into the wall switch plate. Sparks flew out of the wall, and the entire building lost power. The emergency generator eventually kicked in and my patient did beautifully. The skeptics, those people who live in fear, cried that it was a bad omen about the impending internet surgery. Personally, I preferred to think of it as "cleansing" the room of any negative energy. I was criticized by some peers that it was dangerous to perform live surgery. They said, "What if something goes wrong? Aren't you afraid of being

53
~

sued?" Frankly, I was quite confident in my skills and felt I could deal with anything that transpired. I planned to operate just as I always do, as if the cameras were not present on the room. My patients come first and that day would be no different. Patty Derman would be my main focus.

The cleansing must have worked, because on the day of the internet surgery everything went as planned, and even better than expected. The surgery was completed in record time and Patty's results were excellent. With the help of the internet, Rob Skalicky and I, and those who assisted us, performed the first live mastectomy and reconstruction the world had ever witnessed.

A breast with cancer can be removed and reconstructed. Women do not die of cancer in their breasts. They die when the disease spreads outside of the breast. There are women who do not obtain screening mammography out of fear that they may have cancer. To me the fear lies in having cancer that is not found. If you do not look for a cancer it does not mean it doesn't exist, it just means you choose to ignore its presence. A tiny cancer that could be detected on a mammogram can be easily treated. Early detection of cancer leads to less invasive treatments and a greater likelihood of cure.

Knowledge is empowering and fear paralyzes. We wanted to educate women about the choices they have when it comes to caring for their breasts. We were the pebble in the pond whose ripple effect would expand far wider than we had ever imagined. Years later many people still comment on the impact of the event.

I had one patient who came to me two weeks after Patty's surgery who had been ignoring a mass in her breast. She said that Patty's story gave her the strength to seek medical attention. She was afraid of loosing her breast. She indeed had cancer and Patty's journey, shared on the internet, saved this woman's life. I was proud to be part of this event.

America's Health Network filmed a documentary about the surgery and why Patty made the decision to have prophylactic breast surgery. In March of 2000, the documentary and the actual surgery were awarded the prestigious Gracie Allen Award for excellence in women's broadcasting. Rob and I felt very blessed to be part of this event. Hopefully, it made a difference in many women's lives. It certainly made a profound difference in mine.

I felt as though I had the ability to accomplish anything I desired. I was being drawn to help those with breast cancer. I felt there was so much more we as doctors could do to help when someone is diagnosed with breast cancer. Being a part of an event that was transmitted around the world, I experienced the realization that there was no limit to the reach of our message in performing the surgery. I could hear my father's voice saying, "The only limits you have in your life are those you place upon yourself." I knew I had no limits!

## Chapter 5

# *Partnership and Friendship as a Path*

In January of 2000, I reached a point in my career that required a major change. I could not continue on my path of being simply a general surgeon. I knew I needed to do more than just operate on people. In order to treat my patients holistically, I needed to be utilizing even more complementary medical techniques. As I stated previously, holism embraces the concept that the individual is an interconnected being, and all of the elements of that being must be treated equally to address the complexity of the whole person. Holism is the basis for treatment of disease in Eastern Medicine. Multiple systems must be evaluated because they relate to one another rather than existing as individual components. The whole is greater than the sum of the parts. Holistic care includes evaluation and treatment of the physical, mental, and spiritual components of an individual, not just a person's physical symptoms. All three are completely interconnected and intertwined. Complementary medicine offers us a pathway to holism where the therapies promote healing, and work in concert with Western medicine to promote healing. I was embarking on a path that was new to me yet it just felt right. I wanted and needed more time to commit to my new found passion in healing. I also needed more time to be home with my young children who had so much to teach me.

Hiring more physicians to expand our practice was not realistic. Having more time to dedicate to *healing* my patients and making more time for my family was a desire I needed to make happen. It became clear to me that in order to be proactive and follow my heart, I would need to change my practice.

This was one of the most difficult decisions I have ever had to make. My partner was an extremely skilled surgeon. We both trained at excellent medical schools and had completed well-rounded residency programs. Our similarities in the operating room far outweighed our differences. We had one of the busiest and most respected practices in Bucks County. The nurses and physicians at our facility entrusted their family members to our care. But we held different views about what the future held for our practice. Our similarities, of which there were many, would not be enough to keep us together. Sharing a medical practice is like being married in many ways. Lines of communication must be open in order for the partnership to thrive.

When I spoke with my partner about leaving the practice, he was truly disappointed and asked me to reconsider. Because of my high regard for him, and because we both cared about the future of our practice, I agreed to stay. We gave it our best try for six months, but due to all the synchronicities occurring in my life—several events that were unfolding simultaneously—it became apparent that separate practices would be healthier for both of us.

The first incident would be a huge blow. Having lived through the diagnosis and treatment of brain cancer in my dear friend Lauren, I didn't think I could imagine a disease that would pack a greater punch; and then came the knockout punch of Lou Gehrig's disease (ALS). I didn't even have time to put on my boxing gloves when the right cross took me out.

My friend and colleague, Dr. Christine S. O'Donnell, was a real *ball-buster* of a surgeon. She was orthopedic surgeon extraordinaire and was respected by the medical community as one of the best. She commanded respect from everyone and gave the same respect in return. Chris was not easy to work with in the OR, from what I am told. The nurses revered her as a surgeon but were quite intimidated by her when required to be her scrub nurse or circulator. Bottom line, she was a talented surgeon and her patients came first.

Her language in the OR, like mine, has been described as *colorful*. Both of us have been asked, on

59

~

occasion, "Where did you park your rig?" There are truck drivers that Chris could make blush. I think we were both products of male-dominated residencies, and our four-letter adjectives came from our survival training. The foul language let us fit in and be one of the guys. "Oh, darn! . . . fudge! . . . gosh! . . . shoot!" don't quite cut it when someone's life is on the line and you are responsible. (Okay, maybe this is an excuse, but it will make this more palatable when my mother reads this book.)

Chris was one of my role models when I started in private practice, right out of surgical residency. She arrived on the scene in Bucks County only a few short years before me. Her superb surgical skills and her professionalism paved a path of instant acceptance for me when I arrived at St. Mary Medical Center. Women surgeons, still a rare minority in the surgical world, had to be more than just competent to be accepted. Chris O'Donnell was way more than just competent, she was the best.

Chris was born the middle child of three, with an older and younger brother. They had a relatively normal childhood and she was the driven child. Chris had carefully planned the course of her life. She went to college at the University of Vermont, combining her academic drive with athletic prowess on the ski slopes. She was so driven that she could be found sleeping standing up in the middle of a frat party. She loved living and skied the double diamonds of life with confidence and great skill. When she wasn't operating, she was devoted to her family.

Chris was not the type of woman who needed, or kept a lot of female friends. Girlfriends were an extravagance. She had a few very close girlfriends from her past, and chose to spend all of her free time away from her career with her family. She would only let a select few into her personal space.

I first met Chris in the very crowded women's locker room in the St. Mary operating room (OR). The female surgeons, shared the locker room with the nursing staff. I had been assigned a locker in the front row right beside the entrance. There was very little room to maneuver and I had to dodge all of the women as they came into this confined space simultaneously. One morning the nurses and I were dressing for surgery when I heard this loud bellowing laugh coming from the next row of lockers. The voice was deep and the laugh had an almost croup-like nature to it, it could almost be described as ludicrously loud. I had never heard a laugh like that in my life. I asked the nurse standing beside me what the noise was, and she informed me it was none other than Chris O'Donnell, an orthopedic surgeon. I dressed, walked around the line of lockers, and found Chris. She was a petite size zero, with long brown hair, deep brown eyes, and a huge smile. She was wearing size small scrubs, which were baggy on her bony butt, and a pair of knee-high wading boots to protect her from the high volume of blood often present in ortho- pedic surgeries.

61

Later I learned that when she was performing total hip and knee replacements, her petite physique made for quite a sight in the operating room. She possessed the strength of a man three times her size. I was amazed that such a small human being could belt out the kind of laugh I had just heard. I have never met another person who could laugh as intensely and deeply as Chris. Her laugh was a side effect of her love of life. I introduced myself to her that day and we have been friends ever since. She was truly a trailblazer for women surgeons everywhere.

I rarely get the opportunity to watch NBC's *Today Show* due to my early morning schedule, but one morning in February of 2000, I caught a segment about a woman diagnosed with ALS. I remember thinking I was fortunate, as a cancer surgeon, to treat a disease that is potentially curable. I wondered how physicians who treat patients with ALS, an incurable disease, could stay positive day after day.

A day or so later, Chris called to tell me she had experienced some trouble with her foot when she and her husband had been on a skiing vacation. She had a difficult time negotiating the moguls and fell a few times. Shortly after that, Chris rapidly developed a foot drop, a sign of nerve damage that rendered her unable to lift her toes toward the sky, and became concerned that something was seriously wrong.

That very day I knew in my heart she had ALS. I didn't mention it to her—it was unspeakable. How could I speak to my friend of a disease that I knew would be fatal. I was sad and heartbroken. I so wanted to be wrong! I didn't even want to contemplate the thought myself, but I knew. I felt helpless and scared. I had this strong intuition that my dear friend was in terrible trouble.

Over the next few months Chris, the mother of two beautiful young children, was put through a battery of tests: MRIs, EKGs, spinal taps, blood tests, and countless visits with a variety of specialists. During her diagnostic workup, Chris continued to practice orthopedic surgery. An MRI of her neck revealed a thyroid nodule that was suspicious. It had to be removed, but Chris was so worried about missing work that she asked me to do the surgery on Good Friday, which fell in April of that year. The OR is closed for this holiday and it is no small endeavor, in a Catholic hospital, to schedule surgery on one of the holiest days in the Catholic religion. As it turned out, I had no trouble getting volunteers to work an extra day since Chris was so loved and revered by the OR staff. Her thyroid nodule was removed and it proved to be benign. It certainly could not explain her progressive symptoms. Her foot drop became more severe, and Chris began to limp noticeably by late spring.

Watching Chris's health deteriorate was difficult for everyone who loved her. She continued to work full-time during the diagnostic period. It was far too easy to see, and tremendously painful to watch, the progression of the loss of her motor functions. We would have welcomed the diagnosis of Multiple Sclerosis or some other slowly progressive disease. Finding the disease that was causing her problems was a matter of eliminating other neurological disorders which could be responsible for her symptoms. Chris maintained her positive attitude despite her worst fears.

How unfair I felt it was that I could help so many women I didn't even know get treatment for their breast cancer, while I had to watch my dear friend grow weaker and weaker, and could do nothing. I was powerless to help her. I realized again how much emphasis we, as a society, place on curing disease and how little energy we devote to healing.

Things were becoming crystal clear. On so many levels, Chris's malady was already teaching me life lessons. She needed to heal and yet wasn't even diagnosed with a specific disease. Tomorrow waits for no one. If I had any second thoughts about moving forward with my plans for a new practice those thoughts were on their way out the door. I was now committed to combine my surgical skills with my need to promote healing. Chris's dis-*ease* reinforced my inner healing journey, and catapulted my life journey into high gear.

## Chapter 6
## *Reality Sets in*

I have been relatively adept at separating my emotions about a disease, from my role as the physician treating the disease; at least when the disease was in my patients. Lauren's cancer was my first personal reality test, and I pray every day never to have another. Chris's ailment was my second, *too close for comfort,* disease. I knew the diagnosis wasn't going to be good because of the rapidity of her decline. My emotional closeness to my friends made their dis-*ease* part of my inner journey. I was living it with them. It was palpable. With disease in my patients I had always been able to separate my emotions as a method of self-preservation. Lauren and Chris's illnesses had opened an avenue of vulnerability I had not encountered previously.

My emotions were raw, my mind constantly racing. I was struggling internally with a host of emotions that were relatively new to me. I felt I had to leave my old practice to follow my heart, but it wouldn't be easy. I was powerless to help Chris at that point because there was no label for her disease. I was feeling vulnerable and helpless in many ways and at the same time, ironically, I was being honored for being a humanitarian and community leader. I guess my game face was good because no one seemed to be able to tell that my internal struggle was taking place.

The American Red Cross, Spectrum Awards were presented in March of 2000. I had been named the recipient of the Clara Barton Humanitarian Award and a breakfast was given to commemorate the event. Three women were honored by the Red Cross that day and I was fortunate to be one of them. My family, friends, and some of my office staff, were taking time out of their schedules to attend. As a gesture of support, my partner purchased a table at the event for the rest of our staff so they could share in this special day.

I was thrilled to see that many of my patients attended. Patty Derman, my internet mastectomy patient, was there and still living life as a local celebrity. I was surprised to find another patient, Dawn Buck, standing in the room since she was undergoing chemotherapy and had not purchased a ticket for the event. As it turned out, her mother-in-law, Faith, had been hospitalized just two days prior to the breakfast with a pulmonary embolism, and had given her ticket to Dawn. Although I was very upset about Faith's illness, I was delighted to see Dawn.

Dawn Buck was another true gift in my life. She and her husband Kevin had been high school sweethearts and had been married for several years. Their relationship had the energy of true soul mates. They were so connected to one another that everyone who knew them could see it and feel the bond. Dawn was thirty-four years old when she discovered a mass in her breast. She went to her gynecologist who discovered that she was also seventeen weeks pregnant, even though she was taking birth control pills. The mass in her breast suddenly became secondary to her pregnancy.

What a shock for this young couple who wanted children but had wanted to wait until later in their marriage. Her doctor was obviously concerned about the fact that she was on the birth control pill for the entire first trimester of her pregnancy. The lump in her breast was thought to be a lactation adenoma, which is a common condition associated with pregnancy and the hormonal changes of the breast. An adenoma is of little or no consequence, but requires a biopsy to prove it is not cancer. Dawn went about her business planning for the birth of their first child.

Her mother-in-law, Faith, the scheduling secretary for a different gynecological group, wanted Dawn to see the obstetricians that she worked with, but Dawn decided to stay with the doctor she had known for seventeen years. Dawn was thirty-two weeks pregnant when her obstetrician thought the mass in her breast had gotten larger. She sent Dawn for an ultrasound and the mass was indeed solid and irregular. She needed a surgical evaluation and was referred to my practice. And so my relationship with Dawn and Kevin Buck began.

When I examined Dawn, I knew immediately we were dealing with a breast cancer. The mass was suspicious and she already had several lymph nodes palpable in her armpit. I felt such emptiness in the pit of my stomach. I had treated many women with breast cancer who were diagnosed right after the delivery of their babies, but this was the first time I had two patients to treat—a mother and her unborn child. I did a core biopsy in the office the afternoon I met Dawn, and within twenty-four hours my worst fears were confirmed. Dawn was my first pregnant patient with breast cancer. Being a mother myself, I felt the horror of what this diagnosis would bring. My vulnerability from Chris and Lauren was now compounded. Even though I had no prior relationship to Dawn, we shared a very strong bond called motherhood.

The phone call to Dawn and Kevin was one of the most difficult phone calls I have ever made. In one short conversation, I took away all of the joy of an impending birth and changed their world forever. I knew I did not give Dawn her cancer, and I also knew I might not be able to take it away completely. This devastated me. In addition, I did not have enough information, and was unable to perform the normal staging procedures because of her pregnancy. The usual staging process involves x-ray studies and scans that could harm the baby. They would have to wait.

My priority was to make sure Dawn would have an uneventful delivery, as soon as possible. I called my friend Amy Harvey, who was a gynecologist in the practice where Dawn's mother-in-law worked. She took over

Dawn's obstetrical care. Amy needed to determine if the baby's lungs would be mature enough for delivery. Usually, the baby's lungs are ready for life outside the womb by thirty-nine weeks. But we did not have the luxury of time. We wanted to be sure no harm would come to this child, but also wanted the delivery to happen as soon as possible so I could begin treating Dawn. Amy gave Dawn steroids in order to prepare the baby's lungs for life outside the womb. When Dawn was thirty-four weeks pregnant, we felt it was safe to deliver the baby. Kevin Buck Jr. was born April 9, 1999. Baby Kevin was beautiful and healthy. Despite everything that was going on, it was a wonderful day for the Buck family.

Now that I only had one patient to treat, I began the process of evaluating Dawn's entire body with a computer-aided tomography (CT) scan of her chest, abdomen, pelvis, and a bone scan to complete the staging. Her bone scan was negative and I was thrilled with the good news. Before I shared the healthy bone scan results with the family, I tracked down the results for the CT scan. My worst fears were realized when I saw that her liver was riddled with metastatic breast cancer. This staged her cancer as Stage IV, meaning it had spread to distant areas in her body. It was no longer considered curable!

How would I ever be able to break the news to this wonderful young couple who were celebrating the birth of their healthy baby boy? I called Amy to inform her of the news because I needed emotional support before I went to talk to Kevin and Dawn. Amy and I were colleagues, professional teammates, friends, and spiritual soul buddies. That day the home team took a major hit. I could feel the vulnerability creep in again. I was unable to make sense of it all.

It's difficult to believe at times like this that God has a plan. What good could possibly come from this thirty-four-year-old woman finding out she has Stage IV breast cancer after just giving birth? At the time it was beyond my comprehension. I just couldn't understand how this could happen. I felt empty and helpless. I didn't want to let this family down. I wanted to make all of this badness go away for them, but I did not have the power to do so.

So began Dawn's year of chemotherapy, surgery, and motherhood. She was amazing throughout the entire ordeal. Her positive attitude and strength were nothing short of miraculous. She went through each cycle of chemo like a champ. All the while, she cared for her beautiful little son, Kevin, Jr., Dawn's tumors seemed to be responding to the therapy. She went on to have a mastectomy in the fall of 1999, and then started radiation. It was in the spring of 2000 when she was found to have progressive disease and started back on active chemotherapy.

Seeing Dawn at the Red Cross awards breakfast was the greatest honor I could have received that day. She came to thank me for all I had done for her, but it was I who owed her thanks for all she had given me. She taught me about the strength of the human spirit. Dawn persevered through chemo, surgery, and radiation so that she could be well and raise her son. She reminded me of how precious every day of life is, and that my children are my greatest treasures. Even when the cancer returned, she blamed no one. She simply asked what we could do to make it go away again. Dawn's presence was my gift that day. I didn't need to take home the hand-blown glass award. I had Dawn's smile imprinted forever in my memory banks as my award. Someone snapped a picture with Amy, Dawn and me. I will always cherish that picture.

Two weeks later, Dawn was hospitalized; her liver was failing. She had been planning baby Kevin's first birthday party for the following week. She needed an outfit to wear for the party. All of her dresses weren't fitting well because her abdomen had swollen from the fluid caused by the cancer. Amy and I took it upon ourselves to go shopping for an outfit. We were powerless to do anything medically, but we could go shopping and help her cross one more thing off of her list of things to do. We bought a beautiful blue dress for her to wear. We also bought her matching earrings to complete the ensemble. She loved the outfit and couldn't wait to wear it on her baby's first birthday, a party that Amy and I wouldn't have missed for the world. Dawn had a brief trip home from the hospital with just enough time to finish the plans for Kevin's party.

Dawn was re-admitted to the fourth floor oncology unit, which is used for inpatient chemotherapy, as well as for end of life compassionate care. Another friend, and long-term patient of mine, was admitted at the same time. Rosemarie Vassalluzzo, a prominent woman in the community, had been diagnosed eight years earlier with Stage IV breast cancer. Ro was married to Jules, a respected physician in our community. She had experienced a pathologic fracture of her hip that was related to her breast cancer. Occasionally, cancer spreads outside of the breast and is found when it attacks another area of the body. In Ro's case, her cancer caused a weakness in her hip bone that led to a break in the bone. Despite Stage IV disease at diagnosis, she had a long disease-free survival after her initial chemotherapy.

Ro was an award-winning horticulturalist and columnist for a local newspaper. She was very active in the community, specifically on the Foundation Board of the St. Mary Medical Center. A multi-talented woman and a trailblazer in the community, Ro was not shy about any subject and could be counted on to always speak the truth. Charming but not always politically correct, she was able to plan and complete any job single handedly. She was not simply my patient; she was another one of my role models.

Ro had developed an infection during her chemotherapy and was admitted to the oncology floor. She was so ill that we were making plans for hospice care at her home. I was emotionally preparing for her death as she had fought a very long battle with her cancer. I knew that her chemo and radiation had bought her valuable years to spend with her family. Although she was not old by any means, she had been present to raise her children, and see some of her grandchildren grow as well. Saying good-bye is never easy, but I felt closure as I prepared for what I thought would be our final days together. Her entire family had assembled at the hospital, things were far from optimistic. The decision had been made not to resuscitate her in the event her heart stopped.

I had been spending a lot of time that weekend on the oncology floor. I went into Ro's room and sat at her bedside. She was not conscious at that point. Her fever was very high and the antibiotics did not seem to be working. I sat with her, talking to her, knowing full well, on some level, she could hear me. I let her know how much respect I had for her and what a role model she was for me.

I had always wanted Ro's input into the backyard water garden I had been planning. I had purchased the pond kit two years earlier, but never had the time to start the project, not realizing that I had to make time for the things in life that are important. I left her room promising her I would make the time to construct my pond, and would always make the time for the projects and people in my life that make it worth living. I then said good-bye to a dear friend and patient. I ran into her husband, Jules, at the elevator and we held each other and cried.

Needless to say, this was an emotionally draining weekend. Two patients who I was so incredibly attached to were near death. With Ro I could make peace, I knew we had helped her to have seven years with her family that she might otherwise not have had. I had closure. I was willing to accept her death. With Dawn, I was sick, drained, and empty. I felt no closure. I was not at peace—far from it. The wound was gaping and raw.

Rosemarie would surprise us all. She turned a corner the next day and would recover from the infection. By Mother's Day that May my pond was well underway. Ro would not see my pond for another year. She had been doing so well and was busy enjoying the wonderful people in her family who were so important to her.

Dawn, however, would not be as fortunate. She died of liver failure just four days before her baby's first birthday. At the time I did not realize the impact Dawn's passing would have on my life. This would be the one loss that required a long period of healing for all involved. On the day that Dawn had planned for us to celebrate her son's first birthday, we attended a celebration of her life at her funeral.

73

At the time, I tried to rationalize Dawn's death. I didn't have the insight to find closure. It took me a long time to make peace with her loss. Would she have chosen to save herself by terminating her pregnancy if she had known she had breast cancer earlier in the pregnancy? Would it have made a difference? Why did she get pregnant while on the birth control pill? Was she meant to have baby Kevin to help her husband heal and survive her loss? These were questions that often flowed through my mind.

I have gone through my own healing process since the loss of Dawn. She certainly impacted my life in a positive way. I will always be grateful I participated in her care and in her healing. I feel Dawn was a guide in my life, an angel on earth. My desire to focus my practice on treating breast disease was reinforced by this experience. She touched my spirit and I felt her love as a patient, mother, wife, and friend. Had I put up a protective wall and distanced myself I could have been shielded from the pain I felt at her death. The love and energy we shared, however, was a far greater gift than any pain that came from the death of her body. Her spirit is alive and I think of her often when I am feeling overwhelmed. The obstacles in my life are nothing compared to what she faced. Although I would have to take small steps to get there, I knew in my heart I was headed in the right direction. I was keenly reminded once again to stay present in the moment.

On the day Dawn was buried, a gentle white snow fell upon us at the cemetery as we were placing pink roses on her coffin. I knew it was Dawn's way of letting us know that she was all right.

Through adversity we grow as individuals and spiritual beings. The adversity I encountered in treating

Dawn's cancer felt insurmountable at the time. Being an integral part of Dawn's journey took me on my own inner journey. It was a devastating blow to my doctor ego to feel the helplessness her breast cancer dealt me. We gave her the best treatment Western medicine had to offer and it wasn't enough. There are many times in life when we are unable to cure a disease, but even those patients that we can't cure need to find healing. Dawn found healing in her child. Baby Kevin kept her going even during the most difficult treatments. She was very much at peace knowing that her Kevins would have each other, even after she was no longer with them. She had found healing before her death, now I needed to find healing in my life.

In the beginning of May, I read an article about the Avon Breast Cancer 3-Day event. The article was about a woman who had participated in the event and it allowed her to heal the loss of her sister who had died from breast cancer. I needed to heal and I knew I needed to participate in this event. I enlisted my friend Beth Matlack to train and walk the three day, sixty mile event with me. She had known Dawn and knew how much this meant to me. We started to train that spring and began to raise more than $1,700 each to qualify to walk that fall in Atlanta, Georgia.

Obviously, there were a lot of things going on in my head at the time. I was trying to decide if my partnership could, would, or should be saved. I didn't want to make any hasty decisions that I would later regret. I was watching my dear friend, Christine, fall prey to an unnamed disease. I witnessed a miracle in Ro's recovery, and experienced a great loss in Dawn's passing from this life.

My eyes were now wide open; I just needed to exercise my free will. Only I could unveil my destiny and create my own path on this incredible inner journey that was unfolding.

## Chapter 7

## *Universal Energy*

The spring of 2000 brought tremendous change and much personal growth. As I mentioned earlier, I had been introduced to Reiki energy healing by my friends, Lauren and John. They found great comfort in Reiki during Lauren's initial cancer diagnosis and I was anxious to find out about it first hand. Reiki is an ancient form of Japanese energy healing that has been passed down for generations. It was referenced in 3000-year-old Sanskrit writings. Reiki involves channeling Universal (Rei) Energy (Ki) from the practitioner to a recipient. Soon I would become very familiar with this ancient art.

I became involved with the Holistic Health Program at St. Mary Medical Center by yet another synchronicity. A woman who was a Reiki master teacher was admitted to the hospital. I was asked to see her in consult for abdominal pain. After I reviewed her x-rays and completed her physical exam, I was not convinced she needed surgery. I wasn't even certain that she had diverticulitis (a localized infection of the colon). She seemed to be very distressed with her personal life. During my consult with her, I inquired about the stress she was under and its possible connection to the onset of her symptoms.

As we searched a little deeper, we were able to connect the onset of her symptoms with certain issues in her personal life. She had been unaware of the connection prior to our discussion. She felt better very quickly and was discharged the next day. I was not telling her anything that she didn't already know. All I did was help her to look at issues she needed to work on, and see them more clearly. She was amazed that a surgeon would take the time to delve into her life stress in order to find the root of her physical symptoms. She actually suggested that I read *Anatomy of the Spirit*, by Caroline Myss, which became a wonderful, insightful resource for me. Prior to reading *Anatomy of the Spirit*, I never really connected the energy centers of the body with physical disease processes. (I will elaborate on these energy centers later.)

Caroline gave me a new perspective on the relationship between emotional issues and physical symptoms. I had spent most of my adult life reading medical texts, and these lacked information about the connection between mind, body, and spirit. For this neophyte, Caroline's book was a welcome guide to holism.

The patient must have been truly moved by our encounter because she recommended me to the women who were initiating the Holistic Health Program at St. Mary. I was approached by Mary Anders* and Nancy Saxe, two pioneers who had initiated holistic healthcare at our facility. They had been given my name as a physician who would have an open mind to their program. At the time I was certainly open to complementary healing modalities, but I really had no experience from which to draw. I met with them and became interested in learning more about their vision for the future. I agreed to work with them on integrating holistic therapies into our institution.

My friend and colleague, Beth Matlack, who would go with me to the Avon 3-Day walk, had also decided to pursue training in Reiki therapy. She lost her mother to ovarian cancer when she was growing up, and thereafter assumed the role of family matriarch. I became friends with Beth as soon as I arrived on the scene at St. Mary. At the time, she was my partner's very favorite Physician's Assistant (PA) and I understand why. Not only is she an excellent assistant, Beth is a joy to work with. In the operating room, she would pitch in and perform any function to keep the OR schedule moving smoothly. In fact, Beth is so easy going that her nickname is "Pollyanna." I hadn't found out about her registering for the Level I Reiki course at the Holistic Center until the day before the course began. She told me about it while we were training for the Avon 3-Day.

My friend Lauren's experience with Reiki healing had certainly piqued my interest. At the time I didn't think I could train to be a Reiki healer until I had experienced it myself but Nancy, from the Holistic Center, assured me that it wasn't necessary to receive Reiki before learning to give Reiki. So, I enlisted my friend, the gynecologist Amy Harvey, and we signed up at the last minute for the Friday night and Saturday course—even though I was on call that weekend and was certain I'd be paged and unable to finish. As it turned out, I wasn't interrupted once during the course. (*You have to love the universal protection that arrives when you're on the right path!*) My angels must have been running interference with the pager towers.) Amy and I were both still in pain after the loss of Dawn. We hoped that Reiki could be a source of comfort in our lives.

The experience would affect the way I would look at every aspect of my life from that day forward. Reiki is about focusing Universal Energy on what you are doing. For me, one of the first results of the training was that I began to be more present with each patient. I would set an intention for the day and that helped me become more centered and balanced. Before embracing Reiki, I was guilty of allowing distractions in my daily life get the best of me at times. My attention was not as focused or clear as it was after learning Reiki.

Don't get me wrong, when performing surgery my focus and attention has always been with the patient. Patients rely on my judgment and surgical skills, which can be stressful to say the least. Their lives are in my hands. There were times when stress would bring me to a breaking point. Before Reiki became a part of my practice, I was guilty of trying to be all things to all people and didn't know how to set limits. There had been occasions when I was so pushed to my personal limits that the nurses in the OR would give me a time-out to alleviate tension in the room and allow it to dissipate. They would politely tell me that I needed to go to the corner of the room and sit on a stool until I was ready to pro- ceed. (*It was a figurative time-out but I got the message loud and clear.*) I am proud to say that I have not been placed in time-out for years. This may be because I am now able to see when the stress level is rising, and I have the skills to quiet my mind and change the energy in the room.

Now I am able to give one hundred percent of my attention to my patients, whether I am operating on them or evaluating them, without being distracted. Additionally, I practice Reiki on my patients while they are being placed under anesthesia. I don't feel the need to share this fact with them because I find they benefit from Reiki whether they believe in it or not. I have had innumerable patients comment that they have felt what I call the life force just as they drifted off to sleep. They have told me they feel a tremendous sense of calm and peace, which makes the surgical experience a positive encounter. Several studies on the power of prayer or positive intention have shown there is benefit to patients when these modalities are employed. The patients were not told that they were being prayed for but the results are indisputable, they fared better than those not prayed for. Whether you call it prayer, positive intention, Reiki, or whatever fits, the results are real. There is no mistaking the power of two humans connecting on a spiritual plane. I can't think of a better time to share this experience then when someone is entrusting me with his or her life. I am honored and humbled to be a part of their healing process.

After my Reiki Level I course, I was eager to share the experience with my family. My son, Tommy was the first person to receive Reiki from me. I placed a very

81

soothing CD on the stereo and began the session with him. He could immediately feel the energy transfer from my hands, which were two to three inches above his body. The field of energy between us was incredibly strong. At the mid-point of our session the CD player stopped for a few moments and then restarted. My husband thought it was an electrical problem because it was raining outside, but I knew it was a result of the energy transfer between our two energy powerhouses. At this point on my journey, I knew that there are no coincidences; the CD stopping was just confirmation of the energy transfer in the room. Tommy had been lying directly in front of the player. If the storm had caused the player to stop the whole house would have been in darkness!

Later that day, Joe was able to experience Reiki, and although he didn't say much, I think his mind was opened to the idea of Ki and Universal Energy. My sweet little Dean was still young enough to remember what Universal Energy is, even if he didn't know what it was called. He enjoyed the experience of sharing it with me as only a young child, still in touch with the powers of nature, can. One evening around that same time, while I put soon-to-be-four-year-old Dean to bed, he reminded me, "Mom you can heal with your hands, you don't need to use a knife." Out of the mouth of my baby came profound wisdom.

Our society tends to shut down the amazing gifts our children have to teach us. Children's actions come from hearts that are so pure. Sharing Reiki with my sons, and feeling their energy, was such a confirmation that I was well on the way to opening my own heart to healing. As children, my sons had no pressure from society about what they should feel or experience with Reiki. Simply put, they had not shut down spiritually, as so many adults in our society have done. (I used to be one of those adults.) I now remembered my spiritual connectedness and had a voracious appetite for more knowledge. I always tell my patients that knowledge empowers and fear paralyzes. I wanted more knowledge to run full steam ahead.

My days that summer were very full: training for the Avon 3-Day, reading every book that crossed my path on spirituality and healing, being a mom, and making plans for my new practice. I had also reached a deeper understanding about how I could promote healing using complementary modalities like Reiki, hand-in-hand with surgery. I no longer fit in. I was the one who had changed and I didn't expect my old practice to change to meet me. It was during that summer I came to terms with the realization that I needed to move on in many ways. I knew I needed to follow through with a professional change that would require a tremendous amount of effort. Joe was overwhelmingly busy setting up a new corporation, while I was delving deeper into books on medical intuition, energy healing, meditation, hypnosis, and anything else that would enhance my potential as a healer.

My entire extended family went to the beach early that August and stayed in a home my parents rented, one block from the ocean in Bethany Beach, Delaware. Early in the week, while I was walking through a small local bookstore, a copy of *Talking to Heaven*, by James Van Praagh fell off the bookshelf and landed in front of me. I picked it up and after reading the cover, I knew this was a book I wanted to read. It is a wonderful book about

83

the life of a spiritually gifted individual who helped so many people heal from the loss of a loved one. I had embraced reincarnation, and now insight from a medium was the next step in my evolutionary process. I was quite pleased that the book had presented itself to me so clearly by falling off the shelf. My sister who was with me in the bookstore, commented about what a coincidence it was that a book I would want to read fell right in front of me. Was it a coincidence? I think not.

I read this wonderful collection of healing stories in less than a day. What a gift James Van Praagh has to connect with so many people who lack closure after the loss of a loved one. I loved reading stories of James's channeling and the love and peace it brought the families and individuals who went to see him. I was very moved by his work and it helped heal the many losses I have had in my own life. Although I loved the stories and the peace he brought to families, I had never personally witnessed channeling, or messages from a deceased relative given through a human medium. I wanted to completely embrace channeling but the "show me" person wanted to have first-hand experience. Seeing James channel in person was now on my list of things to do. That would be the proof I needed. At the time I had no clue, but I would have more validation in my life that channeling was real in the months to come.

James suggested in the book to keep a dream journal right beside the bed in order to write down dreams. He feels, as do many other gifted healers and spiritualists, that dreams are one way the spirit world and our subconscious communicate openly. All we need to do is to document these messages upon rising in the morning before we forget the content. I immediately set out on a mission to find an appropriate book to serve as a dream journal. As fate would have it, I found a silver covered journal with black pages equipped with a silver pen. The cover read, "My Dream Journal." It was destined to be mine, I was certain. I purchased the journal for myself as well as additional journals for my sister Amy and girl-friends from the Florida trip, Dina and Amy Harvey. I believe that when you find something new that is insightful, it should be shared with friends.

If you had told me just two years earlier that I would be reading books on channeling, regression hypnothera-py or Reiki healing, I would have told you, "That's a nice thought but you've mistaken me for a Woodstock hold-over!" Had I not lived the experiences unfolding right before my eyes I would have been a vocal skeptic. One synchronicity was leading into the next. I wondered how many synchronous occurrences in my life I just glossed over because I simply wasn't paying attention. Once I opened my eyes it was amazing how much I was able to see. My dream journal was my first step toward the chronicle of my spiritual awakening.

I had my dream journal; now all I had to do was start dreaming. The first few mornings after purchasing the journal, while still at the beach, I logged my dreams. I am sure Freud would have had a field day with my dreams. The first dream was about going back to medical school and starting over. In this dream, Joe thought I needed to go to Harvard and repeat my education and residency. *That is what I would consider a nightmare!*

I wonder now if the dream was really about starting my education as a healer. With the shift in focus toward healing, I would need to see the individual as a whole. It would require seeing the mind, body, and spirit of each person as equal and interrelated components. I would need to shift gears and give equal credence to the mind and spirit of my patients, as well as their physical body.

In medical school I was taught to take a history, examine a patient, and evaluate laboratory and x-ray studies. From this I would treat symptoms and work toward a cure. I was now beginning to see the importance of *listening* to my patient's story in addition to examining their physical body and critically looking at their studies. I wasn't getting rid of my Western medical training, instead I was enhancing what I did by looking at my patients as whole beings. Sometimes the root of the real problem is very distant from the symptoms a patient presents. In order to truly find healing, all aspects of the mind, body, and spirit need to be evaluated. My interpretation of this dream was just another confirmation about the future of my path as a doctor.

On August 6, I woke from a deep sleep after having a most vivid dream. Chris O'Donnell, my girlfriend with the failing body and unnamed disease, was calling me, but I couldn't answer the phone. In the dream the phone would ring, and I could see it, but I couldn't answer it. I documented the dream but didn't make an attempt to analyze the message it held. At this point it was not as important for me to decipher the dream as it was to write it down. I wrote the message and then went about enjoying my time with my family on the beach.

When I returned from the beach, I checked messages on the answering machine at home. On August 5, Chris had called my house twice looking for me! She sounded distraught and made it clear she really needed to speak with me. I thought it very odd at first, then realized it was another synchronicity. She had left a message the same night I had dreamed she was calling me and I couldn't answer.

I called her back that afternoon and she was indeed distraught. Her doctors had finally come to the conclusion that her symptoms were definitely related to Lou Gehrig's disease (ALS). To this day I feel the gravity of those three letters and how they destroy a life. Labels can be awful and this ALS label was the worst I had experienced in my medical career. ALS results in progressive muscle weakness and loss of normal function. As the body deteriorates, the mind remains sharp and clear. The individual with the disease, becomes a spiritual being locked in a body that has failed. The disease has no cure. That afternoon, for the first time since she started manifesting her symptoms, we allowed ourselves to cry together.

What do you say to a friend who has just been given a diagnosis that is a death sentence? I could do nothing medically to help cure this disease, but I offered my spiritual and emotional support. Before this, Chris had thought we, my spiritual buddies and I, were slightly *out there*, but now she wanted to go out there with us. Chris, the physician, who at this point could find no answers or comfort in science, needed to understand what was happening to her. She asked if I could give her the "Cliff Notes" on spiritual enlightenment to get her up to speed with the rest of us.

Shortly thereafter, Amy and I made a road trip to Barnes and Noble bookstore to buy Chris copies of the books we had been reading during the previous two years. We gave her tapes on relaxation, hypnosis, and self-healing. We also asked if she would like to participate in our Reiki "shares," group Reiki sessions in which we'd get together and share Reiki energy. She was quite anxious to get involved now. We scheduled a Reiki Level I course to get things moving. This special Reiki session for Chris also included my friends Lauren, Beth Matlack, Amy Harvey, and Barb Schlager, who is a radiation oncologist I worked with at St. Mary. Lauren's neighbor, Sandy, a forty-two year-old woman who was being treated for glioblastoma multiform (an incredibly aggressive brain tumor) joined the group as well. Nancy, the Reiki master teacher, was the facilitator.

There was a period right after Chris's diagnosis when we would talk about her disease and how it could potentially be cured. She had looked into experimental drugs, research trials and also considered that we might be onto something with our new found energy healing. Chris had hoped as did I that through Reiki, or another Eastern healing form, we would be able to eradicate her disease. We had magical thinking of sorts. She thought that perhaps we were going to be able to cure her and share our knowledge with the world. I know now that our lesson was in the healing, not the curing. I support-ed Chris in her decisions to try experimental drugs while, at the same time, we pursued our spiritual sup-port group.

This support group began as a way to take on the process of finding healing for our old friend, Christine, and our new friend, Sandy—a daunting task considering what these women were facing. At the same time, we were all finding support of some kind. Those of us in per-fect health were learning to heal the powerlessness we felt as doctors who could not cure our friend's diseases.

Perspective is an interesting educational tool in life. So often we lack perspective when we measure the magnitude of events in our daily lives. We become frustrated or angry about small things that are really of no consequence in the face of the big picture. "Don't sweat the small stuff," was becoming my daily mantra. My perspective on so many things in my life has been shaped by so few. What Lauren endured with her brain cancer and what Chris was about to face with her disease, were monumental compared to what I thought was difficult in my own life. I had my health, my family's support, and my passion. I had no major obstacles.

I've learned many lessons in my life, but one that now came loud and clear was that we are never guaranteed tomorrow. I needed to make changes in my life right away and not wait for the perfect moment. It was crystal clear. I was making the correct choice to move on professionally. Opportunities rarely just happen; sometimes you need to create your own destiny, and I was now ready and willing to create mine.

After making the decision to leave the practice, and knowing that this time I would follow my heart, I felt it best to move into my new location as soon as it was available. The doctors who were currently in the office suite I wanted were waiting for their new space to be completed. Although I proceeded to move forward with my plans, I wanted to choose when and how I would tell my partner that I was making the change. It was my fervent hope that I could make this as smooth a transition as possible for the staff.

Unfortunately, through a series of events beyond my control, my partner found out about my pending office space before I could tell him myself. My hope for a smooth transition faded away. This was to be a very difficult time for both of us and for our staff. Although I knew I was absolutely making the appropriate changes in my life, I was still very attached and connected to the wonderful elements of the old practice. I needed to let go of what was once safe and move forward with integrity. I drew strength from my Reiki support group. I was on solid ground with a strong foundation; a luxury my friends did not have because of their illnesses.

## Chapter 8

# *Life is a Journey*

# *Not a Destination*

Octuber 1 was our target date for opening the new office. It would be a long six weeks while I remained in practice with my former partner. Change is difficult even in the best of situations. This was a stressful time for all parties involved. We were attempting to have a smooth transition but feelings were at stake. I hadn't realized just how trying this change in my life would actually be.

How difficult it is to not take things personally. *The Four Agreements*, written and taught by Don Miguel Ruiz, a South American surgeon turned healing teacher, are simple yet profound rules that every person could live by:

1. Be impeccable with your words
2. Do not take things personally
3. Do not make assumptions
4. Always do your best

How difficult Number Two is to follow in real life. It is difficult to not take things personally. I was responsible for the changes being experienced by everyone involved in the practice. I knew from a very deep place in my soul that I had made the correct decision. Now I was feeling the impact of my decision on others. (I've made *The Four Agreements* required reading for all employees who work in my present practice and the agreements are plastered on the walls of my office.) I believe the agreements should be required reading for the human race. If we all followed these agreements, we would live in a magnificent world. They are not rules; they are agreements that each individual must agree to uphold within him or herself, leading to personal accountability. If they were practiced, there would be no blame, guilt, lies or suboptimal effort. Utopia! I think that is what they call that place. I certainly need practice upholding the agreements in my life and that is why they are plastered all over my office. I cannot expect my staff to live up to them if I do not try my best to do so. I started by doing my best to pull together a team to work with me in my new practice. I wanted a staff that works *with* me not *for* me.

In the middle of August, while walking through the mammography department in the outpatient facility, I met one of my patients. Donna had been diagnosed with breast cancer two years before, and on this day she was getting her annual mammogram. I took a few minutes to read her films and was happy to tell her that everything was fine. After we hugged in celebration, she made a profound comment: "When you start your own practice, I want to work for you." I was floored by her words because there had been no public knowledge of the impending changes in my practice. She told me she just had a feeling it was coming.

After we spoke for a few minutes, I realized that Donna would be a perfect hire for the new practice. Donna was a woman who had experienced an abnormal mammogram and subsequent treatment; she would know exactly how to handle my patients with compassion, discretion, and empathy. She knew the fear and anguish a woman feels when faced with a potential breast cancer diagnosis. She knew what it was like to wait weeks for an appointment just to be evaluated. She knew what the journey of a cancer diagnosis entails. I went home that day and told Joe we had a new employee and he'd have to meet her. I was convinced that my chance meeting with Donna was anything but accidental, it was synchronistic. Donna was hired as a receptionist. I wanted her to be the first voice my new patients heard when they called the office worried about test results, the first face they saw when they came into the office frightened by what lay ahead.

Joe and I continued to work toward our goal of an October 1 start date for the new practice, and I continued to work on my personal goal of completing the Avon 3-Day. Our support group also continued Reiki shares with Chris while she looked for experimental protocols for ALS. Chris's journey lead our entire Reiki group on a journey to find true healing. My journey included what was to be a very long yet enlightening walk. I had no way of anticipating just how a sixty-mile walk could impact my growth. After months of training and fundraising, the Avon Breast Cancer 3-Day finally arrived. What an amazing event. I am proud to say I not only participated, but I completed the journey. It was an event that empowered healing for all who took part, whether by walking the distance or by providing medical and ancillary support.

The three days began on a rainy Thursday, September 20, 2000—also my husband's birthday—with our arrival in Atlanta, Georgia. Beth Matlack and I arrived at the airport and Beth's sister, Alison, greeted us there. She was responsible for transporting us to Beth's brother, Christopher, who then helped us on the initial leg of our journey to Lake Lanier.

When we arrived, we quickly became educated about the ins and outs of the next three days. It was pouring rain. My clothes and shoes were soaked. I had packed all of my rain gear in my suitcase, which was still in Christopher's trunk. Silly me, thinking we would be indoors to register! We received our ID badges and a checklist of items that needed to be accounted for in order for us to be completely registered. All donation information had to be submitted prior to the event. We turned in our pledge packets and were off to the tent assignment area. After we stood in the rain for another half an hour, we found out we needed to watch a safety video and get our cards stamped before we would be given a tent assignment.

The safety video viewing line had an hour-long wait. Again we stood in the pouring rain and soaked up

Atlanta's wetness. Ironically, the lake we were starting from was nearly completely dried up from a drought that year. Great weekend for the universe to decide to replenish the water supply! On the upside, we had the pleasure of meeting some really wonderful people while waiting in line. The group directly in front of us was clearly a small circle of friends united in a noble cause. The ringleader and instigator of the pack was a woman called Amy (yes, still another Amy in my life). She was the tie that bound this crew together. A stay-at-home soccer mom, Amy had initiated this adventure among her friends. She was upbeat, positive, and always found a bright spot in even the dreariest of moments. Amy had recruited her friend, Laura, who was the proverbial naysayer. She is a diehard democrat who works in Atlanta. She would celebrate her thirtieth birthday during the walk on September 22, which was my little Deano's fourth birthday.

Next we had Judy…Judy…Judy! This woman actually made me look slow, low-energy, and quiet. Ha! She was along to keep things moving and to keep the troops in line. The fourth, and certainly not last, member of this pack was Terry. She was a solid athlete, solid human being, and a bundle of positive energy. The group had trained together, all but Laura, who never really trained. She was going on this sixty-mile, three day adventure cold. These ladies were our safety video pick-ups. Little did we know that they would become our allies and partners.

The safety video should have been renamed the "Watch Out or You Could Die" video. The video portrayed several potential scenarios which could end in death if we were not careful. What viewing this video did for Beth

95

and me, was to allow time for us to bond with these four women. We were about to embark on a three-day journey that had many obstacles and unknowns. I was overwhelmed and didn't quite know what to expect. I imagined how my patients must feel overwhelmed by unknowns when they are about to face chemotherapy, surgery and radiation. Just as my patients need a support team for their cancer journey, I needed my 3-Day support team as well. With the team in place, we moved forward. Completing the safety video got us the stamp we needed to receive our tent assignment. Oh, yes, and allowed us to get out of the rain for forty minutes.

We headed for the tent assignment area and found another line and a thirty-minute wait this time. But we had new friends and interesting conversation to keep us occupied. Had we known then what we knew later in the weekend about the impending weather, we would have skipped this line. We would never see the inside of a tent or the heralded Tent City. The 3-Day is famous for the meticulous set up and organization of the tents. Imagine, 3000 tents arranged equidistant from the next, all made of the same material. Then add surrounding tents for food, entertainment, medical attention and relaxation. We did wait in line, however, and received our tent assignment and all of our identifying tags. We were dismissed and told to return at 5:00 A.M. for our final check-in and the opening ceremonies. By the end of this initial experience it was dark, we were cold, tired, and hungry—and this was the *easy* day!

*Two, four, six, eight, hydrate, stretch and urinate!* This was my mantra during the Avon 3-Day. Arriving at Lake Lanier on Friday morning could best be described as controlled chaos. It was damp, but thank God, the rain had temporarily halted. The opening ceremonies were extremely moving, and all of the walkers participated in a group stretch to get warmed up. Then boom, we were off and walking. (No running allowed—it was in the safety video.) The morning was relatively uneventful. Everyone was just trying to get their walking rhythms. We had hoped to see a familiar face or two in the crowd, but it was virtually impossible to find even one of them in the crowd of 2,700 participants.

We walked the first five miles in a gentle mist and mild breezes. We stopped every three miles to hydrate, stretch, and urinate, as directed by the safety video. As the morning progressed the mist turned into a steady light rain. At about the six-mile mark, the rain began to come down harder and the winds followed. By the time we arrived at the mid-point lunch break, I was soaking wet, cold, and I needed to take off all my clothing in the Jiffy John just to try and get dry. I stripped buck naked and wrung out my clothes, thinking that moderately wet was better than soaking wet. At this point my cell phone, and emergency credit card were the only dry things I owned.

After lunch we had the great fortune to reconnect with the safety video crew, and what a pick-me-up meeting that turned out to be. We were literally fighting the winds and rain, trudging up and down the rolling hills of Georgia, tired, wet, and cold, but able to go on because of the encouraging chants led by Judy and Terry. At every rest stop they serenaded the entire pit crew and fellow walkers with, *two, four, six, eight, hydrate, stretch and urinate.* As we walked they composed our theme chant entitled, "The Twelve Gifts of Walking." It went something like: "On the first day of walking, Avon gave to me…"

It was late that first afternoon when we had our initial encounter with the Lone Wolf, also known as Jaime Butler. (I would not know her proper name during the Avon 3-Day, but a little over a year later we would be reconnected.) She was an independent driven individual who believed in her cause. She chose to walk alone even though her friends had backed out of the event. I was very attracted to her enthusiasm and spirit. Walking the distance alone was the exception not the norm. It isn't easy blazing trails alone. I could completely relate to her desire to make a difference by walking the 3-Day; I felt I was doing the same thing by changing my medical practice. She didn't share details of her life with me that weekend, but she shared her energy, her essence, and that was our connection.

The Lone Wolf was sporting pigtail braids and a T-shirt that was imprinted with large block letters stating:

BREASTS
Now that I have your attention
I am walking
In honor and in memory of. . . .

This was followed by a list names. These were people she loved that had been affected by breast cancer. She was wearing a pair of Birkenstock-type sandals, with gym socks, that made her quite a sight. Best of all, she was a chanter and helped lead our little group of walkers in many uplifting chants. Actually, she had a military style to her chanting which led me to believe that we had missed a turn somewhere along the route and were now in boot camp. We were all walking at the same speed, so we spent a good portion of Day One with the Lone Wolf in tow.

It was also on day one that I became privy to the details of Laura's ovarian cancer. It was clear to me that her treatment experience had been very traumatic for her. It was also painfully obvious that her attending physicians had been so focused on curing her cancer, they forgot about the young woman inhabiting her body who also needed to be healed. Because of her cancer, she had lost her ability to bear children and experienced the emotional as well as physical changes that premature menopause brings. From what she shared, it sounded like these losses were downplayed by those who treated her. My heart felt heavy for all the pain Laura had carried with her. Years after her surgical scars had healed, inner wounds remained that were raw and in need of healing. She needed more than Western medicine had given her to date. Clearly, a surgical cure did not guarantee an emotional or spiritual healing.

Everyone wanted to know what would motivate a surgeon to leave her husband and son on their birthday weekend to participate in this grueling event, and so I shared Dawn Buck's story with them. When I explained that I needed to walk in order to heal from the loss of Dawn, Laura looked at me with a puzzled expression, "What do you mean, heal the loss?"

How *does* a healer heal? I have told myself over and over again that, even though I cannot cure cancer in every person I treat, I can still help them by supporting them on their journey to healing. Laura was reminding me of this important life lesson. I knew that I hadn't failed with Dawn; I just needed to be reminded that healing was equally important as curing a disease. Years after the successful treatment of Laura's cancer I could also help her to reach a safe place. This was also part of my journey, my awakening, and my healing.

The weather that day could only be described as a hurricane. Torrential rain, high winds, and bad road conditions prevailed. Walking was a struggle. I asked myself, *Could this be something like what my patients feel with each and every chemotherapy treatment? If it is, how do they get up and drive to the next session, knowing what lies ahead for them?* I felt I had reached a new level of understanding. This walk was by no means as grueling as chemotherapy, but each phase seemed to add insult to injury. I could only imagine the emotions that would swirl through my patient's minds as they mustered the energy to go back for more chemo, knowing what lay ahead. I realized that they would have to stay focused on the benefits of chemotherapy: the potential eradication of their cancer, overall health, and wellness.

I kept focusing on the fact that at the end of the twenty-four miles there would be hot food, a dry place to sleep, and dry clothing. Dry and warm would be heaven compared to this cold rain. In order to reach my destination, I needed to stay in the moment, taking the miles one step at a time. During the three days, I didn't think about all of the things that needed to be done to start my new practice. I was completely in survival mode.

We arrived at the designated campsite to find it under a foot of water. It was a bump in the road no one anticipated. The area was completely unsuitable for sleeping outside. I was crushed, emotionally and physically. Clearly the company that had organized the 3-Day had not planned for the hurricane. No alternative sleeping plans had been made for the 2,700 walkers. There was a large medical tent set up to treat hypothermia, blisters, and exhaustion. We arrived to find our fellow participants wrapped in foil blankets, huddled together for warmth.

As medical director for our group of friends, I was chosen to take Laura to the medical tent to be treated for blisters. Her feet were in very bad shape. Her blisters were bringing up memories of her earlier cancer treatment. I was becoming involved in her healing process whether I wanted to be or not. Laura's blisters were a reflection of underlying issues. She had never been empowered to find healing after the cancer ordeal she had experienced. No one had taken the time to teach her to look within and find the healing she so clearly needed. Now it was all coming to the surface. She was deathly afraid of needles and she reacted with intense fear when the podiatrist wanted to drain one of the larger blisters. She refused treatment at the medical tent.

We left and waited for transport buses to take us to the local high school, which was to become our makeshift tent city. Tired, wet, and hungry, we persevered. Our bags were lost in transit somewhere between the campground-turned-lake, and the high school that would be our home for the night. We had no dry clothing, no food, and Laura could barely walk because of her blisters. I was able to talk Laura into going back to the medical personnel when we got to the high school. Unfortunately, there was a two-hour wait for treatment. I used my credentials to talk a young podiatrist into giving me a crash course in, Blister Care 101. With the necessary medical supplies to carry out the treatment, I was able to help Laura.

I couldn't believe how deeply afraid Laura was. A part of me wanted to say that they were only blisters, for

God's sake. But I was at a point in my evolution where I realized that these blisters represented so much more to Laura. The needles brought her right back to her traumatic cancer experience. The needles took her back to her surgery and the complications she experienced. Her body had a cellular memory of those events that continued to wreak havoc with her psyche long after the experience had passed. Cellular memory is a phenomenon where certain experiences can evoke a genuine physical response. For instance, patients have shared with me that as they approach a facility where they once received chemotherapy, nausea will again overwhelm them. It is a true visceral response. Cellular memory can occur in a positive sense as well. The smell of bread baking can catapult us back to grandmother's kitchen reminding us of childhood. Laura's cellular memory took her to a place she didn't want to revisit. Laura's fear paralyzed her from receiving the help she desperately needed. I knew that she needed to trust me, allowing me to see the vulnerable young women who still needed healing. As she began to trust, I used Reiki to help get her into a psychological place that felt safe, and it worked. She allowed me to help her. I felt empowered using my Reiki training to put her at ease, and Laura was relieved to have someone attend to her who genuinely cared.

It was 9:30 P.M. It was clear that dinner was not going to be served any time soon; the possibility of getting our bags was bleak. I used my unauthorized cell phone to call a local hotel, and secured reservations for our party of six with my contraband credit card. We would be spending the night at the La Quinta Hotel in God Only Knows Where, Georgia. The next feat was to get a ride to the hotel. The parking lot outside the school was a mad house. The taxi we called had little or no chance of finding us amidst the chaos and rain.

We instituted our own Plan B+. We left the school and found a bus that was leaving the parking lot. We pleaded with the driver to give us a ride to the hotel. She was very sweet and agreed to be our secret taxi. We were about to board the bus when we had the great fortune of collecting our bags from the delivery trucks, which had just arrived. Timing is everything! As we boarded the bus, we thanked our driver for her act of kindness and asked her name. "Angel, dahlins, my name is Angel," she drawled. As if I didn't already know she was an angel! We stopped at Pizza Hut on the way to the hotel and Angel let us buy her dinner. One, Meat-Lovers pizza was all she would accept for her generosity.

At Pizza Hut we encountered two more refugees from the high school, Maggie and her friend, Tina. Their family members had rescued them and brought them out for dinner. We informed them about the chaos at the school, and they decided to follow our lead and spend the night at the same hotel. We were picking up new friends at every turn.

Never underestimate the importance of a hot shower, clean clothing, and a soft warm bed. Not to mention pizza, a slice of heaven from a cardboard box. By the time we fell asleep, it was nearly one o'clock in the morning. We needed to be up, packed, and ready to roll at 5:30 A.M. Peeling our worn bodies from the sheets four hours later was nothing short of miraculous. It felt as though we had just fallen asleep when the alarm sounded and we were off again.

We were dry, clean, and had a few hours of shut-eye under our belts, so none of us complained. We arrived

103

back at the school and were pleasantly surprised to find a hot breakfast waiting for us. Somehow during the night, they had transformed the school into 3-Day Central and were organized. Just before dawn, after depositing our belongings at the school, we started out on Day Two. Our group was now eight-strong and we felt ready to conquer the world.

The weather had shifted. On Day Two we would broil, with one hundred percent humidity, in the hot sun of Atlanta. The medical emergencies for that day shifted from hypothermia to heatstroke and dehydration. Laura's blisters were still the main medical emergency in our group. We made frequent stops to re-assess her feet and rewrap the blisters. Neither rain, nor wind, nor searing sun could keep our group from having fun. We took every opportunity to serenade the police officers, who stopped traffic to let us pass safely. We would each drop to one knee, hand over heart, and sing, "Baby, baby, I get down on my knees for you . . . if you won't love me like you used to do." Well, you get the idea. We were loving life and celebrating the moment.

The day's walk was challenging, we were tired and the sun was cooking our worn bodies. Laura worked so hard to keep up, and at every rest stop I had to drain her new blisters, all the while working with her needle phobia. Each time it became easier to calm her. She knew what to expect, there were no surprises, and therefore her fear was dissipating. The knowledge she was gaining about blister care made it easier for her to face the pain from the needle.

We ended up walking with the Lone Wolf again that afternoon. She had squirt guns loaded with cold water and she loved using them. She reminded me of Pippy

Longstocking. She was walking by herself, yet she was not lonely. She and I never really had an in-depth conversation; we just sang songs and repeated chants to keep up the spirit of the group. I sensed a really genuine energy in her. She was brave enough to take on the sixty-mile adventure all by herself. We learned as we walked together, that the friends she was supposed to walk with had backed out at the last minute. The way I see it, the Lone Wolf was amazing in taking on this challenge alone. We bonded on a very spiritual level that did not require dialogue to make a connection. She was on a mission of sorts and I could relate. Day Two was well underway and our walk was going as planned, that is, until lunch.

That afternoon will always be ingrained in my cellular memory. We had just finished lunch and I had wrapped Laura's feet. We had barely left the parking lot and she was unable to go on. She needed her bandages loosened, and I motioned her to come over to a stone wall so I could rest my back while she sat on the ground. She gave me her foot and I began the process of re-dressing her blisters. A few seconds into the job, I jumped off the wall screaming in pain. An army of fire ants were feasting on my thighs and butt. My companions emptied their water bottles over me as if I were on fire. Within minutes my legs and buttocks swelled and were covered in hives. I broke into my medicine stash and took 75 mg of Benadryl, hoping to alleviate the hives and swelling from the histamine release. I knew full well it would make me tired but my body was in dire straights. I could not help but think: *Here I am at an event supporting breast cancer survivors that comes equipped with wicked side effects, mimicking those of chemotherapy and radiation.* Still, I kept plugging on, thinking that this was nothing compared to what my cancer patients endure during their treatment phase. My awareness was increasing by the minute.

Toward the end of Day Two, Laura faced a difficult time. Her feet were in such bad shape she could not go on. She had to be picked up by the Sweeper Van in order to make it back to the school for the night. She saw this as defeat, but we saw it as just needing to take care of, "de feet!" If she had any intention of completing the third day of the event, she would have to rest her worn out dogs. I would have quit miles before she did if my feet were in that condition. Beth and I were blessed to have avoided any blisters. I think this was Dawn's protection and I thanked her spirit for watching over us on our mission. I wouldn't have been on the walk had it not been for Dawn and I had a sense of her presence with us on our journey.

I found Laura in the medical facility when I arrived back at our camp/high school. She wanted to leave and go back to the hotel. She felt defeated and wanted to run away. I encouraged her to stay within the 3-Day energy and hear some of the other participants' stories. I knew hearing how much others have endured on their paths might help Laura to get a new perspective on her journey. She agreed to stay and it was the right decision. We laughed, shared stories, shared medical supplies, and most importantly, we shared a bond of love and trust that comes from going through something challenging together.

Day Three was much less traumatic, even though we were all physically and emotionally exhausted. The weather was still hot and humid. Our mantra, chanted in unison, *Two, four, six, eight, hydrate, stretch and urinate*, was mandatory at every two mile mark. Our bodies were aching but we could all see the light at the end of the tunnel. We had a deadline on Day Three. We needed to be in the stadium in time for the closing ceremonies. If we fell behind, we would be "swept" and would not be able to walk into the stadium for the festivities with everyone else. The pressure on Laura was palpable. Some of our friends were getting self-centered and whispered hints of leaving the slower people behind if they couldn't keep up with the group. Exhaustion was setting in and the heat wasn't helping us keep our cool.

We ran into the Lone Wolf, and it couldn't have been at a better time. It was after lunch and we were having trouble getting our momentum back. Along came the Lone Wolf and, in her boot camp style, she led our group in singing and chanting to the end. She was a gift that appeared in our hour of need. She was playing such an important motivating role on this journey and we didn't even know her real name.

Arriving at the finish line was anticlimactic. This was because the bonding, that came through shared experience with all these wonderful women, was what had mattered most, not crossing the finish line. Just as I was discovering in my practice: although the treatment of my patient's cancer is the goal of the medical care I offer, the journey the patient and I take as partners, and maintaining focus in the moment, is what allows healing to truly begin. Healing is truly about the journey, not the destination.

We were cheered and welcomed as we entered the holding area. There was a reception area where we received long-sleeved navy blue T-shirts, which identified us as 3-Day finishers. We donned our hot shirts in the brutal Atlanta sun and headed into the stadium. During the procession, Beth and I became caregivers; many participants who weren't adequately hydrated were dropping from heat exhaustion and required emergency medical attention. We had to use our T-shirts as pillows to cushion their heads from the ground. That day we made a promise to one other to work on the medical crew when the 3-Day came to Philadelphia. We could see how hard the medical crew worked, and we wanted to repay our gratitude by crewing ourselves. Beth remarked how awesome it would be if the Philadelphia 3-Day coincided with the opening of our Breast Care Center. I told her I loved the idea, but that my dream of a comprehensive breast care center was years away. She reminded me that there are no coincidences and that she was sure I would make it happen. We were ancillary medical crew that day, but the medical crew directorship was in my future.

I cannot describe the emotions we felt walking into the stadium. They were profound. I still fill up with tears when I see advertisements and video clips of any Avon Breast Cancer 3-Day closing ceremony. That's my cellular memory at work! When we lined the field and the survivors marched into the area—a wall of pink overtaking the stadium—it seemed the entire city of Atlanta was engulfed in tears. Next came the amazing support and medical personnel, and another cheer rang out. We thought we had adversity on this journey, but they had to completely revamp their entire program to accommodate Mother Nature and 2,700 walkers. Sure, we had to camp out in a high school science lab, but they didn't sleep at all. It was a life-changing event for all of us. I am still learning from that collective experience.

The 3-Day solidified my desire to focus my practice on the care and treatment of diseases of the breast. It was a direction I had been slowly drifting toward for years but now I knew I would have to take the leap, strap on my wings, and fly with it. It was as though I had gone through the kind of life transformation that cancer brings, without having to experience the cancer. By relating to my patients, through their disease, I saw that they had become my guides, helping me to come to a deeper understanding of what I needed in my life.

I had reached a cliff in my professional life, just as my patients reach a similar point around the end of their treatment. I teach my patients that when the medical treatment is complete, they have two choices as they look over the cliff into the next part of their lives. They can choose to put on wings and soar or they can close their eyes and fall, not knowing where they might land. No one returns to the life they had before cancer. It is impossible, too much has changed. It is particularly important for caregivers to realize this phenomenon. This is the point in treatment when fear creeps in, and it can take over. When patients are receiving treatment they feel somewhat protected. When the chemo, radiation and surgery are complete, they need to start living and many find this transition difficult. I make a point of seeing my patients two weeks after their last treatment regardless of whether it is after surgery, radiation, or chemotherapy. My hope is to help them put on their wings and soar, avoiding a free-fall.

I had come a long way on this journey of just three days and I was grateful to everyone involved. Laura will always hold a very special place in my heart because of the lessons she taught me. I learned how powerful Reiki could be as a tool to help calm patients during procedures. I realized how vital the connection is between physicians and patients if healing is to take place. I know now that even years after cancer treatment, healing can begin. It is never too late to heal from cancer. Laura was my gift from Dawn that weekend. Laura allowed me to see so clearly the healer that resides within me. I knew from that 3-Day event how much one person can touch another human being's life. I didn't have to be her surgeon to make a difference!

In my experience, healing is the most important aspect in the treatment of cancer. Healing occurs when we reach a safe place within our hearts, release fear, and begin to live again. This translates into any loss in life. Healing is a recurring theme. Without love, we would not experience loss. Without loss there would be no need for healing. Without healing we would not grow and evolve as spiritual beings.

As a physician, I am so honored to be part of this process. I was so glad Laura let me help her on her journey. When I called her apartment from the airport the day after the walk ended, she was rested and had just single-handedly drained the remaining blisters on her feet. My sweet friend, who just seventy-two hours earlier was unable to look at a needle, let alone touch one, had learned how to treat her own injuries. The scars from those blisters would be a reminder of her healing process for some time.

Healing takes time. In some cases it may take an entire lifetime to complete. I really understood that patients need tools to begin, and then continue through the healing process. By looking within her heart, Laura found some answers to help her on her path. She began the process that weekend, and continues to flourish. When I returned to Pennsylvania I saw that my patients, particularly Dawn, my friends Chris and Lauren, my 3-Day family, and my family, had all helped me to put on my wings and soar into my new practice.

That weekend brought a sense of peace as I viewed my future. I looked into my heart and found out things about myself that I had been denying. I could no longer deny my desire to focus my practice on breast cancer. I realized that treating all of my patients holistically, and specifically my breast cancer patients, would make a difference in so many lives.

Breast cancer is such a devastating disease on so many levels. It is a physical disease yet it has an even greater psychological and social component. If I am able to "cure" a patient but leave them paralyzed with fear that the cancer may recur, I have reached my goal with the physical body, but I have failed on an emotional and spiritual level. Their life will be robbed of precious moments as they cease to function, waiting for the cancer to return. Although I cannot cure every patient I treat, I know that I can make a difference in their lives. I was unable to bring about a cure for Dawn, yet I knew I had helped make her journey one that was focused on healing. She found peace in her heart knowing that her Kevins would be there for one another long after she was gone. I have often been asked, "How can you treat cancer day after day and not get depressed?" I remain optimistic because I think I make a difference in my patient's lives. I know in my heart it is the journey that is truly important.

The way I approach my life carries over into my career. If I live life looking for positives, even in the face

111

of adversity, then I can impact and teach those around me, leading by example. The Avon 3-Day reminded me that even through all the adversity I faced on the journey, I had developed relationships, learned to be resourceful, and discovered I had a physical reserve I had not known before. As humans, some of our most needed growth comes out of our greatest trials and tribulations.

There were angels on my journey that lifted me up when I was in need: the Avon crew, the medical crew, the Lone Wolf, and lest we forget, Angel our bus driver. In the journey of breast cancer, I knew I could become an angel on earth for my patients. I was no longer content to sit back and treat the disease without also healing the spirit residing within each body. I had found the strength to move forward on a path. I was gaining wisdom, strength that comes from experience intertwined with knowledge. The vision was clear but still slightly out of my reach. I wanted to impact breast cancer care in a major way and the first step would be to step out of my comfort zone and into my new solo practice.

## Chapter 9
### *Dragonflies and Transitions*

My return from the Avon Breast Cancer 3-Day led directly into the start of my new practice. I had secured temporary office space for October 1, since the permanent space I wanted would not be available until January. The temporary office was small but would afford me the opportunity to spread my newfound wings and soar into my future.

Making the change quickly was important to me; I didn't want to loose my momentum. The timing of the 3-Day was perfect. I needed that experience in order to prepare myself for the changes that were about to occur in my life. I was walking my talk about adversity bringing opportunity for growth. Starting a solo practice would be difficult, and it would require strength and vision to keep going day after day, no matter how difficult the storms I might weather. Luckily, my hurricanes and heat waves were manageable that year. I was fortunate to have a hard working staff, and a loving, supportive husband/parenting partner/business manager/office manager. We were all so busy the days just seemed to fly past.

I was overwhelmed by the number of patients who needed surgery, and the time it took to offer the kind of holistic care I was committed to giving each of them. It wasn't long before I realized I would have to make some tough decisions about the future of my practice. I could either limit my practice to breast care or I would have to find another surgeon or two who would come on board with the philosophy of treating the whole person.

During this time of tremendous change in my life, I became aware of the presence of dragonflies every-where. I wondered why, all of a sudden, they seemed to be all around me. I looked them up in *Animal Speak*, a book about the Native American perspective on animals and their presence in your life. The book said that the individual who sees the dragonfly is typically emotional and passionate. That was a good start, and dead on. It went on to state that the presence of dragonflies in one's life indicates either a beginning or ending of a two-year period of change. In my case I believed it signified a commencement, and also a culmination, in my profes-sional career. I was secure in my career as a surgeon, and now I was embarking on my soul's career as a healer. I was in a transition.

The book went on to say that dragonflies are the most adaptable of insects. They can fly with just one pair of wings if needed. This helps them survive in harsh environments when necessary. Dragonflies also remind us that we are light beings, spiritual entities, and can reflect the light in powerful ways if we so choose. *Let there be light*, seems to be the divine message of the dragonfly, prompting us to use our creative imagination as a force within our lives. Life is never quite what it appears to be, and change is constantly floating on the fringes, but no matter what life might seem to be presenting, it is always filled with light and love if one chooses to see it. The dragonfly is a messenger, telling us to see through illusions in life and allowing us to let our own light shine through. Like the dragonfly, I choose the light and, therefore, the dragonfly has taught me a very valuable life lesson. I would look for positive outcomes in all my life experiences, regardless of the apparent adversity.

Joe and I had worked day and night making the new practice a reality. I also felt compelled to stay connected to the spiritual world that had become my center. I wanted to share this passion with my husband. In November, Joe and I departed for Florida to attend a weekend conference offered by the Omega Institute, a provider of holistic education. The conference was called, "The Adventure of Being Alive." We were joined by several of our friends who were also tuning into the amazing experiences of being present in the moment.

During the month before our departure, I had completed Reiki II training with my Reiki group from August. Nancy, our Reiki Master Instructor, was present in Florida for the conference. Sharing some of the workshop sessions with Nancy allowed Joe and me to experience a level of connectedness with Universal Energy that we would not otherwise have experienced. Nancy could sustain very deep meditation. In a session with a Shamanic healer, the vibrational energy Nancy emitted during the meditation was palpable in the room. She sat between Joe and me and we could both feel the energy shift that occurred during the session. The experience left me feeling like Joe and I were just at the beginning of our inner spiritual journey. How fortunate we were to have such a gifted teacher/healer in our lives. This was turning out to be more than an interesting weekend; it was an important chapter in my adventure of being alive. I was able to reach a truly peaceful state through meditation. With all of the change going on in my professional life, I was remarkably calm and contemplative.

On the second day of the conference, several of us were sitting by the swimming pool reading flyers. One that resonated deeply was an advertisement for a trip, scheduled for August 2001 titled, "The Voyage of Enlightenment." Ten days in the Greek Islands with James Van Praagh and Brian Weiss. Say no more, I was sold. Joe wasn't as easily sold when he looked at the cost of the trip and calculated the time away from the practice. We were in tremendous debt from having just started a new practice, and he worried about who would cover my patients while I was away. I, true to form, was used to trusting that things would take care of themselves. I didn't sweat the details. I knew that I needed to be on this trip and the rest would work itself out. As it turned out we signed up for the trip. It was to be my fortieth birthday present.

The rest of the conference that weekend was equally interesting. Joe and I particularly enjoyed John Cabot-Zinn's session on mindfulness-based parenting, which confirmed for us we were on the right track in the way we were raising our children. Other sessions we enjoyed that weekend were those involving James Van Praagh and Brian Weiss. Joe had just read *Many Lives Many Masters* but had not read anything about James's channeling abilities. He was open, and at the same time he was still slightly skeptical.

On the final day of the conference there was a spiritual painter set up in the hallway of the conference center and we stopped to watch him for a few minutes. We learned that he was Dr. Pak Lee, a physician from Taiwan who specialized in physical medicine and rehabilitation. (The kind of doctor who directs physical therapy and also help patients regain function after physical changes such as stroke or brain injury.) He was also a very gifted spiritual artist who painted "guided messages" in the form of beautiful pictures and ancient Chinese symbols. The paintings offered spiritual guidance for the recipient. The messages were not from Dr. Lee, he was just the messenger. He was present at the conference to teach a course in spiritual painting. During the weekend he would produce paintings for people in attendance whenever he received a message for them from spirit. I found the paintings intriguing and beautiful.

The good doctor did not speak English so he had an entourage of translators. His staff educated us about his paintings and the history surrounding them. While in his fifties, he had awakened one morning with a spontaneous ability to paint. His father, also a physician, had this gift as well. Each work of art held a message depicted in both symbols and pictures. The symbols are over two thousand years old and require translation from ancient Chinese to modern Chinese. These are then translated into the language of the person or persons for whom the messages are meant. No one can commission a painting, nor are they for sale. If Dr. Lee has a message for you, the painting and interpretation are free. We were mesmerized by his work and purchased a book that contained paintings by both Dr. Lee and his father, to bring home to our son Tom as a gift. Tom had always been very interested in Eastern philosophies and traditions. He had just attained his first level black belt called Bo Dan, and we felt this book would be the perfect gift.

Dr. Lee autographed the book for Tom and as we were turning to leave, Dr. Lee's sister stopped us. "Just a minute, Miss," she called to me. "My brother has a painting for you. He said that he received this message in his morning meditation and that you need to take it with you." I was very surprised and grateful. I waited as she unrolled a very large and beautiful painting. The paintings we had watched him do that day were on smaller, thinner paper than what she was presenting to me. This one was large and at the bottom he had painted the words, BETH D. We waited as the translators looked at the symbols and the picture. Both Joe and I were amazed that this art was produced from his meditation and that the message was for me. The interpreter said, "The green dragon that is adorning the page represents the Emperor's precious blessing. It is a symbol of tremendous strength and leadership. You are a very strong individual and are very blessed." He continued by saying, "I see that you are a healer, a physician." At this point, Joe's eyes were wider than I'd ever seen them. There was no way Dr. Lee could know I was a doctor. The interpreter went on, "You chose to be a physician in this lifetime in order to be able to do your work in healing with the least resistance. As a physician, you are able to easily transition into your work as a healer." Wow, was I hearing this or was Rod Serling going to come walking around the corner to let me know that I had entered the Twilight Zone? He continued, "The changes you have made recently in your professional life were timely, and you are on the correct path. You now need to become more prayerful and quiet your mind."

No kidding! I would love to quiet my mind, meditate and regress, but attempts at calming the chatter in my mind usually gave way to sleep, not meditation. I was further instructed with, "Start every morning with a meditation prayer ritual." I was told to take a cup of water and place it at my feet. Sitting in a chair, I was to place my hands on my knees and ask the universe for the answer to any question I wanted answered. I was told not to close my eyes completely as this could allow a lower vibrational energy to penetrate my consciousness. "Leave a small slit for the light to enter," he said. "Do this every day and within fifteen days you will have the answer to your question."

I was stunned by the accuracy of the information that had just been given to me. I was willing to follow through and give the meditation ritual a try. Joe made a comment that the dragon would look great in the room he had just added to our house, but the interpreter insisted, "No, this painting must hang in her office behind her desk as a reminder to keep her energy balanced as she works." It seemed I had my work cut out for me. I needed to start my prayer ritual and the answers would come. This sounded a little too easy to me but who was I to judge? What I wasn't totally clear on was the question that needed to be answered through prayer. I knew I needed balance in my life between career and family, but how I was to go about that remained unclear. I hoped that through my meditation, the answer to this question would become clear to me.

Omega's "Adventure of Being Alive" ended and Beth's adventure of being alive continued. We returned from our weekend retreat and I jumped back into my crazy life of over-booked office hours and long surgery days. I did, however, remember to perform my meditation prayer ritual. I can't admit to doing it every day but I was probably about seventy percent on target, which was pretty good for me. I would wake up, find my way down the stairs to the new room, have a seat in front of the pellet stove, and place the water at my feet. Keeping my hands on my knees and my eyes open just a slit, I would ask the universe for a clear sign about what I should do about my practice. Should I remain a general surgeon and find some additional help, or limit my practice to working with breast cancer? I never expected to get such a clear and profound message in response. I guess the universe wanted to be sure that there was no question about what I was to do with my future.

Nearly two weeks had passed since Omega, and I was still transitioning into solo practice. On November 18, Joe and I were to attend a medical staff dinner dance at Philmont Country Club. We made the trip with Lisa and Rob Skalicky, the plastic surgeon who did the reconstructive surgery with me on the internet. His wife Lisa is an emergency room physician at St. Mary Medical Center. We arrived at the dinner dance in time for dessert, and quickly made our rounds, greeting colleagues and friends. At the end of the evening, Lisa told me she was on duty in the Emergency Room the next morning and asked me to come and get her for a coffee break after I'd finished making rounds. I agreed.

The next morning started as any other normal day. I can't remember whether or not I did my meditation that day. I do remember that when I completed rounds, I forgot about my plans for coffee with Lisa. I was preoccupied with getting home to spend time with my boys. I thought if I hurried I could make it home in time to get the boys to Sunday school. I was delayed in the parking garage when I was caught in a conversation with someone, and realized I couldn't get home in time without speeding.

I decided I could at least stop at the store and get milk so my children could have their breakfast cereal in style. I am a creature of habit and always shop in the same food store close to home. This particular day for some reason, I stopped instead at the supermarket in Newtown, which was just a half-mile from St. Mary Medical Center. I walked in the door, purchased a cup of coffee, and suddenly realized I had forgotten to call Lisa. I grabbed the milk from the cooler near the door and got in line to pay. Just at that moment my beeper went off—it was the emergency room. I thought it was Lisa reminding me about our coffee date when I saw that the beeper read STAT. (A shortened version of the Latin word, *statim* meaning, IMMEDIATELY.) I called back and Lisa answered saying, "Where are you? I need you right now! Tom Shultz is trying to die and I need a surgeon immediately." I dropped the milk on the check out counter and rushed to my car. I was back at the hospital within minutes.

Tom Shultz is an internist at our hospital. I had just seen him and his wife, Linda the night before at the

121

dinner dance and he had looked like the picture of health. When I arrived in the ER, Tom was on IV fluids and headed to a CT scanner. (The CT scan is an x-ray device that can evaluate the abdominal cavity non-invasively. It would give me valuable information about what was causing Tom's illness.) His blood pressure was initially 60 palpable in the ER and this was a very dire sign. His pressure was so low that it could barely be perceived by the medical personnel. After three liters of intravenous fluid, his pressure increased to 100 systolic; better but not perfect. As I took Tom's medical history on the way to the CT scanner, it was apparent that whatever had happened did so after wrestling that morning with his five-year-old daughter, Jaclyn. When I felt his abdomen, it was obvious that he had signs of peritonitis or peritoneal irritation, surgeon speak for badness in his abdominal cavity. Something was absolutely broken! At that moment I knew Tom and I were about to be professionally introduced as surgeon and patient.

Emergency surgery is always stressful, but operating on a colleague, when his life was hanging in the balance, was tough. A presentation like this was most consistent with a rupture of the aorta, the main blood vessel that courses from the heart and traverses the abdomen. I had last repaired a ruptured aorta in residency some eight years earlier. I was not a vascular surgeon and had no intention of practicing on a colleague. A ruptured aortic aneurysm is a blow-out of an enlarged and thinned aorta. It was one finding I didn't want to see on the CT scan as it comes with a very high mortality rate. Most patients with a ruptured aorta do not survive the surgery and those who do often have many complications. Tom's wife Linda had no idea what was wrong with him that morning so she had called Fran Metkus, Tom's partner. Thank God, Fran was also their neighbor. After a brief exam, Fran put Tom in the car and drove him to the ER, making the executive decision not to wait for an ambulance since Tom may have died waiting for it to arrive. Tom was in and out of consciousness on the drive to the ER. When he arrived at the hospital, Lisa skillfully resuscitated him and then called me, STAT.

I perched myself in front of the CT scan screen along with Fran and Charles, a cardiovascular surgeon who had been called just in case Tom had a ruptured aortic aneurysm. Several images into the scan I could see a football-sized mass compressing his stomach and what appeared to be blood floating freely in his abdomen. We couldn't finish the scan because Tom's blood pressure dropped precipitously and he became unstable. He was trying to die right there on the CT scanner. I needed to take Tom to the operating room immediately or he was going to bleed to death. I called the operating room and thankfully they had a room already set up to do a hip replacement but that patient hadn't arrived in the holding area yet. Stella, one of the OR nurses, paged the other OR nurse, Gisel, calling her from Mass in the hospital chapel. We went directly to operating room seven.

I descended upon the OR with Tom's intravenous bags compressed to my chest trying desperately to pump the fluid from the bags into his failing body as quickly as possible. There was no time to fill out the consent forms for surgery, we were nearing the end of our grace period. Tom was close to death. He needed to have the source of his bleeding stopped and his blood volume replaced, there was no time to waste on paperwork.

Gisel and Stella were my nurses and I couldn't have asked for a more top-notch team. They never questioned me about why I needed to bump the hip surgery from the schedule. I think they could hear the sense of urgency in my voice when I demanded an operating room. I have never been one to cry wolf so they knew this was the real deal, life and death. At that moment the surgeon in me was in command. I was focused on saving Tom's life. I didn't have time to think, *what if he dies?* That didn't surface until later. My adrenaline was flowing but I was in control. I was suddenly thrown back into my Trauma Surgeon days, in residency and early private practice, when these life and death moments were more common.

The team followed my lead, working collectively to save Dr. Thomas Shultz's life. Matthew Choi was my anesthesiologist, who, along with his nurse anesthetist Clare, started prepping Tom for anesthesia. We received blood from the blood bank, which I had ordered while watching the CT of Tom's abdomen. Additional intravenous access was obtained and we started the blood infusing before we put him under. I was concerned that he would crash and his blood pressure would drop once I opened his abdomen and released the pressure. After opening his abdomen, I would have only a small window of time to control the source of the bleeding before his heart would pump out his remaining blood volume. In the operating room we got his blood pressure back with blood and IV fluids but he was far from out of the woods. We had stabilized him enough to tolerate the anesthesia. I stayed in the room with him as he went off to sleep.

As Tom went under, I held his left hand in mine and placed my right hand over his heart. I was sharing Reiki with him and I knew then that he would be all right. I had a tremendous sense of peace as I thought of the impending procedure. It is beyond my ability to explain but he put me at ease as he drifted off to sleep. I told him to go to sleep and that I knew in my heart he would wake up and be fine. He looked into my eyes and as he spoke, he reached my soul and said, "I know that I will be fine. I was told this in the car on the way to the hospital."

Tom later recounted that during his life-and-death ride to the ER, he *was* told he would be fine, though he wasn't sure how he received this message. His wife Linda later shared a similar message she received on her drive to the hospital. Her parents, who were no longer in physical form, let her know that it was not Tom's time to leave. She heard this message loud and clear as she drove past an empty field en route to the hospital.

For a man who was bleeding to death from a tumor, Tom's surgery was uneventful. I opened his abdomen and quickly identified the small arterial vessel that was pumping out his blood volume. It took me all of two minutes to find the bleeder and suture it closed. Once the bleeding was under control, I was able to take my time and meticulously remove the football sized tumor and a portion of his stomach. He remained stable during the operation, but required a transfusion of nearly his entire blood volume. The tumor, a gastric stromal tumor, with unknown malignant potential, was the size of a football and had grown off the greater curvature of his stomach. The tumor was not considered a cancer, but it is so rare that experts cannot say whether it will recur. He had started to bleed from the tumor while he was wrestling with Jaclyn. A small arterial blood vessel had

125

broken and he nearly bled out his entire blood volume at home. The surgery we did was essentially curative and the likelihood of the tumor recurring was incredibly low. To date he has had negative CT scans and we celebrate his good health every year.

As Tom and I have recounted the events of that day, we have thought about the many synchronicities that put all the players in the correct place, beginning with little Jaclyn's fist hitting the exact place in his stomach that started the vessel bleeding, right down to the operating room being set up and ready for surgery, and all the others in between. It was the tiny fist of a five year-old that set off a chain of events that would lead to finding and removing a tumor that could have taken her father's life. Thank God Fran was home that Sunday morning and answered Linda's call. He followed his instincts to scoop Tom up from the house and hightail it to the ER. Had he waited for the ambulance, Tom's fate may have been different. Lisa's intuition to call me, before she even knew what was wrong with Tom, was the next intervention. She knew I would be near as we had planned to have coffee that morning. My proximity to the ER when the call came in was uncanny. I never stop in Newtown for groceries, so being at the store half a mile from the ER was way out of the ordinary for me. Then to have an OR room with open instruments and the best nurses you could ever hope for was beyond belief. It was divinely orchestrated; I was just one of the players.

I went home late that day, but as family days go it was pretty much the usual Sunday. I enjoyed time with Joe and the boys. They were not upset that I was gone most of the day or that I had forgotten the milk. They didn't even know that I had the honor of saving a life that day. After all, it was just my job, or as I prefer to phrase it, my passion. All Dean wanted to do was get to work on our family project of painting the floor in the new addition to our home that Joe had just built.

As I was painting beautiful blue squares on the floor, I started to relive the events of the surgery. It isn't every day I get to save a life, let alone the life of a friend and colleague. Tom was alive and I knew I was partly responsible for that. I also knew that if he had died I would have felt responsible as well. I was acutely aware of the importance my Western medical training had played in the outcome. I had trained in one of the best residency programs in Philadelphia and all of those years had paid off.

I had saved lives before but Tom's was unquestionably the first life I had unequivocally saved in my new solo practice. As wonderful as I felt about saving his life, I became ever so aware that a bad outcome would have had a devastating impact. With unquestionable certainty I realized I was not meant to walk away from general surgery at that point. I also suddenly realized that it was the end of day fourteen of my fifteen-day meditation from Dr. Lee. I had asked the universe what to do with my future, and here was my answer loud and clear. It was not yet time to give up general surgery. I still had lessons to learn and paths to follow before I dedicated my career solely to the treatment of breast cancer. It was a very strong and direct message to me but I would have preferred a gentle tap on the shoulder to emergency surgery. Tom's surgery felt like a two-by-four smacking me on the head.

Looking back now, I can clearly see I was meant to be exactly where I was and doing exactly what I was

127

doing. I was to be a general surgeon available for all who needed my intervention. Although I knew in my heart I wanted to focus completely on treating breast disease at some point, I knew it wasn't my time yet. Isn't it amazing how that works?

## Chapter 10
## Revelations and Trust

The New Year ushered in a new set of challenges. My long-awaited office space became available at the end of December and my staff and I began the process of creating a space that resonated with the energy of the healer I was becoming. I was clear about how I wanted the office to be decorated; all I had to do was get all my support staff to support me in this project. I didn't want the office to feel sterile, or even like a physician's office. I wanted it to be safe and inviting. From the moment patients stepped in the door, I wanted the space to help alleviate anxiety. We needed to create a healing environment. I chose dark green carpet for the floors and Queen Anne chairs paired with love seats for the reception area. The room ended up being as inviting as my own living room. It felt like a space for the living. The walls were adorned with prints I chose, giving my patients and their family members something beautiful to look at while they waited. Each room had a slightly different theme, but throughout the office the warm embrace of a hug could be felt. I brought in several water sculptures adding water's soothing serenity to the space. It became known as the Living Room, which to me has many different meanings. Patients often comment that it doesn't feel like a Doctor's office. Mission accomplished!

The space felt so good, I kept going and put up wallpaper borders in every room, making it feel even more like home. With the help of my dear friend and OR nurse, Lee, we completed the task of wallpapering in one day. Lee is my resident interior design and advisor so she made sure every detail in design was perfect. Matted and framed above my desk was the amazing green dragon painting from Dr. Lee, a reminder to keep my life in balance. I look at it many times a day and smile. Whenever a patient asks about its meaning, I take the time to share with them the story of my spiritual journey. It certainly is a conversation piece offering my patients a bridge to another dimension.

By late January, I knew I needed additional help to run my day-to-day practice. I convinced Beth Matlack to give up her glamorous position on the open heart team and join in on all the fun I was having in solo practice. I didn't

think I could afford another surgeon at that point, yet I
was desperately in need of one. Beth was ready for the
change and decided it was the right time. She was tuned
into her own spiritual awakening and it seemed to make
sense to both of us for her to join me. I remember how
sick she was about giving notice to the operating room
that she was leaving. As it turned out, she received total
support from everyone. Keith, Beth's friend and fellow
physician assistant from the heart team, told her, "If I had
tits, I'd have DuPree hire me instead of you!" It was Keith's
attempt at letting Beth know that he understood why she
was leaving and that he thought it was a great opportunity. Beth would not be able to start until April, but at least
all the groundwork was set for our new arrangement.

I was working long hours. Many weekends I'd work
straight through from Friday to Monday without much
of a break. On one hand it was really flattering, and a
wonderful confirmation that I had become a respected
surgeon, as other physicians wanted me to care for their
patients and family members. On the other hand, I wondered just how long I could keep up the pace and maintain my sanity. It wasn't the amount of work that concerned me. I was missing out on moments in my children's lives I could never replace and that pulled on my
heart strings. I needed more physicians in my practice,
but I was not willing to have just any warm body fill a
void to cover a call schedule. I had gotten my message
loud and clear to stay in general surgery and now I
needed to figure out a way to make it work. I needed to
find someone who was at least open to "healing" and
was willing to learn. Where was I going to find a surgeon
who needed a job, let alone one that would be willing to
embrace the healing consciousness?

The angels were conspiring in my favor and they enlisted the help of old friends to assist me on my quest for an associate. Amy Harvey's nurse called my office looking for advice. Her husband had just been diagnosed with prostate cancer, and she wanted to know about nerve-sparing prostatectomy surgery. I told her the physicians I knew locally were excellent, but I didn't have statistics on their nerve preservation rate. I agreed to call around and see what I could find out for her. I called my Chairman from residency, Bobby Somers, at Albert Einstein Medical Center and asked him for some references. As luck would have it, he was sitting at his desk, which in itself was a miracle since he rarely sits at his desk. I told him I had two questions. The first was about prostate issues. Once that conversation was complete, I asked him if he had any residents who needed a job in general surgery after completing his program. "Not this year," he told me, but he didn't elaborate. I wondered if it was because he was not alone in his office. I told him I was extremely busy and really needed help. I asked him to check at the program directors' meeting to see if there were any good candidates looking for a practice. I reminded him that he still owed me from residency.

That was when the old Bobby I know and love stepped in and said affectionately, "Listen, you, stop reading my mind." He went on to tell me that he was sitting in his office at that very moment interviewing a woman for a position in his own practice at Einstein. He said she was really great, and he knew this firsthand since she had completed her first two years of residency at Einstein. I demanded to know what was wrong with her if he was willing to offer her up to me! With a laugh, he admitted there was nothing wrong with her. He thought she might be a good fit for my practice. I asked him if he would have called to tell me about her if I hadn't called him. "No," he told me, "I want to hire her myself. But since you called, I'll give her your name and number and she can decide if she wants to call you. If she calls you, then may the best man win!" He added, "Her name is Stacy Krisher, and if you tell Mark, Richard, or Lisa that I gave her up to you, I could loose my life." Lisa, Mark, and Richard were his partners and they were hoping to attract Stacy to their practice. I assured him, "Mum's the word."

I wasn't sure if Stacy would call or not. At the time she was completing her residency at Maine Medical Center and was only in the Philadelphia area for the day. I alerted the front desk that a young surgeon, looking for a job, might call and if she did, they were to interrupt me. Just two hours later Stacy called the office. Bucks County is only thirty minutes from Philadelphia so I knew if she called I could convince her to drive to the suburbs.

We spoke briefly about the practice, and I found out she had grown up in Bucks County and was a graduate of Council Rock School District, where my own sons attended school. It was bizarre, yet another synchronicity. I lived in her hometown and her family still lived in the area. She just happened to be interviewing at Einstein with Bobby the moment I called out of the blue. She tells me now that she knew she was in the right practice just by walking into our waiting room. It felt right.

My staff escorted her into my office and my first impression was that she was too good to be true. Here was a female surgeon, who wanted to be part of a general surgery practice and had grown up in Bucks County.

133

The universe was conspiring in my favor and I just needed to be open and receive this gift. I could tell immediately upon meeting her that she was pure of heart and a
perfect fit for the practice. Here was yet another Rod
Serling moment on this path I was following.

Stacy had a flight to catch back to Maine, so we
talked for a little while and then she left to catch her
plane. My office staff weighed in on the interview and
they gave me a group thumbs up. All she could give me
was a photocopy of her original curriculum vitae that
she had taken to Einstein for her *official* interview. Her CV
was impressive and she certainly had the right credentials. I had the feeling I had just spent the afternoon with
my future partner. Stacy had no idea when she came to
Philadelphia that she would have two interviews, let
alone one in her old backyard.

The next morning I called the operating room and
intensive care nurses at Maine Medical Center to inquire
about their opinion of Stacy as a surgeon, and as a
human being. In medical matters I always ask the nurses' opinions before I ask the doctors because nurses will
give you the real dirt on someone if there is any dirt to
find. Stacy was clean as a whistle. Then I called the surgeons whose names she had given me and she checked
out with them as well.

Later that morning when I went to the emergency
room, Gary Glassman, an ER physician, told me he
thought my new partner was really nice. I'm sure I
looked surprised. He then said, "Stacy? The surgeon from
Maine Medical Center you interviewed yesterday?" I'm
sure I looked as though I didn't know what he was talking about because I was surprised he had met her.
Apparently she left my office and headed right for the ER

to check *me* out with the nurses. I liked that quality in her. She was young but she already knew how the system worked. That was the moment I knew our partnership would definitely work.

The buzz was all over the hospital that I had hired a new partner. Stacy and I hadn't even sat down and talked about the logistics of her coming to St. Mary Medical Center. Stacy didn't want her family to get their hopes up about her moving back to Bucks County if the logistics didn't work. As word spread, I came to realize that one of Dean's caregivers, Eileen from the Child Development Center at the hospital, had told me about Stacy two years earlier. Stacy's sister, Kim is married to Eileen's son, Jack. Eileen had told me that her daughter-in-law's sister was completing a surgical residency and that it would be great if she could find a job in Bucks County. Back then I wasn't in my own practice so I let the information go in one ear and out the other.

I needed a surgeon and one appeared! Not just a warm body, but a real, live, feeling human being who was well trained as a surgeon. Although this seemed too good to be true, I knew this was not a coincidence, it was divine timing at its best. Divine as it was, I had to face the reality that I was running a practice and had to make ends meet. How was I going to pay for her?

That night when we were at our friends the Beveridges for a group haircut—Marlene gives all of us a haircut at the same time and then we have dinner together. Mike Beveridge gave me an inspirational 2001 calendar. When I opened the page to February, the current month, I saw that the picture was similar to one hanging in one of my exam rooms. My picture had been photographed by my children's pediatrician and friend,

135

Bob Sasson. It is a photograph of Antelope Canyon and its similarity to the picture in the calendar was amazing. I read the caption: "Take risks based upon what you have to gain, not what you have to lose." Another message, loud and clear: Stacy Krisher would have to become a part of my new practice. The signs were everywhere and all I had to do was make it happen.

My logical, rational, analytic mind needed to move over and allow the trust factor to take charge. The signs were right there staring me in the face. She was the one. I just had to take the risk. I had so much to gain. I released any fear I had surrounding this decision, and surrendered to the signs before me. It wasn't until years later when I read *The Alchemist* by Paulo Coelho that this lesson became so crystal clear. When you are following your heart's passion, the universe conspires in your favor. With each synchronicity more astonishing than the last, I had surrendered to a higher power. Had I not been open to this higher consciousness, I could have easily rationalized Stacy right back to Maine. Seeing the signs may be easy but learning to trust in them adds a whole new dimension to the word TRUST.

I called Stacy to arrange a return visit in order for her to really get a sense of what my practice was all about and decide if it was right for her. I had arranged for her to fly from Maine to Philadelphia for a dinner meeting. I wanted my husband and some other close colleagues to meet her and get a feel for whether I was making a sound business decision. We met for dinner as a group and the evening went very well.

The next day Stacy joined me at the hospital to look around. We had a long discussion about the future of my practice and the future of medicine. She had interviewed at several hospitals that wanted her to limit her specialty to breast disease, but this was not what she wanted, at least not at the outset. She had extensive training in advanced laparoscopic procedures and wanted to pursue those areas of surgery. Although I was performing all aspects of general surgery, I was upfront about my significant emphasis on breast care. We agreed that we would attempt to secure two additional surgeons in the practice within the next three years to allow her to focus on advanced laparoscopic procedures. I could then shift my focus totally to diseases of the breast. From the time I completed the 3-Day, I knew that a practice focused on breast care was my destiny, but my journey required a small detour. Detours aren't difficult to navigate as long as you follow the signs.

The sequence of events that transpired to place Stacy in my life were beyond chance. They began with my painting from Dr. Lee and were followed closely by Tom Shultz's brush with death. Saving his life solidified my decision to stay in general surgery. Then there was the divine timing of the phone call to Bobby. I felt that Stacy was meant to be in my practice.

I wanted to be exclusively a breast surgeon within two years, but I would continue with general surgery until that time in order to enable Stacy to become established in the community as a competent surgeon in her own right. My spiritual messages from Florida were right on the money. Had I limited my practice back in November to breast cancer care, I would have missed the opportunity to work with this talented, pure-of-heart individual.

Stacy took the job and we decided we would work out the details later. I had gone from being a solo practitioner to a senior partner in the course of two weeks. I put out the intention, that I needed help in my practice, and my prayers were answered. I was manifesting my own destiny by surrendering to a higher power. There were signs all along the way that I was moving in the right direction. I was truly beginning to listen to my inner voice, my intuition, or my heart's passion. If I had chosen to focus on the concrete things such as lack of money, lack of office space or any other excuse, I would have missed these opportunities. I was open and listening. What would come next?

# CHAPTER 11

## *Divine Timing is Perfect*

I plugged along in my solo state counting the days until I would have help. Somehow, just knowing that relief was on the way made each daily hurdle easier to jump. I kept going by staying focused on the big picture, envisioning how my practice would be, knowing I would be making a difference, and helping all of my patients on their quest to find healing.

I was still trying to find the spiritual key to help Chris O'Donnell. I was looking for resources to connect the disease in her body with her spiritual being. I read, *Medical Intuition* by Mona Lisa Schulz looking for answers. I thought that as a physician, Mona Lisa might be able to shed some light on how I could help Chris. The book gave me insight into how internal processes develop and manifest as external symptoms, but didn't give me the answers I was searching for in Chris's case. Her disease process was progressing rapidly now and we, as friends and physicians, were powerless to halt that progression. I felt inadequate as a physician and wished I had more to offer. There are so many diseases we can cure, or at least halt in their tracks, and I wanted to be able to deliver for my friend. What I was overlooking was the importance of my friendship throughout her disease process. I was powerless as a doctor but powerful as a healer. I did the best I could to support Chris emotionally. Amy Harvey stepped up to the plate as she became one of Chris's primary caregivers. Despite her hectic life, Amy made time to provide Chris with loving competent care. Though powerless as physicians, we were powerful as girlfriends. We supported Chris in every way we could. Chris flew to Puerto Rico to start an experimental protocol. There had been some promising data on the reversal of symptoms, and Chris was willing to give it a try.

As a community, we pulled together to raise funds to support ALS research in honor of Chris. Dede Calkins, a nurse from Lower Bucks Hospital and an old friend of Chris's, spearheaded the event. I knew Dede from my residency at Einstein. She was an OR nurse and I was a surgical resident when we were simultaneously pregnant with our first children. (Since our move to the farm, each of our sons, Tom and Tom, play football together at Newtown Junior High.) Dede pulled together an amazing collection of people and donations to raise money for ALS research. The event raised more than $125,000. This was clearly a reflection of the respect and love the community had for Christine S. O'Donnell, M.D. Local celebrities along with all of Chris's family and friends came to the event to show their support.

Dede had organized a huge Chinese auction as part of the fundraiser that evening. There were a variety of extraordinary items ranging from bicycles, baskets of fine wine, trips, and original artwork. People could vie for these by placing raffle tickets in buckets near each item. The more tickets you placed in the bucket, the better your chance of winning. My children had me place my tickets in all the boxes with items for kids, hoping they would take home one of the treasures. I saved only two tickets for myself.

I was drawn to two pieces of original art. The first was a watercolor painting. Its vibrant use of colors attracted my eye and the artist's technique gave an impression that the painting was melting off of the bottom of the piece. It was a bouquet of burgundy, pink, and crimson flowers with an unabashed placement of multicolored brushstrokes around the flowers. The painting was very much alive. The second was an oil painting of a vase of daisies. Its perfection lay in its simplicity. The frame was a plain, almost box-like, structure that appeared hand made. I love original art because it retains the artist's energy. I placed one ticket in each bucket and returned to the festivities.

It was wonderful to see the tremendous support for Chris and her beautiful family. This was the first time since October that many of her colleagues and friends had seen her. It was difficult for many of the nurses and

141

~

physicians she worked with to see the deterioration in her body. Still, what was obvious that night was the growth of her spirit. The light and love that surrounded and emanated from her was intense. I knew that I would not have been able to move so rapidly into my new practice and my new healing space, if it had not been for the lessons I was being taught by Chris. She modeled for me how our time on this earth is precious and every day should be cherished and used to its fullest potential. I had no reason to delay changes in my life. Chris had already been able to help me see just how important my healing work was for my patients, and for myself as a physician. She had no hope of cure and was no longer able to stand, but she stood tall in my eyes as my guide to the importance of helping patients find a safe place within their own heart.

As the evening drew to a close, it came time for the auction drawings. I was standing with Dede when the first painting was brought to the stage. It was the oil painting of the daisies. I held my ticket tight as Lynn Doyle, a popular TV personality, drew the winning ticket. I said to Dede, "I really need one of those paintings to remind me every day of the wonderful lessons my buddy Chris has taught me." Before the words were out of my mouth, I realized I was holding the winning ticket in my hand. Dede was surprised by the coincidence since there were hundreds of tickets in that bucket and I had placed only one. My husband was not surprised; he felt this type of synchronistic event was happening to me all the time now, and Chris concurred.

I got my new painting and headed to find Chris with Dede in tow. When we found her, she was shaking her head in a way she does when she knows that something is perfectly right. We were all together when the watercolor was brought up to the stage. A local artist, Kate Bernstein, who possesses the delicate hand required to be skilled with watercolors, had painted it. She knew when to stop and allow the creation to live on its own. I appreciate works of art that resonate with the energy of letting go. Even though I had just won a beautiful piece of artwork, I couldn't let go of the fact that I wanted the watercolor, too. I had such respect for any artist who could stop before the vision was overworked. I had to fess up to my friends that the watercolor was my favorite of the two paintings and now that I had won the oil painting, I probably had no chance of winning the watercolor.

Another ticket from hundreds of tickets was about to be pulled, and again I had only placed one in the mix. Dede told me she knew just about everyone in the room and she promised she would try to work a trade with the winner of the watercolor if I wanted to trade. It was tempting, but I felt I was destined to have the painting I had just won. Before I could respond, Lynn read the winning number—it was mine again! As I walked up to collect my second painting, I saw Joe's face. This time he was amazed. This wasn't luck. It was a case of divine intervention. Serendipity! The hair on my arms was standing at attention and I was in a state of awe. I felt there was a reason I was to have these beautiful pieces of art. They would serve as a constant source of inspiration. Because I have Chris in my life I am reminded of just how blessed I am to have my health, my career, and my family. I would now have cellular memory of this moment every time I looked at these paintings. I would always be reminded of the powerful connection the human spirit has with the divine.

143

When we arrived home I placed my new watercolor in the place of honor overlooking my kitchen table. I wanted this to be the first painting I would see every morning while drinking my coffee. Before I had this level of awareness, I would sit and drink my coffee wondering how I would cram all of the activities of my day into ten short hours. Now, I would sit in my kitchen and prepare for my day by setting an intention: that my day be focused on the highest healing for each and every patient.

The watercolor would be a daily reminder of the strength Chris exhibited during her healing process. These paintings were a gift—a reminder of the beauty and intensity of the human spirit. I went to bed that night with a sense of calm, feeling the perfection of the universe. The events of the evening were confirmation of the divine in my life.

Sunday morning I headed to the hospital to see my patients, and placed the oil painting in my car. After completing patient rounds, I went to my office and looked for just the right spot to hang the painting. There is a phone hanging on the wall in the main hallway of the office. This is an area I walk past all day and if I hung the painting there I would see it between each patient. I grabbed the hammer, hung the painting, and stood back to see how perfect it looked. I promised to always remember that these paintings symbolized the gifts that Chris had given to me. These came through witnessing her spiritual growth as she navigated her dis-*ease* process. I would never forget her precious gifts.

Chris has been one of my greatest teachers. When she was healthy, she taught me how to be a surgeon and how to balance being one of the guys without loosing my femininity. She showed me that juggling family and career, while difficult at times, was certainly manageable. Through her disease process, she showed me how quickly someone can open to healing. I believe because she knew there was no cure for her disease, she became aware of the need to focus on that which she could control—her spirituality. She wasted no time saying, "Why me?" She taught me to savor every moment with my children and helped me to move forward to a place in my professional career that would honor who I am.

The Monday morning after the fundraiser, Joe told everyone about my great fortune in winning not one, but two paintings. My staff wasn't surprised. They knew it was not just good luck, but rather a divine synchronicity. If they didn't buy into the concept of the divine timing, they wouldn't be working in my practice. I feel divine timing is guidance from a supernatural or spiritual source, not necessarily a religious source, that brings about occurrences in our lives. These occurrences have a deeper meaning than we often attribute to them. My next experience with divine timing was only hours away.

Late that morning I received a phone call from a referring physician that one of his patients had a Bi-rads IV mammogram and needed to be seen as soon as possible. Bi-rads IV, is a radiology classification indicating a high suspicion of cancer. After making certain she could get her mammography films, reports, and the doctor's referral, I made space for her in my schedule.

That afternoon, a gentle older woman with the Bi-rads IV mammogram was called from the waiting room. Her name was Elizabeth Ruggles. As she walked into the hallway en route to the exam room, her face lit up. She stared at my treasure from Chris's fundraiser. I could sense she had a familiarity with it. "I painted those daisies in 1987 when they were sitting by my kitchen window," she said. "They have been in a private gallery since then." I was floored. This was too much, even for ME! I leaned over and hugged this sweet woman and told her that I had a story to share with her. I then shared with Elizabeth how I had come to acquire the painting and the significance it had on my journey. She too was amazed at the synchronicities that had unfolded around us.

Because she was my final patient of the day, we were able to spend extra time chatting about life. She had never had children and felt her paintings were her legacy, her mark on the world. I believe she was pleased that my office would be home to her child, and so was I. She was also delighted that her daisies would be my connection to my dear friend Chris long after Chris was gone.

What were the odds of this happening? Just thinking about how perfectly interwoven the pieces of this story ended up being, places me in a state of grace. The best part was that the speculated density thought to be cancer on her mammogram was just a benign sebaceous cyst. (A non-cancerous growth in the skin.) I excised it in the office that day. Her follow up mammogram was perfectly healthy. As Elizabeth walked out of the office, she stopped in the hallway to stare at her baby. She was mesmerized by her own work, and then commented that she would like to make another appointment to come in and, "touch it up" so that it would remain perfectly preserved for years to come. I was so touched and honored to be a part of this story. It was a happy ending all around. She thought she was coming to my office because she had breast cancer and instead she was reunited with one of her children. Now that is what I call divine!

## Chapter 12

## *Angels in My Future*

After Chris's fundraising event, I received a call from Lee Ellen, one of my best friends from kindergarten. Lee and I grew up together in a small neighborhood called Elmwood in York County. Emily Morris, another life-long friend, was also a member of the Elmwood Rat Pack and our threesome was unstoppable once we got started. We spent many a day exploring the creek and riding our bikes all over east York. There are actually seven friends from this period of my life who are the women I credit with being part of my, at times, charmed childhood. We had so many experiences together that shaped who we have become. Our group was active for several years and didn't disband until we reached high school. Through the good, the bad, and the ugly, we all have shared a tremendous love and respect for one another. We are the kind of friends that when one in the group is in need, it doesn't matter how long we have been apart, we drop everything to be there for our friend.

Lee couldn't have been closer to me had she been born into the same family. We were sisters by childhood rights. Now Lee was calling from Wyoming and I could hear by the tone in her voice that something was terribly wrong. For the first time I was on the receiving end of an awful phone call involving breast cancer. Lee had been diagnosed. I sat in my kitchen, feeling numb, and asking myself what my patients and their families must ask every time I call them: "How could this be happening to someone I love?" She was only thirty-nine, and with the exception of those awful cigarettes, she was healthy. There was no family history of breast cancer (at least not until two months later when her aunt was diagnosed). Lee proceeded to make plane reservations to come to Philadelphia for her treatment. I went into doctor mode, separating my emotional self from my professional self in order to give my new patient, Lee Ellen Judge, the best medical care the world had to offer.

In the past I have had to separate emotion from medicine when operating on acquaintances, friends, and relatives. In the operating room, I am able to step back as a friend or relative and step in as a surgeon. It might seem strange, but I can be present with my friend as they are going off to sleep so they feel a friendly embrace. Then, during the scrubbing of my hands, I become centered on the operation I am about to perform. When I return to the room, the prepping and draping of the patient is the ritual that begins the operation. Once my patient's face is covered by drapes, I focus on the procedure and perform the best operation I possibly can. This is exactly how I approached Tom's life and death surgery. I am sure that there are those who would criticize performing any surgery on a relative or friend, but I have found a method that works for me.

I knew that for Lee, peace of mind would be priceless. Simply knowing I was someone who loved her enough to cut off my own right arm to cure her of cancer would put her in a safe place. The most difficult part of the process would be getting her to understand where I was spiritually, and how I wanted to marry techniques from the East with the technological advances of Western medicine. I could perform the medical treatment for the disease, but I wanted her to move into a place where she would be able to heal her dis-*ease*. For that I would get some well-timed divine guidance.

Lee Ellen's stay in Bucks County was short. She had her preliminary surgery and we determined that she would need chemotherapy, more surgery, and radiation. The groundwork was laid for her treatment. She would return to Wyoming to complete chemotherapy, and then return to St. Mary for her definitive surgery in the summer. Lee's tumor was one that had spread throughout her breast, so she would need to have a mastectomy to adequately treat the cancer. Because we knew she would need chemotherapy, we decided to treat her whole body with the chemotherapy first and have her return for surgery a few months later. Before she left for home, we bought her a wig (or as we call it for insurance purposes, a total cranial prosthesis). This was a new experience for me. I was usually the one

149

prescribing wigs, not the friend who goes along for the purchase. It was a new world for me, one that I knew I needed to experience first hand.

I became adept at switching hats back and forth, friend to surgeon. I learned to listen very closely to what Lee Ellen was saying and also how she said things. I had to determine if she wanted her girlfriend Beth's input or whether she wanted Dr. DuPree's medical answer. She shared her fears and concerns with me at a deeper level than many patients did at that point in my life. Losing her hair and a breast was hard, but her greater concern involved who would raise her children if the cancer stole her prematurely from them. She loved her husband very much but knew the vital role she played as the primary caregiver. I realize now that this is the biggest concern for any young mother who is diagnosed with cancer. Lee helped me become a better listener. When my patients voiced their fears and concerns I learned I didn't always have to have all of the answers, I just needed to listen!

When Lee left for home, our plans were firm. She would receive her chemotherapy in Wyoming and we would reconvene for her bilateral mastectomies in July. She chose to remove both of her breasts based on her newly discovered family history and because of the particular type of cancer she had. Infiltrating lobular cancer has a habit of extending farther in the breast than can be detected. Her cancer was not found through her mammogram and she did not want to live with the fear of missing a cancer in the other breast. Her young age coupled with family history, played a role in her decision process. Her Aunt Peggy was diagnosed and treated for breast cancer in Florida at the same time Lee was diagnosed.

The year before, the Elmwood Rat Pack and four other high school friends had made plans to celebrate turning forty together. When we made these plans, we had not imagined that one of us would be about to have bilateral mastectomies. Lee's surgery was not in the original plan, but it helped us nail down a definitive time to get together. Lee headed home to Wyoming and it was back to life as usual for me, or so I thought.

That May, an interesting woman and her loving husband walked into my office. Helen Sheehy and her family would provide yet another experience in my evolutionary process. I was quite open to spirituality at this point, but never expected an angelic intervention to come as a result of a colon resection. Helen had recently been diagnosed with colon cancer. This was yet another operation I would not have done had I limited my practice to breast care back in November.

Helen had been scheduled for surgery by another surgical practice. When she disclosed the surgeon's name to her daughters, they informed her that he was not the surgeon she should have perform her colon resection. I would later learn that they did not base this decision on his surgical abilities, but on the prayerful advise of a divine being. A call to her gastroenterologist led Helen to me. That recommendation, and the confirmation from her daughters that I was the right surgeon, was all Helen needed to cancel her surgery with the other surgeon and make an appointment with me.

When Helen walked into my office, she and her husband Bill knew instantly they were in the correct place. You see, Helen was greeted at my reception counter by a beautiful angel doll that my neighbor Jane had made. To Helen, this was an important sign that she was in the

151

right hands. She shared this information with my physician assistant, Beth, during their initial medical interview. When Beth related the history to me, she finished by saying, "You aren't going to believe how cool this couple is, or the divine interventions that got them to your office!" I thought nothing could surprise me at that point, after having such an amazing year already.

My spring began with the loss of Dawn, the young mother with breast cancer, which lead to the Avon 3-Day and my vision of a practice focused on breast care. Reiki healing became one of my tools to help patients heal, and Chris's disease was given a name, but no hope of cure. A timely start to my new practice, a trip to Omega's Adventure of Being Alive, and a spiritual painting, complete with meditation advice, were additional adventures. Then came the lifesaving surgery of Tom Shultz, putting the brakes on the breast practice so that I could attract my new associate, Stacy. Chris's fundraiser reminded me that divine guidance is everywhere in my life. My girlfriend, Lee is diagnosed with breast cancer, giving me insight into what it is like on the other side of a diagnosis. During this year, healing had taken on a whole new meaning. I think it is safe to say a lot was happening around me.

I reviewed the medical information and results from Helen's physical exam and asked Helen and Bill to meet me in my office so I could review all the details of her impending surgery with both of them. They sat on the loveseat in my office, and I sat across from them in my high-backed chair. I talked to them about the risks and benefits of the colon resection. Helen seemed very comfortable with the entire process. She had been through several surgeries in the past, and had experienced more

than her share of complications, yet she seemed resolute in my taking care of her problems now. As is usual,
I asked if they had any questions for me. They had no
questions, but Bill asked if he could tell me a story. I was
all ears and ready to receive. Having learned to be completely present in the moment with my patients, I knew
he needed to tell me this story, so I sat back to listen.

The story went back to a time fifteen years earlier.
He recalled that his daughter Kelly, who was a senior at
the University of Delaware at the time, had come home
unexpectedly in a state of near panic. She told her parents she had started having, "strange and indescribable
experiences." When she came into the house that night,
she asked her father if he had a blue sweater. He told
her he did, and she asked him to put it on. He wanted to
take her into the den to continue their discussion, but
she demanded that they go upstairs into a blue bedroom in the house. Once there, Kelly began to relay
details of the day Bill's father died eighteen years earlier.
She had only been four years old, and could not have
known the things she was telling him. She also relayed
details of Bill's life that only his father could have
known. "I need to give you a message from your father,"
Kelly said. Because of what she told him, Bill was convinced that something supernatural was happening to
Kelly.

The message Kelly had was that Bill must forgive a
family member for something that had occurred years
before. Bill's father had forgiven that individual and he
wanted his son to let go of the pain and anger as well. It
was a very difficult subject for Bill to discuss, but he
shared that the information from his dead father was
complete confirmation that the messages his daughter

was channeling were real. Later, it would become known that his other daughter was also spontaneously receiving the same kinds of messages. Both women told their parents they were channeling an Archangel named Raphael. This lovely older couple believed that it was Raphael who had guided them to me. This was my first experience with a patient who felt she was divinely guided to me, or at least the first to admit it.

I had witnessed channeling during the conference in Ft. Lauderdale with James Van Praagh. The messages he relayed at the time were not for me, yet I saw the profound effect they had on those who were given messages. This was proof enough for me that there was something to channeling. I don't doubt that a spiritual realm exists that allows the essence of spirits to communicate with us and protect us. I believe there is a very thin veil between that realm and our own. To gain access to it, we only need open our minds a little wider.

I will admit that I was a little taken aback by the story Bill was telling me. Sitting in the safety of my office and listening to Bill, I was certain that the Sheehy family was about to become a part of my spiritual path and that this story would somehow affect me deeply. At that moment I could not have known what a wonderful gift they would be to me.

Helen came through her surgery beautifully and had an uneventful recovery. She had no complications, a shorter than average stay in the hospital, and a wonderful pathology report. She would not require chemotherapy or radiation. The surgery was considered curative. Helen felt that the event of her cancer was simply a means for me to meet her daughters, and possibly Raphael. Indeed, through the wonderful gift her daughters possess, I would eventually be introduced to a new field of possibilities in my spiritual development. Helen gave me Kelly's telephone number and I put it in my Palm Pilot so I wouldn't lose it. Then I tucked the whole idea away in my memory banks for when the right time presented itself.

I was not up on my Archangels and their realms or spheres of influence. I didn't even know there was an angel named Raphael. As it ended up, Raphael was the Angel of Healing. I thought of how appropriate it was that an angel of healing would want to touch my spirit at a time when I was broadening my spirituality. I looked for information about Raphael and I will share some of it in case you are not *angel savvy*.

My research unveiled that the name Raphael means, "God cures," and Raphael is charged with the mission of healing the Earth and its inhabitants. *(I believe that angels are genderless, but since this one is channeled by a female, I refer to Raphael as "she.")* Raphael first focuses on uplifting thoughts and erasing negativity in a person. Then she works at a cellular level, repairing cells, tissues, and purifying the bloodstream. Unconditional love is the result of an opening in the heart's center, which comes from the nourishment of one's true essence. When this happens, areas of the body are awakened and bodily sensations that are unimaginable are experienced, revealing amazing gifts that have been dormant. I felt this must be the reason why I was introduced to her during this time of awakening in my life. I knew that I had been slumbering in some respects and needed to awaken further to my healing consciousness. I was being guided by synchronistic experiences that seemed to be increasing by the minute.

155

I have experienced miracles at many times in my practice. In spite of my inability to explain how they occur, they are still miracles. As Albert Einstein once said, "There are only two ways to live your life. One is as though nothing is a miracle. The other is as though everything is a miracle." There are elements at work in the universe that I do not comprehend, nor can I explain. Does that make them miracles or uncertainties? Although I am a scientist, I began to realize that I no longer needed to look for logic in events that appeared illogical. "Science without religion is lame. Religion without science is blind." Again, I quote my friend, Albert Einstein.

I now believe that hospitals and medical practitioners are under the watchful eye of Raphael, and she is delighted when our minds and hearts are open to healing. I came to learn that angels of healing act to clear congestion in the etheric body. This is the part of the body, consisting of physical matter, that is shaped and anchored in form, as well as the form's energy matrix. When congestion is cleared from the etheric body, the flow of universal healing energy can work to heal both the physical manifestation of disease and the cause of the dis-*ease*. Those who work in the healing professions could ask Raphael to influence and direct the healing process. This can be done by setting an intention for the highest healing as you work.

When called on to assist, angels can direct the healing process by providing a blanket of comfort, acceptance, and love. They prefer to work at night when the life forces are lowest and therefore offer the least resistance. We must remember healing cannot be equated with cure. For some, highest healing may come from passing out of this dense body into a much lighter being.

Most of us are given a vital, beautiful body at birth that is maintained by the natural flow of universal energy. As children we are tireless and spontaneous. We eat when hungry, sleep when tired, and express our feelings without filters. Children love to live, laugh, and play. It is only as we grow older that we begin to change our behaviors. Life experiences tend to breed negative habits. These habits may benefit us in day-to-day survival, but they also halt our natural flow of energy. Constant negativity becomes reflected in chronic fatigue, pain, and minor illness. When we are unable to recognize this pattern, we fall prey to major illnesses. If we continue to ignore the messages, we often experience a serious or fatal result. We have the choice to do whatever it takes to find healing in our phys-ical manifestation or to give up the physical body, enabling our souls to heal in spirit form.

We need to listen to and love our bodies. Many of the signals our bodies give us are masked by medicines that treat our symptoms. Treating symptoms can result in a quick fix of disease manifestation, yet mask the under-lying dis-*ease* that needs resolution. Take as an example, obesity induced diabetes. We treat the high blood sugars, the symptom, with pills but often ignore the life style changes required to truly heal the underlying dis-*ease*. In this treatment protocol, patients are not required to do the work that would allow them to identify the root cause of their dis-*ease*. As a result, they are denied access to knowledge they need to heal completely.

The natural state of our bodies is one of health and vitality. When a state of imbalance exists, the cause of the imbalance must be identified. In many ways there are clues to the source, if only we can quiet our minds long enough to hear the answers. We have the ability to

157

surround ourselves in healing light and create the balance we so desire. The source of the healing energy will
vary from individual to individual. It may come from
meditation, guided imagery, Reiki, yoga, exercise, or
numerous other modalities. We are unique individuals
and therefore each one of us has to find what works
best. Understanding the energetic makeup of the body
can be helpful in discerning what modalities will be
most beneficial.

The Human body is made up of seven energy centers, each of which is associated with a particular color
and can be visualized as an aura enveloping the human
form. This is well described in Barbara Ann Brennan's
book, *Healing Hands of Light.* The seventh or crown chakra
is called the ketheric template or spiritual self, and is
represented by the colors violet or white. When we bring
our consciousness to this chakra, we become one with
Creator or Source. The sixth chakra, or third-eye, is associated with the celestial body, spiritual ecstasy, and the
color indigo. This chakra brings a connectedness to the
universe that is most often reached through meditation.
The fifth chakra is associated with the throat. It is at this
level that sound creates matter. The chakra is represented by the color blue. The forth energy center, or astral
body, is associated with the heart and the color green.
When relationships are formed between two individuals,
there are cords of energy that are shared from one heart
chakra to the other. It is an unmistakable bond. The third
center is the solar plexus, or mental body, and is represented by the color yellow. It represents the individual's
emotional connectedness to gut feelings. Orange represents the second chakra or sacral plexus, and represents
the emotional body. It is an area that embodies love,

excitement, joy, and anger. The first, root or base chakra is associated with the color red. It represents the etheric body, the region between energy and matter, and is felt to house the relationships of family and belief systems.

Suppressed emotions may be felt in the chakra from which they originate. A part of the body may cease to vibrate at its normal frequency becoming numb or frozen and a hard lump may result. The lump may represent many different things energetically: an abusive relationship, an unhealthy work situation, fear of change or anything that prevents nourishing of the soul. If the mass is physically removed but the fear or issue remains, then the healing process will be incomplete. These areas may require specific energy work with a healer who is trained in body energy healing. Surgical removal of the area will treat the current process, but if the underlying source of the dis-*ease* is not alleviated, another symptom may surface. In order to process those feelings, allowing transformation back to healthy vibrational frequencies, work must be done on an energetic level as well as the physical plane.

This is why I was so receptive to the messages of Raphael. Raphael asks that we evaluate our lifestyle as a whole. Eat when hungry, rest when tired, fill our bodies with healthy foods, and take action to honor our bodies by maintaining a state of balance. It may require changes in our habits: giving up tobacco, alcohol, junk food, and stress. It may require leaving jobs and relationships that dishonor us. We have the power to change anything in our lives if we choose to do the work and go within ourselves to find our soul's purpose and our heart's passion. If we deny what we know to be true in our hearts then dis-*ease* may be the tool that awakens us to our higher self.

The messages I was exposed to from this angel of healing were simple yet profound. There was no surprise that this angel's energy was trying to contact me. I had already heard all of these messages in my daily life. It was simply the way in which these messages were delivered to me, at this phase of my spiritual development, that was life changing.

Understand, I was by no means ready to scrap Western medicine. I am biased when it comes to treating illness as I have been trained in some of the greatest health care institutions in our country. I was, however, being called to look at medicine in a more holistic way. I was willing to be open to a new level of understanding about the human spirit and its relationship to the physical body. If disease is really a reflection of a deeper issue within our make-up, then treating only the symptoms of the disease within the body would result in a void in the spirit. If disease in the physical body is also a reflection of what we have done to our planet, then we need to take a hard look at how we have treated Mother Earth.

Many forms of cancer and illness are linked to environmental sources and I believe even more of these connections will become apparent to us. Some environmental triggers are under our individual control, while others are under the control of our government or large businesses. We need to be in conscious command of those factors that are within our power and work to change those under the control of others.

We too often take our health for granted. Only when we are confronted with a disease that threatens our lives do we begin to take a much deeper look into ourselves. Many of us choose to ignore the obvious when it comes to our health. Look at the level of morbid obesity in our society. Obesity is linked to heart disease, diabetes, breast cancer, joint disease, and many other aliments. It is unfortunate that it often requires the threat of losing our lives for life changing behavior to be permanently adopted. Many premature deaths result from not taking control of those factors that we can control and change.

I have worked with health care professionals who have turned away from traditional medicine as their home base for the care of their patients. That is their choice and their path. I pass no judgment but know in my heart that my path is to continue my practice of Western medicine, and to enhance that by being open to modalities that complement and complete the healing process. Accepting that there are forces at work in the universe beyond those under my control required a certain amount of letting go. I was truly beginning to surrender to the higher power that exists in the universe. I had many experiences where I felt I had encountered angels on earth, but now I was open to a new world of communication with the angels above.

## Chapter 13
## *Let There be Light*

The fortieth birthday celebration with the girls was slated for the last weekend of June 2001, and would coincide with Lee Ellen's definitive breast cancer surgery. Of the seven life-long friends, only four of the group could attend. Joe took the boys to visit his parents so we could have uninterrupted girl time at my house. Emily arrived from Boston on Friday evening with her baby daughter. Amy arrived from Virginia on Saturday morning after a detour to York to drop off her two young daughters at her mother's house. Lee flew in from Wyoming sporting the red wig named "Tess" that we had purchased for her during the first phase of her chemotherapy. This one was a sassy change from her straight, blonde, everyday wig.

Lee's breast cancer was certainly a wake-up call for our group. We were all affected because of our love for her. We chose to keep what Lee was facing the following Tuesday at a safe distance during the weekend. Just being together was giving Lee, and the rest of us, the comfort and support we needed. We focused our conversations on the positive experiences of childhood, the things that had really shaped us; and we celebrated the wonderful gifts that had been given to us during those times, especially our connection with one another.

During the course of our weekend, the topic of my patient Helen and her daughters came up. We were all intrigued and thought an angelic message was something we were interested in experiencing together. I was excited to share my spiritual world with my friends and since I was new to angel channeling, the thought of having them at my side was comforting. Amy and Emily were very open to the experience and Lee Ellen was neutral.

We wondered if Kelly, Helen's daughter, was available. I had only met her briefly during Helen's post-operative period, and had no idea that people who visit her usually make appointments weeks in advance. In my ignorance, I called to ask if she could channel for our birthday group. The planets must have been aligned because all the elements fell into place. We secured Katherine's sitter for an additional hour and made our way to Kelly's house. I was not familiar with the area she lived in, yet we arrived on time and without difficulty.

A gracious woman greeted us in front of her beautiful home, with its walls of windows looking out onto woods surrounding the property. None of us knew what to expect. Had it not been for our long-term friendship, lending each of us a sense of security, we certainly wouldn't have been in Kelly's living room preparing to listen to an angel. I knew I would have gone to visit Kelly on my own eventually, but having this core group of friends with me was perfect.

We watched as Kelly, a sweet, quiet, down-to-earth soccer mom, seemed to absent herself mentally. She intoned unrecognizable songs and simple sounds. She breathed in deeply several times, making hand gestures toward each of us as though trying to sense the energy of our spirits. We were anxious, and felt the urge to giggle. We sat on the edge of our seats, filled with tension, unsure of what we were doing, and to be honest, feeling some doubt.

And then, at first gently as a cloud falling upon the earth, and then thunderous as a storm, Raphael presented herself to us. "Hello!" she shouted. Looking at each other with surprise, and some amusement, we replied, "Hello." Kelly had instructed us to do this before she had entered her trance. This greeting was followed by a very hearty laugh and another, "Hello!" Thus began our visit with Raphael, the Angel of Healing.

I have looked back on that first experience with a sense of amazement and awe. It's almost indescribable because it touched each of us on so many different levels. So many times in our lives we know there are changes we need to make, but there is fear associated with those changes. The confirmation we experienced during this channeling session would eventually help each of us release that fear of change and move for-ward, acting on what we already knew was needed in our lives.

There was a different message for each of us, and each of us came to the session with unique confusions and questions. Lee Ellen, who was about to undergo sur-gery, had questions and fears about her health and what her future held. For Emily, there were family issues sur-rounding the death of her father and her relationships with her siblings. Amy needed answers about her career. And I—a doctor, a scientist, a "show me" person—wanted to know why an angel wanted to talk to me. I knew in my heart I was being summoned and couldn't deny it or shrug it off.

Raphael spoke to us in a beautifully simple, uncom-plicated manner. She explained that she was meant to teach us—to teach us about love—and to bring us knowledge about healing, about living on this planet *you call Earth*. Our session wasn't heavy or mystical as we imagined it might be, nor was it eerie. It was light, fun in fact, and she encouraged us to enjoy laughter and the joy of being alive. (I am able to relate this to you verba-tim because the entire channeling was tape-recorded. Kelly has no knowledge of what was said during the channeling session so she keeps a record of the mes-sages.)

Raphael told us we were beautiful and then she said, *It is so special for me to speak to beings who find themselves at this time in a female body.* She went on to say that the planet Earth was moving toward a balance between female and male energy. She told us we are moving into a time of enlightenment, a time of remembering, a time of awak-ening; moving into a place in which we can begin to

understand who we are as a human race. She explained
that those with female energy, because we bring forth
life from our wombs, find it easier to remember and
thus come closer to the miraculous origin of our being.
She also said women move more easily into a place of
understanding and compassion. She continued, "I am so
very happy when beings, such as yourselves, are remembering who they are and opening enough to be able to
remember me; for I am you, and you are me; for we are
the same and we are one, and we have always been
together. I am simply a part of you. A reflection of who
it is that you are. What you have chosen to do at this
particular time is to come to me in order to remember
a part of yourself." Raphael added that we as a planet
are ". . . moving into a time of enlightenment, a time of
remembering, and a time of awakening. Moving into a
place in which you can begin to understand who it is
that you are, and remembering that it is the female energy in this particular time on your planet that will be
bringing such great change forward. And raising the consciousness to a level in which you will be able to create
an easier flow, and resistance and fear will be able to be
eliminated, as well as war."

Questions started flowing from us, and they were
answered in simple language, spoken very quickly and
almost without pause, one sentence running into
another. In between there was singing in a most beautiful voice, it *was* angelic. The beauty of the words we
heard and the explanations we received that evening—
from the simplest of questions to the most profound—
were enough to forever sustain my belief in the angelic
realm. It was personal and it was life changing. I connected to this reading in a way I had not connected to

anything else I had read about or experienced in my spiritual life. Because of this connection, I would return to Kelly's home several times in the next few years to hear messages that supported me on my path of being a more intuitive physician, a better wife and mother, and a more spiritual human being.

One message I received that evening with my friends related directly to my being a physician. I asked Raphael if the positive outcomes I had been noticing from sharing Reiki energy with patients were all in my head, or if Reiki was really shifting the process of their healing. She responded with, ". . . the act [surgery] you do in particular situations is very much minor compared to the connection that is made between you and other human beings . . . and it is important for you to know that each being that you touch, when it is touched with love, creates change in that being. That creates change in their structure, and changes in their life forever. Whether it is that the physical healing occurs or not it is not for you to judge; for it is that which must be surrendered to something that is a part of yourself, that is a higher part of you and them; for judging what is best is something we cannot do at this time. But giving as much love and as much light in the process, in helping to remove resistance, is something which you can do, and it is so very needed at this particular time here on your planet, and I am so very honored to be around your presence for this particular work."

So, here it was, a message from an angel that I needed to give up my attachment to *outcomes*. I had heard this before: I am not the one who decides who will be healed and cured or who chooses to pass over into spirit to continue their work. My inability to cure all disease does not make me a failure as a doctor; it makes me a spiritual being having a very human experience. Again I experienced an element of surrender. As a doctor, I am not playing God. The fate of a patient's soul is not in my hands. These were unlike any lessons ever taught to me during medical school and residency.

Western medicine created a model with the vision that everyone be cured from every disease, or we as physicians are thought to have failed. I thoroughly believe this misconception is one factor contributing to our current malpractice crisis. We physicians have stopped valuing our connection with the human spirit in our patients. We have, as a group, started to simply treat the disease in the body. We are pushed to see more patients in order to meet the financial needs of our practices, and in the process we have less time to con-nect with the human spirit of our patients. This leads to a feeling in our patients that we are not invested in them and their healing process. When there is an unexpected outcome or a complication, they in turn are often quick to place blame on the physician who "doesn't seem to care." They want someone to be responsible for their process and physicians are the easiest targets. As physi-cians, we must understand the role we have played in getting to this place and regain our ability to connect with each person we help. We need to once again touch the human spirit in our patients, not just examine and operate on their bodies.

I also learned from Raphael that a patient has to be in the right frame of mind before we can approach the topic of healing the spirit. I had asked Raphael how Lee could find healing, and Lee quickly and firmly corrected me, let-ting me know she wanted the best modern medicine had to offer to cure her body, before we would even begin to talk about healing! It was clear that my friend was going to teach me I couldn't choose her path for her. She would have to find healing in her own time and in her own way. I needed to honor her and let her healing unfold at its own pace.

Most patients aren't ready to focus on the internal work of healing until they have completed the therapies on their physical bodies. I thought because she was my buddy, I could catapult Lee into her healing process. I had to learn to surrender my need to control that part of her process. Lee needed to take it at her own pace and I needed to honor her for that. Lee reminded me that she was the main character in the movie she was producing, and I was just an extra. It's a lesson I try to remember with all my patients.

When we left Kelly's house, we felt charged and awakened, although Amy and Lee were still skeptical about the experience. The rest of the evening our conversations involved supernatural experiences and how we each perceived our connections to the divine. We even talked about electric energy being easy for the spirit world to manipulate, and that it is often the way messages are received. How many stories are there about lights turning on or off when no one is even near a light switch?

When we went to bed that night, I slept in my room, Amy and Lee were in the guest room, and Emily and her baby slept in my son Dean's room. The skeptical Amy and Lee were a little spooked by the events of the day and decided to sleep with the bathroom lights on. They were lying in bed talking about what had gone on that day when a light bulb over the bathroom mirror spontaneously exploded and scared the pants off them. Their conversation had involved wanting some sort of proof of the existence of the spirit world. Ask and you shall receive! When they related the story to Emily and me the next morning, we weren't all that surprised. Signs like this were happening to me almost on a daily basis at that point, or perhaps they had always been there, and I was just awakened to them and paying close attention.

Lee's surgery was two days later. While we were in the middle of her bilateral mastectomies, I was recounting the events of our interesting weekend to my OR nurses. They were all very intrigued. I explained about how spirits often use energy, specifically light, to send messages. As I was telling them about the bathroom light incident, we suddenly lost all power in the OR. It took a few seconds for the emergency generator to kick in and restore our lights, but it was long enough for all of us to get the message. My scrub nurse, Lee asked me to refrain from telling stories involving energy manipulation during surgery in the future; losing power in the OR was just too stressful for her. We all had a good laugh and I obliged by keeping the conversation *light* after that. Lee Ellen had an uneventful cancer surgery and reconstruction in spite of the illuminating incident.

I choose to believe that the electricity event was a message to me that Raphael, the angel of healing, was hanging out right there in the operating room. How comforting it is to know that I am never alone when I'm operating. The channeling experience didn't change how I do what I do as a physician, but it did reinforce my belief that we are not alone as we course down the river of life. Each and every day of our lives is filled with moments like those I described, if we choose to acknowledge them.

# Chapter 14

## *Confirmation*

I have to be honest; I was intrigued with the whole angelic intervention concept. Although I was still skeptical about how all of this would fit into my world, I wanted to experience more. The whole realm of the spiritual or the supernatural, the world beyond what we can actually see, was at my fingertips. All I had to do was remain open to possibilities. Today, television shows about mediums and psychic interventions are extremely popular, and every station boasts at least one spiritually based series. This is a topic that is clearly of interest in our present day culture. Even my son Dean can't get enough of the old "Twilight Zone" episodes. All of these possibilities encourage us to look beyond our five senses toward another dimension. During his lifetime, Dean has lived through enough of my personal Rod Serling moments to believe that other dimensions exist.

I had been present during channelings by James Van Praagh but had not been given any specific information about my life. I had never had a personal confirmation that an afterlife existed. At times I still craved concrete proof. I felt compelled to return to Kelly again and find out what personal messages Raphael had for me. The session began with Kelly settling into her chair. She wrapped herself in a blanket and closed her eyes. The intonations and singing were very calming and also familiar. It gave me time to relax and slow my breathing.

There are those who will be skeptical about the experiences I share. My goal in recounting these events is not to make anyone a believer but to share the inspiration I received. I can only imagine how Christopher Columbus felt in 1492, when he took off to prove the world was round. In my mind, he sailed for the right reasons: to prove his theory to himself before sharing what he'd discovered with the rest of the world.

The messages seemed profound and in retrospect, served as confirmation of things I already knew about myself. I was beginning to be honest about where I wanted my life, and my career, to go. I knew I had the internal strength to follow my heart and my passion, but having a *divine* source as a guide sure felt comforting. Being a trailblazer in the medical community could be a difficult path yet I was feeling protected. Raphael told me that there was no limit to my "tank." The word tank referring to my entire being: mind, body, and spirit combined. She said I have an opening at the top and an opening at the bottom. Because of this unique design, I have an endless ability to welcome many "energies." This enables me to have no limit to the number of "energies," or beings, that I can assist in healing. I took this to mean that as I work with my patients, I can do so without depleting my personal energy. I can facilitate and partici-pate in their process without harm to my being. Over the years I have been asked by patients and others, "Where do you get your energy? It seems endless!" I have always had boundless energy but now it was feeling more focused and less scattered.

Raphael told me that those beings or souls who chose to be closest to me in this lifetime, needed extra attention, and that I could not be effective in my profes-sional life if I was out of balance with my family life. My sons were young and although Joe was always there for them, I wanted to be much more present in their lives. I remind my patients to find the simple pleasures in every-day living, and for me there is no greater pleasure than seeing the smiles on my son's faces when they are enjoy-ing life. This is one angelic message I replay in my heart and hear on a daily basis. It is so easy to get caught up in all the other aspects of life that seem important.

175

I had for many years been totally driven to attain my goals of becoming a college graduate, then a doctor, then a surgeon. I had set my sights so far in the distance that I forgot exactly where I was in the moment. I am not alone in this, as it seems to be the way of our world. Balance is a verb not a noun in my case. I had to learn to slow my mind and my body. Then, and only then, would my spirit have a chance to catch up! I was hearing the messages but could I really listen and learn from them?

After Raphael gave me her thoughts, I asked questions. I asked, "Why do we have so much cancer on our planet?" She said that cancer in the physical body is simply a reflection of a process occurring on the earth. She reminded me that the planet is very unhealthy and in great need. Both the earth and our bodies come from the same source. At times we have such disregard for the planet, that a state of chaos is created in our bodies. Cancer is the chaotic or disorderly growth of cells in the human body. The human body is reflecting what is occurring on the planet. I look at the number of cancers now linked to environmental sources. We truly reap what we sow.

Raphael reminded me that alleviating the great fear that surrounds cancer is essential in the healing process. She said that when care is rendered from the place of love, and from focusing on the wellness in my patients, that love and positive energy will spread out in a way that is far-reaching, having an exponential effect on everyone it touches. It will expand to a distance far beyond my comprehension. As long as I am healing with complete love and without fear; seeing wellness, joy, and perfection in my patients, and even seeing perfection in the disease that is enabling them to grow spiritually, then I will begin to see a true shift in the consciousness of that patient. The release of fear, and the resulting shift in consciousness, was a lesson about the spiritual/emotional growth that can come out of the dis-*ease* process. And the patient is not the only member of the family who can heal. The patient may be the teacher or facilitator for the larger family to heal as well. It is a state of love that brings about healing. Those individuals living in a state of lack require the lessons that love teaches.

We then discussed my children and their role as healers in this lifetime. I sensed they both have gifts beyond my perception. Tom and Dean are so similar in their ability to connect with the human spirit, yet so different in their personalities. Raphael reminded me that they chose Joe and me as parents in order to be with beings of a certain vibrational frequency. She said they are both very old souls and incredibly wise for their years. I know that people are drawn to my energy but they are attracted to my children like magnets. These are wise men in boy's bodies. My children are with me to remind me to be in the moment for they, like their father, specialize in *being* rather than doing. The analogy Raphael gave was that my children are beautiful flowers that exist and create great joy for others by just being. I on the other hand am the butterfly that flits around, landing for brief seconds for a visit before I'm off to my next task. (This can be a source of frustration when things need to get done around the house and I am the only one in doing-mode while they are all in being-mode.)

I next asked about my brother Bart. I wanted to know if she could channel his spirit, as many mediums can. She said that his spirit was inaccessible because he had re-entered this physical plane quite quickly. She reminded me that his essence is with me as I do my healing work. I asked if he would recognize me in this current incarnation as his sister from his past life. She told me that his subconscious was aware but it was not the time or place for this information to be shared with him. It was not necessary for him to have this information because he was here to be joyful and to play. This message served as confirmation that Bart's spirit had returned to earth as I had thought. I admit, I was disappointed to not be able to communicate with his spirit; part of me dearly wanted to talk to my brother again.

I then asked Raphael how to facilitate the transition for my patients who were about to pass over into spirit form. I wanted to help them and also their families. I already had compassion and empathy in my armamentarium, but I wanted guidance from an expert on how to ease the pain. She suggested I visit the delivery room and remember that birth is but a transition back into physical form. The process of birth can be very difficult for the mother but when the transition occurs, there is an amazing transformation that takes place. New life is born. Just as birth can be difficult, the transition out of physical form can be painful as well. I am to remind patients of the light that surrounds their being. Remind them that they are so much bigger than their physical selves and that they are brimming with love and light. I am to remind them that it is as though they are moving to a new home, where they may experience a difficult transition until they are unpacked and settled. It is like removing a set of clothes that are worn and tired. Once these are removed, they can go naked into the light and absorb that healing energy, remembering who they are. They are releasing a decayed body, a body they have been locked inside, and once it is released, they will be free to fly.

I am to remind them that they are moving into a place of all-knowing and that their sense of peace will be indescribable. At that point they may choose to put on new clothes or they may choose to remain in that state of bliss. They are simply being born to a new world, one that they will remember once they are there. As I looked at this process from a spiritual vantage point, I was amazed at how birth and death are so similar.

I know in my heart that knowledge is empowering and fear is paralyzing. I truly believe that once you embrace the eternal nature of the soul or spirit, then you can release the fear of death. Once you accept that we are spiritual beings having a human experience, then you can embrace death and birth as transitions of the spirit as it grows. As an earthly exercise, Raphael suggested I start encouraging my patients to maintain "gratitude journals" to document things they are thankful for. When I write in my journal on a daily basis, I find I am in a constant state of grace and love. Every day the focus is placed on the positive aspects of life and the negative is released. For my patients I added another suggestion: to keep a stack of three by five cards for the negative things they wanted to write down, release, and then discard.

The spiritual growth of a being is not measured in terms of time. Living more years than another being does not guarantee spiritual evolution. Seeing the beauty, the love, and all of the wonderful things there are to enjoy and experience in life, can promote spiritual growth far beyond a person's years. A being that exists in a state of love and abundance can move leaps and bounds faster than a being who has been around for many years in a state of lack. So I discovered that one way I can help my patients on their path to enlightenment is by filling their consciousness with more love. I do this by being able to sense and to appreciate *what is*, rather than to fear *that which can be*. If someone spends time worrying about cancer returning, they are paralyzed by that fear and their life is consumed by it. Someone who chooses to enjoy every moment of every day is empowered and living in the moment. Since none of us are guaranteed tomorrow, we could be basking in the gift of the present.

There was nothing in this session that was earth shattering or groundbreaking in the field of cancer cures. I wasn't given any information that was off the wall. On the contrary, the messages were profound in their simplicity. I knew I needed to listen to the messages and spend more time with those beings, my sons, who chose me as their mother. I knew I needed to create balance between work and home. But in order to find balance I needed to simplify my life. I was pleasantly confused. According to Raphael, I had the ability to care for so many patients yet I also needed to make more time for my family. Something would have to give. I hoped the addition of Stacy and Beth to my practice would be helpful in this process.

There was so much happening and so much information coming to me. I suppose we all have angels in our lives, but I felt fortunate to be able to communicate with one. I was excited and overwhelmed. It is daunting to think about being a medical trailblazer, as Raphael referred to me in part of the channeling. I hoped I could rise to the occasion. I knew I needed to listen closely to the messages I had just heard. Knowledge would empower me. Releasing fear was essential to moving forward on my path of enlightenment.

# Chapter 15
## *The Messages*

The summer of 2001 seemed to fly by. I was having amazing experiences and was looking forward to the expansion of my practice. Stacy finished her surgical residency in Maine and would start her career as an attending surgeon in August, immediately after she returned from a trip to Greece. Before I had even met Stacy, I had planned my own birthday trip to Greece for August 2001. I was concerned about leaving Stacy alone after only one week in private practice. It wasn't that I didn't trust her, it was just that private practice is challenging compared to residency. This would prove to be baptism by fire for her. I reminded myself that surrender was the name of the game I was now engaged in.

I decided to prepare Stacy for her future adventure at St. Mary Medical Center before she left on her trip. I organized a happy hour to introduce Stacy to the nurses she would be working with in the OR, pre-operative, and recovery room areas. I wanted the staff to have an opportunity to get to know Stacy outside of the work environment. I knew she could handle any emergency that came her way if she had the right support system. The nurses at all the hospitals I have worked in have been my greatest allies and I wanted to afford them the opportunity to embrace my new associate.

The event was a huge success. She was introduced to the nursing staff she would be working with on a daily basis in her new practice. The ball was now in Stacy's court to further those relationships. What I did for Stacy is similar to what I do for my patients. I open them to opportunities that promote healing, but I can't do their inner work for them.

I wanted to properly welcome Stacy into the larger medical community as well. When I had joined my partners many years earlier, they had thrown a wonderful welcoming party, introducing me to the physicians with whom I would be working. I invited over 300 people to meet and greet both Stacy and Beth Matlack who had been working in the practice since April. It would be Stacy's debutante ball in Bucks County and also an introduction for Beth.

The morning of the party, I was busy getting things ready in the backyard. As it turned out, there was a torrential downpour until one hour before the party. Then the rain stopped and the sun came out. I felt this was a very positive sign. While making my last minute rounds in the back yard, I went over to the water garden to check the skimmer and noticed a water lily I had put there a summer earlier. It now had a large and beautiful pink bloom. I knew there had been nothing there the day before. I hadn't even known it was a pink lily because the plant had never bloomed before.

Pink is the color of the breast cancer awareness ribbon, and so this was a very special find on the day that my new partner would be introduced to the medical center community. It was for me a precious gift from the universe to bless the occasion. I sat on the bench Lee Ellen had given me for taking care of her while she was with me for her surgery. I reflected on how fortunate I was that I had found another physician I could practice medicine with. I was particularly thrilled that Raphael had confirmed that Stacy was in the right place at the right time, and was open to the "healing consciousness." I thanked the universe for this gift and proceeded with the business of being a hostess.

183

The party was a great success. Stacy met and talked with many of the doctors she would work with in just forty-eight short hours. Her life as she had known it as a resident, was over, and she was about to be initiated into the world of total responsibility. As a resident you always have a superior, known as your "Attending," who has ultimate responsibility when it comes to the care and the management of a patient. As an Attending, the buck stops with you. I remember

the first patient I saw in consultation as an Attending.
The gentleman had a strangulated hernia. (His small
intestine was stuck in a defect in his groin area.) I
knew he needed emergency surgery, but it took me
several minutes to process the fact that I didn't need
my superior's permission to operate. The first
moment, when you realize that you are totally responsible for the patient, is overwhelming.

The most important guests at this party were my
dear friends, and inspirations, Chris O'Donnell and Ro
Vassalluzzo. Chris was able to communicate with her
specially equipped laptop and her unmistakable laugh. It
was wonderful to have her there. Many of the physicians
she had once worked with were present and had not
seen her for some time. For many, it was difficult to see
Chris in a wheelchair, unable to communicate verbally.
Chris was undisturbed, however and she was beautiful,
confident, and happy to be seen. She would never get to
practice medicine with Stacy, but knew that her presence
at this event was her gift to both Stacy and me.

Ro and Jules arrived at the party for a brief visit on
their way to another function. Ro, who was now using a
cane, looked beautiful. A limp from her hip fracture and
thinned hair were the only visible signs that she was
undergoing treatment for her disease. Ro was radiant
and her internal strength was overflowing. She hadn't
yet seen my water garden even though she had been the
inspiration for its completion. She didn't recall our bedside conversation while she was in the coma but it was
very seated in my memory banks. After her discharge
from the hospital, she'd been too busy living, writing,
loving her family and tending to her own gardens, to
make the trip to my home.

That night, I escorted Ro and Jules to the back of my house and showed them the pond. We sat on the bench and gazed at the beautiful pink lily. It sat just above the water's edge and was surrounded by the most perfect lily pads. I explained to them that this was the first time the lily had bloomed, and now that they were there to share it with me, the experience was complete. Ro described to me in great detail how I could preserve the lily the next morning when it reopened. I planned to cut it and give it to her as a gift.

The morning after the party, I went out to the pond to drink my coffee and reflect on the previous day's events. The lily was gone. It had not resurfaced. I checked every day for a week, hoping to catch the pink lily and preserve it, but it was not going to bloom again. It has never bloomed again in the many years since that day. The beautiful pink lily truly was a gift, just as the company of my dear friends, Chris and Ro, were gifts to me that day. The flower was the gift of that moment, never guaranteed to come back, a fleeting yet precious gift.

The next two weeks went by incredibly fast as Stacy became acclimated to the practice and I prepared to go on my "Voyage of Enlightenment" to the Greek Islands. I was busy making sure Stacy had the appropriate orientation before I left. I was also continuing to provide support for Chris. Our Reiki group was anxious to get together with Kelly for a group channeling as they knew I was having amazing experiences in my channeling sessions.

We set up a time to get together with Kelly at my house. Although we had set this up as a group session, early on it was clear that it was a session for Chris to receive messages, and for the rest of us to listen quietly and learn. The tape recording of that evening went home with Chris and I have not listened to it, but the messages were so clear and profound that I will never forget them.

When Raphael came through, she motioned for us to bring Chris very near to her. Raphael started by stating that Chris was very near the portal of transition from the physical body to the spiritual realm. This was nothing we didn't know already, but it sent a wave of tears throughout the room. Then Raphael spoke directly to Chris, and let her know that when the time came for her to transition, Raphael would be there in the light, waiting with open arms so Chris would feel safe and loved. It would be a familiar energy for Chris and she would recognize it. After Chris was able to control her tears she prepared to ask questions of Raphael.

Chris asked why she had gotten ALS. Raphael told her that she had chosen to have this particular disease in this lifetime to teach those of us in her sphere of influence about the importance of healing. All of us were in the medical profession, but we needed to learn about healing through Chris. We needed to know that when we are unable to cure, we must continue to empower our patients to heal. In addition, we all needed to learn that healing must be paramount over curing. One cannot truly be cured unless healing is an integral part of the process. Chris's tears were contagious and we all shared in the moment of this revelation. Chris was the sage who had chosen this life lesson to empower others. If Chris ever had, "Why me?" moments, she never shared them with us. She maintained a very strong and incredibly resolute attitude toward her disease. It would not get the best of her. She was so much bigger than ALS. This was the ultimate gift Chris had given us as physicians. She had chosen to be our teacher, our guide, and to awaken us to the healer that resides within each of us.

Chris wanted to know what other life lessons she'd need to return to earth to complete after she transitioned. The answer was that she would not need to return to an earthly plane unless she chose to do so. The lessons and sacrifices in this lifetime were so great that when she passed into spirit, she would be able to do her work from the other side.

Our channeling ended and I was once again filled with a sense of love and light from this beautiful healing source. I believe this session gave Chris great comfort as well. Patients often say, "What did I do wrong to deserve this disease?" Here was the answer from a divine source; disease is not punishment for actions done or undone, it is simply a means for growth and spiritual development. The growth and development can be personal or more far reaching as in the case of Chris's ALS. We would all learn life lessons from Chris that we might not otherwise have learned in this lifetime. Her ALS was our scream from the universe to awaken to a better understanding of healing.

## Chapter 16
# *The Voyage of Enlightenment*

I had been looking forward to the trip to Greece ever since the first day I found out about it. It was a once in a lifetime opportunity to spend ten days with James Van Praagh and Brian Weiss on an incredible voyage. Two talented teachers and a small spiritual group on a sailing cruise ship appropriately named, "The Wind Spirit." The Greek Islands were not a shabby destination, but the company we would sail with would turn out to be spectacular.

Our flight to Turkey was relatively uneventful. In line at JFK, we met our first of three "trip pick-ups." This is what Joe called the three women I became close to over the next two weeks of the voyage. Gretchen stood in front of us at the airport check-in counter. She was sporting a baseball cap, a white fluffy sweater that came to be known as "The Poodle," and a backpack that looked as though she borrowed it from one of her preschoolers. She was slightly disheveled and this was part of her overall charm. At this point we realized she would be on our airplane but did not know that she would be on our ship.

We boarded the charter and were off to Athens on the first leg of our flight. I began to browse through my reading assignment from a friend, Bob Sasson. He had encouraged me to bring along *The Tibetan Book of Living and Dying*, by Sogyal Rinpoche. I soon realized why Bob was so adamant about me reading a book on life and death. As spiritual beings, we chose an earthly mortal experience to grow and learn. What we need in order to be successful in our endeavor, and to be fully alive, is complete release or surrender of our fear of death. Once knowledge of our eternal essence is embraced, then and only then, are we free to fully experience life.

As Joe and I departed for Istanbul, Turkey, I began reading the book. Bob felt it was a *must-read* on my journey, both my journey to Greece and my spiritual journey. Bob is my children's pediatrician, which obviously makes him an important person to our family. He is also well read and years ahead of me in his spiritual development. He has been a guide, on my journey, an angel on earth, and every book he has ever suggested has had a major impact on my life.

The book is from the Tibetan Buddhist tradition, written as a manual for life and death and filled with sacred inspiration. It hit home with lessons that I think all of us need to learn. It is only when we conquer our fear of death that we truly begin to live. From Sogyal Rinpoche's book: "How sad it is that most of us only begin to appreciate our life when we are on the point of dying" (p.10). "What more chilling commentary on the modern world could there be than that most people die unprepared for death, as they have lived, unprepared for life" (p.11). So often we focus so intently on where we are going that we forget where we are. Rinpoche states that Eastern laziness "consists of hanging out all day in the sun, doing nothing, avoiding any kind of work or useful activity." Western laziness, he writes, "consists of cramming our lives with compulsive activity, so that there is no time at all to confront the real issues" (p.19).

Here again was a powerful reminder of the gift of the present moment. I realized that having an illness, a potentially fatal disease, could result in a shift in thinking about life. When this happens, the present moment is all that is guaranteed, and our experience of life becomes more precious. Cancer, or another life-threatening illness, can act as a catalyst by helping us re-connect with the preciousness of the present. I was being reminded of the importance of the present through the experiences of my cancer patients, and the diseases affecting my dear friends. I was blessed to awaken from my slumber without a disease of my own!

Our first evening in Istanbul was uneventful. Joe and I had dinner overlooking the Bosphorus River. We could see the lights on the shores of Asia as we ate our authentic Turkish meal serenaded by a zither and harp. It was an interesting dinner, especially since we did not speak the language and didn't know what we had ordered from the menu. Exhausted from traveling and not used to the time difference, we retired to our room early. We wanted to be fresh to tour Istanbul the next day.

The buses were out in front of the hotel early the next morning. Our luggage would go to the ship while we had a prearranged tour of the major sites in the city. While we were standing outside waiting for the buses to load, we met Penny and Ed, a nice couple from Houston, Texas. Penny, too, was on a spiritual adventure, and we began exchanging stories about how we ended up in Turkey. Penny had experienced things in her life that were beyond earthly knowledge, and she was searching for more. Ed was along for the ride, just as Joe was.

Everyone has a story and I believe it is very important to listen to the details. Each person is the star of his or her own full-length feature movie. I've realized that listening to my patients' stories is as important as the surgery I perform on them. Validation of their life and their journey is an incredibly important part of the healing process. Penny disclosed the story of her awakening to me as we toured Istanbul by bus. Joe and Ed became acquainted as well.

Penny was an interior designer, astrologist, and numerologist. Her son-in-law was in the midst of his surgical residency, and her daughter, Jen, was busy raising their child, Jordan, who had been born with Aperts Syndrome. Aperts Syndrome is a rare disorder, easily diagnosed at birth because of obvious craniofacial (head and face) malformations. Jordan was a significant player in Penny's awakening. At a very young age, he had required several corrective surgeries for his disabilities. He was the reason Penny began to wonder what the whole family had to learn from Jordan's dis-*ease*. Penny and Ed chose not to look at Jordon's syndrome as a disability, but rather as a special set of circumstances through which he would thrive. His gifts to the world just came in a very different package than the world was used to seeing.

The pregnancy had been trying for Jen, but Jordan was a gift to her. He was here to teach her how to be a mother. He was here to teach his father, a surgeon, about the perfection in imperfection. He was a guide on earth for his grandmother.

Before lunch, we headed in to the Basilica Cisterns. This was one place Joe was interested in seeing since it was used as a set for one of his favorite James Bond movies, *From Russia with Love*. The Cisterns were damp and pleasantly cool in the August heat. It was difficult to hear the tour guides because the walkways were narrow and the place was packed with tourists. While we were walking back toward the entrance, I overheard a couple in front of us having a conversation that clued me in to the fact that they were also from Pennsylvania. We struck up a conversation with Ron and Sharon, a lovely couple from Central Pennsylvania, who lived only a short two-hour drive from our house. Here we were halfway around the world, meeting up with people who lived so close to home. We discovered we were all in the medical profession. Sharon was an anesthesiologist and Ron was an emergency room physician.

Sharon worked, "passing gas" as she called her job, with a surgeon named Jay Bannon. I had completed my five years of residency with Jay. Although I didn't see Jay often, the bond we had from five years of experiencing life and death together was stronger than that of many friendships. He is one person I would do just about anything for if he asked.

We then discovered that I was working with Sharon's medical school roommate, Cathy, who was also an anesthesiologist. Cathy didn't just work at the same hospital I did, she was a dear friend who shared in many aspects of my life. We had the same friends, piano teachers, personal trainers, and social schedules. Not to mention the fact that I had operated on her when she had appendicitis! Cathy was one of the people who had opened my eyes to spirituality. She is a practicing Buddhist and she walked the talk of her beliefs. I was halfway around the world, meeting people who were connected to my life in some way. It reminded me that we are all connected as spiritual beings.

As the morning progressed, Penny and I found ourselves listening to Sharon's story of spiritual awakening, while Joe, Ed, and Ron were commiserating about being, "the guys who had been brought along for the ride." Cathy, my roommate from medical school, had introduced Sharon to Buddhism. Not unlike Cathy, Sharon had a very strong sense of self and was centered and spiritual. Sharon related to us that an incident she had while on call many years before, had catapulted her into a quest for further enlightenment.

She had been called in to give anesthesia to a pregnant woman who needed a Caesarian section to deliver her child. This was a relatively routine request. The surgery proceeded without incident. It was Sharon's usual routine to go home after a case and answer any messages she had from home. She told us that on that night, while she was in the changing room, she heard someone tell her to stay at the hospital. When she turned around to see who had spoken, no one was in the room. She decided to heed the voice and announced to the nurses that she would be staying if they needed her for anything.

She found an empty hospital bed and fell asleep. A few hours later she was awakened by a nurse who told her the Caesarian patient was dead. Sharon flew out of the call room, into the patient's room, and began to run a code in an attempt to resuscitate this young woman. (Code is hospital lingo describing a process that medical professionals go through in an attempt to bring a patient, who is near death, back to life.) She established an airway, began CPR (cardiopulmonary resuscitation), and administered the appropriate drugs in an attempt to start the woman's heart.

After nearly twenty minutes of resuscitation, Sharon noticed an elderly nurse in the corner of the room she did not recognize. The older woman told Sharon to get the woman's baby. Sharon quickly ordered another nurse to go to the nursery and retrieve the newborn. They put the baby on the mother's abdomen and continued the resuscitation. Sharon told the nurse to make the baby cry, and as the infant cried louder and louder, the mother's heart began to beat again. After nearly thirty minutes, the mother's heart restarted at the sound of her baby's cry and continued to beat. The woman required surgery to control bleeding from her uterus, but she recovered.

Several months later the mother came back to the hospital to see Sharon and thank her for all she had done to save her life. While visiting with Sharon, she described in detail the code and the layout of the room. At the time she was in this room and the code was run, her heart had not been beating. She described the tank top and scrubs Sharon was wearing, and recounted that

Sharon was barefoot. She described exactly how Sharon had demanded that the nurse bring the baby into the room and that she had told her to make the baby cry. It was at this point the mother decided to re-enter her body, knowing that she was needed to care for her small infant.

Sharon had a tremendously strong spiritual base and had long ago accepted the fact that there is life after death. Still, hearing her patient, who had been in cardiac arrest, describe what had transpired in the emergency room, shook Sharon. For Sharon, this event was truly beyond this earthly plane, just as was my experience with Tom Schultz. This is the kind of experience physicians are sometimes privileged to witness.

Sharon and I now felt inextricably connected. Our unique experiences had culminated in our being on this voyage together. Sharon, Penny, and I bonded all morning, and just when we had finished strolling through the market, the person who was to become our fourth buddy joined us outside the covered marketplace. Spooked by stories of pickpockets and thieves, Gretty, in her poodle sweater, joined us. Our group of four was virtually inseparable for the remainder of the trip.

Gretty was the owner of a preschool in Reading, Pennsylvania. She lived about and hour west of Joe and me, and an hour south of Ron and Sharon. Gretty was on a journey of spiritual growth and felt so drawn to be part of this voyage that she embarked on the trip alone. She dropped one of her sons off at college the day before we left New York and never looked back. Gretty's story could be a made-for-TV movie in its own right. She had experienced the premature death of her mother in a motor vehicle accident and, like myself, had searched for

answers to the questions of life and afterlife ever since.
She grew up twenty miles from my current home. I
would know Gretty for over a year before she would
share with me the existence of a daughter she was forced
to put up for adoption. Part of Gretty's healing from that
traumatic experience was what she chose as her life's
work. She now provides a safe and loving environment
for children in her preschool. She has also reconnected
with her daughter, who is a part of her family now.

The four of us had such a connection that everyone
who boarded the ship that afternoon must have thought
we planned this trip together and had known each other
for years. We had probably spent many former lifetimes
together and this was just our soul reunion. I'd like to
believe that we had all gotten the universal invitation to
attend this retreat. All 140 passengers aboard the ship were
on the voyage for something more than the allure of the
Greek Isles. Well, at least most of the passengers were
there to become more enlightened. I can't speak for some
of the spouses, or as James Van Praagh dubbed them, the
*conscientious objectors*, who were there by virtue of marriage.

With our mandatory muster drill ahead of us, we
joined our new friends on deck and prepared to set sail
out of Istanbul. (A muster drill prepares the passengers
for any emergencies.) As we pulled away from the dock,
the sun was setting behind powdery clouds atop the
Blue Mosque. Beams of light shone from behind the
clouds illuminating the sky and this revered house of
worship appeared as a dark shadow in the forefront. The
sunset was a beautiful parting gesture from Istanbul.

During the first day at sea, we traveled toward
Kusadasi, Turkey, for a visit to Ephesus and the house
of the Virgin Mary. Brian Weiss led an introductory

regression hypnotherapy session in the late morning, but the afternoon was free for us to do as we wished. I spent the time in the spa for a massage and facial, and found out from the massage therapist that the crew members were intrigued by the spiritual enthusiasts on board. They didn't quite know what to think of such a diverse group of people who appeared to have so much in common spiritually. (Their awareness of their own spirituality was to grow during that week. Many of the crew joined our sessions with Brian and James, and in turn began to awaken themselves.)

I will remember the visit to Ephesus and the house of the Virgin Mary for the rest of my life. There was such amazing energy associated with those hallowed grounds. The bus maneuvered over many hills and around turns as we climbed the mountain to visit the place where Mary is reported to have lived out the latter years of her life after the death of her son, Jesus Christ. A chapel stands over the site where her home had been and was constructed of irregular sized stone in a very regular pattern. While we waited to go into the Chapel, we had no idea we were about to be deeply moved by its power.

My three soul friends were with me, and our husbands followed, as we entered into the building. Within the shrine existed a unique and intense energy. It was so compelling we were overcome with tears upon entering. The men seemed uncomfortable in this energy and quickly and quietly left the building.

Only one of us, Gretty, was raised in the Catholic faith, and in fact, the rest of us were unfamiliar with Marian worship. Yet, in unison, we began to recite the Lord's Prayer with a nun who stood in the chapel near us. I can only describe it as an incredibly moving and heart rending experience. I lit candles for Lee Ellen, Lauren, Gloria, Chris and Ro, one candle representing all the persons I had treated, and another candle for everyone I would treat in the future.

We left the chapel, reluctantly, and walked down a pathway to a place where water flowed from a spring. No words were spoken between the four of us. The wells here were said to be blessed with healing powers. There were three separate faucets at the spring from which to retrieve water. I chose to collect water from all three, representing the mind, the body, and the spirit, for they are inseparable. (My Catholic friend pointed out that this most likely represents the Trinity: Father, Son and Holy Ghost.) Regardless of the interpretation, the healing power of the well water was the true message; the water was to be used to heal the sick and dying.

I purchased a small bottle decorated with a medallion of Mary and the infant Jesus to keep my holy water safe. I also bought rosary beads for Gloria and a handful of Miraculous Medals to take home to those who needed them. The Miraculous Medal is a devotion believed by Catholics to have been given to a French nun in 1830, in a vision she had of the Blessed Virgin. It contains several important symbols, including images of both the sacred hearts of Jesus and Mary. Catholics wear the medal to remind themselves of Mary's importance in the history of Christianity and to pray for her protective graces.

We left this holy site and headed back down the hill to tour the town of Ephesus. It was amazing to realize I was walking down the same street Alexander the Great had paraded down centuries earlier when he captured the city in 334 B.C. The earliest information about Ephesus dates back to the Seventh Century B.C. This ancient city had, throughout the ages, been under Persian, Greek, and Roman rule. Therefore it has a rich culture and history.

We learned that the Saints, Paul and John, spent much time in this city after the death of Christ. In 431 A.D., the Third Ecumenical Council met in the Virgin Mary Chapel in Ephesus and it was there that the Council accepted Mary as the mother of God. At some point after the fourteenth century, the city, which was no longer a port, had been completely deserted. When I departed on this voyage, I had no idea I would be retracing the magnificent steps made in the history of Christianity, and I was humbled by it. Our tour guide drew symbols on the stones in the street, I X Θ Σ, which, when placed together on top of one another, formed a wheel with eight equal spokes. Our guide explained that this message symbolically spells out, "In Christ we are all one." This was not a new message, yet it suddenly resounded in every fiber of my being with a new significance. Such a simple lesson, taught to the youngest of children, but for the first time I truly understood it. The Christ Energy, which is love, is within all beings. Now I knew I would never be able to deny the Christ Energy. It is within me and works through me. Whatever I do, whomever I help to heal, I know I am merely the instrument of this energy.

I was very drawn to the symbol our tour guide had drawn, and as were leaving Ephesus, I found a gold pendant that had been pounded by hand to create the spokes of the wheel. To me, this would be a reminder that in Christ we are all the same energy. This is the energy I call, *Source*. A higher power that is undeniable. It was a message I didn't ever want to forget.

That evening when we set sail for Rhodes, Greece, we had a wonderful meditation with James. The engines of the ship had been turned off and we were quietly sailing our way across the Aegean Sea. During the meditation, James revealed to us that we had all been brought together at this particular time for a reunion of "like" energies. He told us that our world as we knew it was about to change forever, though he gave no details. He did tell us that something was about to happen and we would never look at our lives in the same way again. Strangely, we had all felt this before he said it, though we had no idea why. We were half expecting something miraculous to happen while we were on the ship. Little did we know what was to happen when we returned home to the United States.

At around 10:00 P.M., while our group relaxed on the aft deck of the ship, we noticed how pitch black the sea was. We noted how it seemed as if we were alone on the earth with just the moon and the stars above us. We were laughing and sharing stories, feeling light-hearted after such a moving day. We heard two women on the deck above us say they had heard a cry for help. They informed the captain and he immediately sent out a search party. They flooded the water around the ship with light, and a short time later, the crew returned from the sea with two very waterlogged and frozen men, wearing only white briefs and life vests. The crew brought them on board and the men were given medical attention and warm dry clothing. The captain pulled down the sails and started the engines to get into Greek waters as quickly as possible.

The two men were Afghani refugees who had fled their country in a raft with nothing more than the

clothes on their backs and their lifejackets. Apparently
their raft had deflated while at sea and they were cling-
ing to the center baffles for their lives. We were told they
had paid $5,000 for the chance to escape and they knew
if they were caught and returned they would be execut-
ed immediately. It was an eye-opening experience for us
to see firsthand how horrible conditions must have been
in Afghanistan. These men were risking their lives in a
tiny raft hoping to make it across the Aegean Sea and
gain asylum. What were the odds of our ship being jux-
tapose to their raft in the middle of the Aegean Sea? I
often look back and think if we had had our engines
running, we probably wouldn't have heard them.

At one o'clock in the morning we heard a great
deal of commotion outside our cabin and I awakened
to find the Hellenic Coast Guard alongside our ship.
They were escorting the refugees, who were now
dressed in the white uniforms of our crew, from the
ship. Apparently the cruise line had arranged for these
men to be transferred to safety in Greece, and it must
have been imperative that it be done before we docked
in the morning.

I fell back to sleep only to awaken an hour later with
a feeling of urgency that I had to write a book about
what was happening to me on my spiritual journey. It
was screaming in my head, although I kept telling myself
that I didn't have time to write a book. Additionally, I felt
I didn't have anything that needed to be taught or
shared on such a grand scale that would require my
writing a book, yet the pressure to do so wouldn't ease. I
couldn't fall back to sleep. I began writing in my journal,
which became the basis for this text. I put my journal
away that evening knowing it was just the beginning.

We arrived in Rhodes early the next morning, and Joe and I spent the day exploring. We visited the Colossus of Rhodes, the windmills, and the Knight's Palace. We experienced the culture of Greece firsthand, and it was marvelous. The day ended with a reading from James, who had a message for a geologist and his wife who were from Kuwait. The message was from their son who had died a year earlier while attending school in Miami. Faten and Abdullah Al-Sharhan had unresolved issues surrounding his death, and they desperately needed answers. The loss of a child is by far the greatest loss a human can experience. For this beautiful couple, closure was what they were seeking on this voyage. James brought them answers that were incredibly healing and gave them the closure they needed. There was no doubt in their minds that James was channeling their son's spirit, for he mentioned that they had the boy's Curious George doll with them on the trip. Faten had packed it at the last minute, but had not taken it out of her suitcase. No one knew they had it with them. Through James, Faten's son told her she would find a necklace made of Arabian shells, and that when she found it, she would know it was a gift from him.

203

Our next port of call was the gorgeous island of Santorini. We took tenders (small transport boats) to the island, and started the day exploring Akrotiri, a city that was once believed to be the lost city of Atlantis. The ancient city was still being unearthed from an excavation begun in 1967. The ruins proved to have a powerful effect on several people, so much so that they needed to leave and sit in the bus. They complained of an uneasy feeling in the pit of their stomachs as though they had been there before and knew the fate of the culture that had once inhabited this city. Some people suggested that they were experiencing a cellular memory from a previous lifetime. (Joe and the other conscientious objectors thought it was something in the water.) The energy was palpable to me.

Our mission for the afternoon was to search for a gold Athena Medallion that Penny wanted. Penny felt a connection to Athena and had it in her head that she would find the perfect keepsake if she just kept looking. I think we hit every jeweler on the island. During our search, we walked into a tiny, out-of-the-way jewelry store that sold handmade jewelry. Faten had entered the shop, too. She was determined to find the shell necklace her son had told her she'd find. She asked the owner if there were any shell necklaces in the store. The owner replied that she did not use shells in her jewelry but she had just received a shipment by accident and thought it contained a shell necklace from the Middle East. When the jeweler pulled out the necklace and placed it around Faten's neck, it was evident how light this grieving mother's spirit suddenly became. Before our eyes, she became a new woman. She'd been given an inconceivable gift from a son who had passed over at such a young age. Her picture was taken just as she put the necklace on for the very first time, and I often look at it. I can see the sparkle it re-ignited in her eyes. It was validation that the messages she had received from James were really from her son. She felt reconnected to his energy. In her heart, Faten knew that his spirit was alive. She wore the necklace every minute of the trip. Looking for Penny's treasure was anticlimactic after the shell necklace find, but we were successful, even without divine intervention.

Late that evening when we sailed away from Santorini, Joe and I were sitting on the aft deck. James was socializing when he suddenly began to do a psychic reading for Joe. He said that when he looked at Joe, he saw numbers, many numbers, all round him. He accurately revealed that Joe is a Virgo, and then very quietly he told Joe that his father, Jack, loved him very much and was proud of him even though it was difficult for him to express his feelings. Joe runs my practice and performs all the bookkeeping, billing and coding duties in the office. Of course this involves numbers . . . and more numbers . . . and more numbers. So that made sense. But the part about Joe's father was difficult to understand at first. Then I remembered that because Joe had been home with the kids, his father had some issues regarding the fact that his son was a stay-at-home parent. We knew that Jack's feelings about a man being the primary supporter of the family were normal for his generation and it didn't affect his love for his son.

James apologized for blurting this out and explained that he did not make a habit of doing personal readings like that. I believe that this information was important for my husband to hear, he was still deciding how much of this spiritual stuff he would buy into. At any rate, it was a beautiful message. I was thrilled that Joe had this mini reading with James as it added a level of validation for him. Joe always seems to be waiting in the wings as amazing things happen to me, and it was perfect that, without solicitation, James chose to give him a message.

The evening ended with salsa dancing on the deck with our new friends. While all of these amazing spiritual experiences were unfolding, we remembered to be present in the moment. I couldn't possibly imagine this trip

205

~

getting any better—it had already exceeded my expectations. The Wind Spirit was underway to Mykonos, having completed half of our voyage of enlightenment but the universe was just warming up.

## Chapter 17
## *Elevation*

The seas were smooth and the skies were clear every day and every night. Beautiful weather was our great fortune for the entire trip. Not a drop of rain or a rough day at sea—just sun by day, stars and a bright moon by night. I felt very blessed to be part of this incredible voyage.

We explored the island of Mykonos by bus and then spent the afternoon on a beautiful beach. After returning to the ship, we continued sessions practicing regression and meditation. My ability to relax was improving. Although I was still unable to have a regression experience, I was experiencing incredible meditations that included vivid colors in varying shades of indigo and violet. I had a sense of moving into other dimensions. It was an awesome experience, yet I felt I was missing something by not being able to regress to a past life. When I discussed this with Carole and Brian, they suggested I consider training with them in one of their seminars back in the states. They were offering a course in early October at the Omega Institute in Rhinebeck, New York. Even though the course was already filled, Brian assured me he would help me enroll. The next chance I had, I called my office from Mykonos to have them restrict those days so I could attend the course. I could feel the momentum building as I was connecting more deeply with my essence. I was eager to continue my spiritual education.

I was experiencing a spiritual shift and I wondered what impact it was going to have on my day-to-day life. I was experiencing a major change in the way I viewed the world and I was sure Brian and Carole could relate. Brian was initially hesitant to publish his findings because they were not consistent with mainstream psychiatry. I was interested in how Brian's peers viewed his openness to past life regression and hypnosis. Brian had a practice based on traditional psychotherapy, and Carole was a busy social worker before their amazing spiritual transformation occurred. They had a shift in their belief systems that not only embraced reincarnation, but went so far as to promote hypnosis as a tool for accessing past lives. In so choosing, they were stepping out of the world of traditional psychotherapy. Their answer to me was simple: their true friends remained friends. When it came to their colleagues, time would tell. In the years since Brian published *Many Lives Many Masters*, his work has been accepted by psychiatrists, psychologists, and many other health care professionals.

As it turned out, some of their friends were on the cruise with them and it gave me an opportunity to meet one of Carole's best friends. Donna had decided to come on the trip even though she had recently lost her husband to ALS. He had been a radiologist in Miami, who coincidentally specialized in mammography. I was beginning to believe that the entire medical profession was awakening along with me. I was able to talk to Donna very frankly about Lou Gehrig's disease and its progression. She was open and honest about the decisions she and her husband had made regarding which battles to fight and which battles to surrender.

ALS is a disease that has difficult rules. There is only one option: to accept it and heal. Donna's husband had decided against a tracheotomy and a feeding tube. These would have prolonged his earthly existence at what he believed would be an expense to his family. Amy Harvey, Chris's husband Bob, and I had also been having these discussions with Chris. When the time came to make decisions like these, we wanted to know what interventions Chris wanted. The interventions of a *trach* and feeding tube are not to be taken lightly. They can prolong the life of a person affected with ALS by several years. Donna said her husband was very clear about not wanting to linger in a state that required total care, and I believe that he viewed this as a gift to his family. I wondered if he was a spiritual person as this would explain why he was able to handle the transition from this earthly plane to life beyond so generously. Donna answered by telling me that she had felt his presence very strongly on the trip. She had even found a heart necklace in a shop in Mykonos that had been designed by the same jewelry designer who had designed a piece her husband had purchased for her back in Miami.

Donna helped me understand what to expect as Chris's disease progressed. She was very clear that the decisions about whether or not to perform surgery to prolong life needed to be Chris's decision. Whatever Chris decided, we needed to give her our total support. The choices Donna's husband made were his own, and they were part of his healing process. Donna had to surrender to her husband's higher power. She was helping me with my healing process by being so open with her story. I needed to let go of decisions that were beyond my control. I needed to learn surrender even more. I was blessed to be introduced to Donna as one of my earthly teachers and doubly blessed to be learning this lesson in one of the most beautiful places on earth.

We were docked on the island of Mykonos for two days and we used every minute to take in the essence of the Greek Islands. On the first evening, a group of twenty of us disembarked and headed for a café at the water's edge. The moon was full and the sky was glistening with stars. As we enjoyed the time together, each of us seemed to experience some level of healing. We were basking in the moment, quite aware of its precious nature. Our group walked all over the city that night and we grew closer as friends. It seemed impossible that we only had two evenings left together. I felt as though we had been together for a much longer period of time.

The last day on Mykonos, Joe and I planned to explore the beaches, but we never quite made it to the water. We kept running into interesting people and unique shops to explore. For days, I had been looking for something to give my three new friends from the cruise. We had grown so close. I was looking for a small piece of jewelry to serve as a reminder of our voyage. I wanted a token of the Greek Islands to make the journey home with us. In a little out-of-the-way shop, I found three wine-chalice pendants hanging in the display window. I realized immediately that these would be perfect. I asked the owner if he had a fourth chalice and he told me that he didn't believe he had any others. He tried to give me something similar and I pleaded with him to take a look in his inventory. I felt very strongly that this was the charm I was to have. After searching, he found a fourth chalice.

The charms were different colors: green, indigo, red, and light blue. Joe asked me how I would determine who would get each color, and I replied that the universe would have to decide that. I placed each chalice in its own leather pouch and didn't look at them again. I was certain these would be a pleasing reminder of the lessons and healing that took place on this voyage. Mission accomplished.

We headed in the direction of the beach. Joe's favorite sunglasses cracked and fell apart while we walked, so we took a detour down a previously unex-plored street in search of sunglasses. Joe found new sunglasses, but what was most amazing was an unusual ring in one of the windows that caught his eye. Joe doesn't shop, and he's not one to wear jewelry, other than his wedding ring and watch. But the ring—shaped like a gear—intrigued him and we went inside to look at it more closely.

While Joe tried on the ring, I was drawn to a sculp-ture in the corner. It was a female form cast in bronze—a very thin sculpted body rising up to breasts and incredi-bly strong shoulders. The right arm jutted at an acute angle, and it elevated the woman's head off of her body.

I loved it. To me it represented the need to elevate one-self out of the physical body while on a journey of enlightenment, and I said as much to Joe. He replied, "Good try, Honey, but I'm not carrying that back on the airplane." I was so drawn to it—it resonated with my soul. There were other small pieces in the shop, and I purchased some items for friends. I took information about the artist, whose name was Yianni. I was very drawn to the large sculpture, but Joe was adamant about not carrying it back on the plane and so I left without it.

Our intention had been to have a quiet day on the beach, but our journey had come to an end without ever reaching our intended destination. We finished our after-noon as the only patrons of a small coffee shop over-looking a bay full of windmills. We sat on a small porch over the water and basked in the afternoon sun. This relaxing time evoked a lesson I always need to be reminded of: life is about the journey, not the destina-tion. I knew I needed to stop flitting around *doing*, and make time for *being*. I had spent so many years doing . . . and doing . . . and doing, that I needed to be repro-grammed to just be. I was forty years old and just begin-ning to learn how to stop all the chatter in my mind long enough to meditate. I really believe that this is one of the lessons I was meant to learn in this lifetime, and I feel as though I am supposed to be teaching this to oth-ers as well. If I can get myself to *wake up* and slow down then I guess there is hope for anyone!

Our final evening on the ship was magical. I had left a message for each of my girlfriends to meet us on deck before dinner. When we were all present, I pulled four burgundy leather pouches out of my purse and held them out in my hand. I asked each woman to choose a pouch. They had no idea what was in the pouches and therefore no way of knowing the colors of the chalices inside. With smiles of anticipation, each friend in turn selected a pouch. We were all keenly aware that different colors represent the different chakra energies; the energy centers of the body that are an integral part of all forms of energy medicine. I had been introduced to the chakras in my Reiki training.

Penny chose first and was excited to see that her pouch contained the light blue chalice. Light blue is the color of the throat or fifth chakra, which represents dealing with issues in speaking the truth. It was her message to begin to speak her truth about her own spiritual awakening. She had held back her spiritual beliefs in the past—afraid of the judgment of others. Tears filled her eyes when she saw the necklace.

Gretty chose next and pulled the red chalice. It was perfect for her because her issues involved the root chakra and the family. She needed to deal with the truth about her past. She needed to forgive herself for things that were beyond her control and love and accept herself. Gretty clutched the chalice to her chest and then gently kissed it with her lips.

Sharon chose third and received the indigo chalice. Her face beamed with exuberance, knowing she had received the correct color as well. Indigo represented the opening of her third eye to energy healing which she was being called to do. Sharon was moving into a place of spiritual ecstasy, feeling her connection to the universe. She was reaching a point of *knowing*, and seeing light and love in everything that exists. She was about to embark on a journey away from Western medicine into the world of energy healing. Her indigo chalice was perfect.

I received the green chalice, which represents healing energy and the heart chakra. The lesson I was to learn and live was that it's the heart that matters most. All energy passes through the heart on its way to either the spiritual realm or the physical realm. The heart is the area in which cords connect individuals in relationship. Once again I was being given the message that *the energy I shared with my patients in our relationship was tantamount to the surgery I performed.* I was learning that the heart is at the center of all transformation so this was the perfect symbol for me.

The channeling I experienced with Raphael had confirmed for me that I needed to do my work from a place of love and empower my patients to do so as well. I was opening more to the metaphysical world. I was still a spiritual neophyte, and I was blessed to have such profound and powerful experiences.

The final evening aboard the Wind Spirit seemed timeless. We knew this cruise was a once-in-a-lifetime experience. Our group had forged a bond that would last throughout time. Both Brian and James remarked that this was a voyage like none other they had been involved in. There was something unique about our group. It was as though we were summoned on some sort of a "soul reunion." Certain relationships just transcend the physical world as we know it. We talked, danced, and took photographs under the full moon until the early hours of the morning. It was like the last evening of a very large family reunion and we wanted to savor every remaining moment. The group would be disbanded in the morning, but our fondness and closeness would always remain with us.

Our ship docked in Athens the next morning and we were taken on an all-day tour of the city. The afternoon ended at the hotel pool where we met an interesting couple from Manhattan, Joy and Bart, who were owners of a vegetarian café in the city. They had been with us for the entire week but it wasn't until that afternoon that we really connected. My conversation with Joy turned to the healing process after a diagnosis of breast cancer. Her mother had died of the disease and she was familiar with the sadness and frustration that breast cancer causes, not just for the patient, but for the entire family. We discussed the fact that there were numerous organizations supporting research, but few organizations promoting healing for those affected by the disease. We talked about how wonderful it would be to establish a nonprofit organization to support the healing process. This chance meeting at the pool with Joy and Bart helped me realize there were others who felt as I did. It was important confirmation from others that my dream of a Center for Healing might be embraced. I would continue to be tested as I tried to discern how to marry my medical world with my spiritual world. That would be my ongoing assignment when I returned home.

Our only evening in Athens was spent with the group of friends we had gotten to know best on this incredible trip. Gretty, Sharon, Ron, Joe, and I walked through Athens to the Plaka—an area below the Parthenon that has unusual charm and offers the flavor of the local culture. We weaved our way through the open-air market on our way to the taverna that my partner Stacy had recommended. Having just been there a few weeks earlier, Stacy had told the owner that she would send us his way on our journey through Greece.

What a wonderful choice. We were dining outside enjoying a full view of the Acropolis above, illuminated in the darkness. As strange as it may sound, with all the customers he must have, the manager of the taverna, called the Tepina Café, remembered Stacy from her recent visit, and he treated us as though we were royalty. The meal was excellent and we toasted the new and very powerful connections we had made with one another. It was ironic that every member of our dinner party that evening lived within two hours of one other back home in Pennsylvania, yet we had to come on this voyage to be united.

Due to other commitments and early flights the next morning, Ron and Sharon dispersed early that evening. Saying goodbye to each other was sad, yet we knew it was temporary. Our friendships in this lifetime were just beginning. Joe was tired and wanted to return to the hotel. He was uncomfortable walking the dark streets of a foreign city. As we walked down the street, Gretty spotted a very thin undernourished woman holding her infant son on her lap. Gretty's eyes filled with tears, and she searched her bag only to find she had no cash. Without a word spoken between them, Joe handed Gretty twenty dollars, and Gretty gave the money to the woman. Seeing Gretty's satisfaction and her feeling of fulfillment at this simple good deed made us all feel good.

I made the decision to take a left turn down the next dark street, assuring Joe that I knew we could catch a cab at the end of the next block. He had learned through our many years together to trust my instincts; they have often led us to the places we needed to be in our lives. As we walked down the incredibly dark alley, we could see a light coming from the left at the street corner. The closer we got, the more clearly I could make out an illuminated sculpture—it was the one that I had been so drawn to in Mykonos! A very large version of this amazing female form was displayed in the window of a gallery. I could feel my heart begin to race with excitement.

The energy I felt walking through the doorway is beyond description. I began to explain to Gretty how I had seen the sculpture before in the shop in Mykonos and as I spoke, my interpretation of the magnificent sculpture just tumbled out of me. I told her that it represented a spiritual journey, beginning at the feet, traveling upward over the twists and turns of the female body, reaching the breasts, where it expands still further, and then continues upward, reaching an apex at the head, where she realizes that her body is not the center of her existence. Our spiritual center is elevated above our bodies, just as was the head on the sculpture. I shared, "Our essence, our soul, is the spiritual center; our bodies are merely the vehicles for inner growth. Once we have reached this realization, there is no going back to an earth-bound existence."

A handsome gentleman sitting behind the counter stood and walked over to me. His gentle demeanor was palpable. He looked directly into my eyes and took my hand in his, saying, "I feel you on a cellular level, every part of your being. You know exactly what I was saying when I created this sculpture. I call it *Elevation*. It represents to me climbing over the curves and turns of life and then reaching an angle, or turn, when you need to move out of your physical body into another dimension to become in touch with your true spirit."

Here again, as had been happening to me on a regular basis now, I felt I had been guided by divine intervention, and I ended up in the presence of this amazing artist whose work I so admired. His name was Yianni Souvagiolou. He was a wise and gentle being who emanated knowledge about his own essence. He had what I call, *soul memory.* His spiritual nature came not from an awakening, but from a true knowing of his essence. He didn't need to read books or be regressed to know that his soul was eternal. He remembered innately what so many of us have forgotten. I was on a journey to discover, or better yet remember, my true essence, and there was no way this sculpture was going to escape coming home to Pennsylvania with me this time. I had to sit down and rest a moment as the energy flowed through me.

While I waited for Yianni to prepare the sculpture for transportation back to the United States, I took a moment to admire his other work. I was drawn to a sculpture of four naked women running, leading with their breasts. Each one could move in different directions on its own axis. Yianni told me, "I call that piece *The Winners.* To me it represents women finding healing from breast cancer. The breasts are prominent to project the position of winning the race. The feet are light and graceful, and each woman can turn in any direction she needs in order to find healing." I knew at that moment this statue would also be traveling across the Atlantic Ocean with me in the morning. I pulled out my business card from my purse and handed it to Yianni. It read, *Beth B. DuPree, M.D., FACS – Diseases of the Breasts and General Surgery.* The look on his face spoke more of familiarity than of surprise, as though he had created these works of art specifically for me. It was as if he knew I was a breast cancer surgeon before I told him.

Gretty and Joe were both in a state of surrender to that moment.

Yianni proceeded to impart the wisdom of his spiritual essence to us that evening. His soul was so true and genuine. Because of this man, I was reminded once again, of the importance of the moment and the need to create balance between mind, body, and spirit. Yianni reminded me, "You must never forget . . . we are all connected as one with the universe." As a token of this momentous occasion, he gave each of us a piece of art to take home with us so that we would remember.

Gretty's statue was called, *The Little Prince,* and was a representation of a story of a pilot who was shot down and crash landed in the desert. This represented for Gretty a confirmation that one of her regressions during the voyage had been accurate. During the regression she visualized a former life where she had been a pilot in WWII and I, her navigator. We had been shot down over England and died. She felt responsible for my death because she had been in control of the airplane. I assured her that I forgave her for any errors in judgment in that lifetime.

Yianni gave Joe a mask, a replica of an ancient Greek statue. We weren't quite sure of its significance but it sits prominently above his computer screen and he looks at it a thousand times a day.

To me, he gave a replica of an ancient Greek coin that he said signified a bringing together of the old and the new, the past and the present. The message for me? To create a shift from relying solely on the technology-based medical model to treating my patients with love and respect; intertwining the best healing modalities of both East and West to bring about a shift in the consciousness of healing.

The evening turned out to be the truly magical moment on my voyage of enlightenment, and not a day goes by that I do not think of Yianni and his work. The statues are in my view every day as I practice medicine. Although I spent all of an hour with this gentleman, his spirit is forever connected to my soul. We have a connection that transcends the physical plane. It is not the amount of time that you spend with another person that matters, but the connection with their spirit.

## Chapter 18
# *Spiritual Emergency 911*

We returned from Greece in early September 2001. Although nothing in my practice had changed, everything had changed in my vision of the world. I felt a sense of connectedness with the universe. The trip had been life affirming.

The changes needed in my professional life were becoming clearer by the day. I knew I had to focus more energy in the process of healing. I needed to be more than just a competent physician. It was time to lead by example and follow my heart, my passion. I would have to come up with a plan to integrate all of this new inspiration with my surgical practice.

Stacy's general surgery board exam was coming up in October and she left for New York City on September 10, to take the board review course I had taken ten years previously. She was happy to have the study time, and left for New York at five o'clock on Monday morning, prepared to stay in downtown Manhattan for the week.

On Tuesday morning, I was in surgery at St. Mary Medical Center. I started my cases at 7:45 A.M. as I do every Tuesday and Thursday. Since this was my first day back in the OR since the trip, I was excited to share my experiences from the cruise with my staff. I gave them details of the synchronicities and the rescue of the Afghani refugees from the sea. The minutes flew past as I recounted the amazing events of my journey.

When I came out of the operating room to talk to my patient's family in between cases, a news alert caught my attention. Out of the corner of my eye I noticed the smoke pouring from the World Trade Center on the TV screen in the waiting room. I thought at first that it was a movie trailer that just looked realistic. My patient's family explained to me that a plane had hit one of the twin towers just minutes before. I don't know why, but I assumed that the plane was a small private plane, not an airliner. As we watched the news broadcast, the second plane hit the other tower. We were in complete shock, staring disbelievingly at the television. Before long, the towers crashed to the ground, and our world had forever changed.

The premonition James had expressed on the cruise was now a reality. Our world *had* changed forever. My heart was very heavy and I wanted to be home with my husband and children. Then, with a horrible feeling of dread, my mind jumped to Stacy in Manhattan. She was there at a review course that I had insisted she take. I became sick in the pit of my stomach. I knew that the hotel hosting the course was just blocks from the towers. I called my office and told them to turn on the TV to follow events as they unfolded. I returned to the OR to tell my nurses of this horrific event. I called Stacy's cell phone from the OR but there was no answer. I desperately wanted to know that she was okay, that she was safe.

Stacy recalled later that she was sitting in the course and her cell phone was ringing in her pocketbook. She realized that it was not on vibrate and she was too embarrassed to reach down and turn it off. If she reached down to touch the phone, everyone would know it was hers. She remembers that shortly after her phone started ringing, the news of the twin towers being hit and collapsing was announced. The roomful of 300 surgeons started to discuss what to do. Should they continue the course or offer to help? They had no understanding of the magnitude of the drama taking place just blocks from where they were, or there would have been no discussion. This group of skilled surgeons were ushered out of the hotel and taken by bus to as close to Ground Zero as possible. There, triage centers, where the injured could be evaluated, were being set up and Stacy was placed in one at Chelsea Pier.

The unfortunate truth is that there were so few survivors needing medical attention that the triage centers weren't necessary. The hope of finding people alive continued for several days, but the ultimate truth would have been too devastating to fathom at that point. Stacy stayed at the center for the remainder of the day until replacements came at 10:00 P.M.

223

My day had to go on as though we had been watching a television show and not the news. I had responsibilities to my patients and needed to remain focused on their needs. I went on, knowing that I needed to set the tone for my operating room and remain calm. I did take a break with my nurses and surgical assistant between cases. I wanted them to know that they were important to me, and we needed to pull together and stay present in the moment for the sake of our patients. I had every member from my operating room team come with me to the hospital chapel. We chose to pray for those people who had obviously perished in the twin towers and on the airplanes. We then prayed for the family members who would soon realize their loved ones were missing or dead.

I can't even recall the specifics of the events throughout the rest of the day. I just wanted to get home to be with my family. I picked up Dean from kindergarten at the Child Development Center at the hospital and headed home to meet Tommy. I wanted to protect my children from the truth, but there was no way to make this go away. How do you explain to a child that the safety, security, and protection we had always taken for granted were now in jeopardy? After Tommy and Dean were safely tucked into bed that night, the events of the entire day finally hit me. I cried as I had not cried since the day the drunk driver killed my brother, Bart. I felt devastated as this unexpected and senseless event rocked my world. I needed to grieve and allow my emotions to run their full course.

As a physician, I equated this catastrophe in this way: The events leading up to September 11 were like a cancer that had been growing undetected in the confines of a foreign land until it metastasized to our country. We were powerless on the day of diagnosis, but as with any cancer, we would be able to heal. Like a disaster, cancer can be the turning point in a life that allows for growth of the spirit. It teaches not only the person with the disease, but all the people that person touches. When we are confronted with mortality, we must learn to fully live in the present.

Stacy was unable to get through to anyone in Pennsylvania until late that evening. She was relieved of her triage duties and walked back to her hotel with others who had been working with her. The ambulances and fire trucks were coming from Ground Zero through what she described as a layer of dirty snow. Already people were placing flowers around the emergency vehicles as shrines to those who had passed. Stacy was emotionally and physically drained. She went to her hotel only to be evacuated because of a bomb scare. Her hotel was near the Empire State Building and security was high. She walked to a street corner several blocks away and sat there with others who had also been evacuated in the dark of night. She met a man who had narrowly escaped the collapse of the twin towers. He had been sitting at a bar all day. He was not able to get up and go home. It was a surreal experience, and Stacy took pictures of what she had seen that day. She has not been able to have that film developed. The images are locked away in her disposable camera.

Our world as we knew it prior to September 11, 2001, will never be the same. The sense of loss—not only of human life, but the loss of our security—will take decades to heal. At that time I felt a tremendous void in the heart of our nation and a sense of helplessness. We were millions strong, paralyzed by the hatred of a few men. The energy that was required to create such hatred toward our nation is incomprehensible. What had we done as a nation to incite such anger? How can we as a nation heal ourselves, and what can we do to spread love and light to those individuals who found themselves in such a state of hatred?

There is no going back to change the past. We had just been graphically shown that one individual could change the world. I needed to move forward into the future. I knew I had the ability to create change in a positive way. Change created with love and light can reach farther and illuminate even those who are in darkness.

After September 11, I began to feel an even greater calling to create a safe environment in which my patients could heal. I treat people with cancer, and with cancer—no matter how advanced it is—there is always hope. Those who lost their lives on September 11 had no hope. Their futures and their dreams were stolen by the darkness of hatred. Again, this is a reminder that we do not know what tomorrow will bring, and so we must cherish the gifts of today. It is my opinion that all physicians and healers need to impart this message to anyone who places their wellbeing in our hands.

## Chapter 19
## *Somewhere Over the Rainbow*

After 9/11, I was drawn more than ever to Brian and Carole Weiss' regression training course. The month of September is a blur in my memory for the most part. My emotions were running rampant and there was so much that was suddenly unknown within my world. I was afraid and saddened. I was not afraid of being killed by a terrorist attack, I was afraid of what was happening to our world as a whole. I was saddened when I thought of the loss of life from the attacks and the loss of life that would result from our country's repercussions. I kept thinking about the two Afghani refugees we had rescued just two weeks earlier and how horrible conditions had to have been in their country to escape as they did in a life raft. What was so clearly happening on our planet was diametrically opposite to what I was experiencing spiritually. I tried to maintain my balance. I went to work every day trying to make a difference and trying to keep hope alive for my patients, my staff, my friends and family, and myself.

I have never wanted to live in fear, and that didn't change. If I allowed those who lived in a state of hatred—in a total state of lack—to keep fear alive in me, they would have accomplished their goal. My friend Penny felt the same way, for she was still planning to fly to Philadelphia from Houston and make the drive to Rhinebeck, New York, with me for the conference.

Near month's end, Rosemarie Vassalluzzo became very weak again and required hospitalization. Just six weeks earlier we had been sitting by my pond enjoying the spectacular pink water lily. Ro had been doing so well, but then she seemed to slip away. I knew this was her time to move to another spiritual plane. She was admitted to the oncology floor at St. Mary and was sur-rounded by family and friends.

In the room next door to Ro's, another long-time patient of mine was also transitioning to spirit. Karen had been a friend since I began my practice at St. Mary Medical Center. She was an Emergency Room nurse who was always, I thought, a little bit *out there*. (Translation: She was into some metaphysical things that I couldn't embrace at the time.) A few years earlier, when she had been between jobs and uninsured, she developed a very large and rapidly growing squamous cell carcinoma on her chest. She hid this growth for months because she was too proud to ask for help and too embarrassed that a nurse did not have medical insurance coverage. It was only when she could see it growing on a weekly basis that she came to me for help. I performed her surgery without financial compensation and was able to get the hospital and the anesthesiologist to greatly reduce their charges so that she could have the procedure. She recovered completely from this surgery and returned to her passion of nursing. Karen subsequently developed breast cancer in 2000 and despite my efforts to convince her to have a mastectomy and chemotherapy; she elected to pursue alternative treatments. I am not referring to *complementary* therapies, which work in conjunction with standard medical treatment. Karen wanted to try to change her diet and use a variety of modalities that I believed could not adequately treat the cancer already infiltrating her body. I knew that all the changes she was making in her life were important in her healing process and wellbeing, but I did not feel they could adequately remove the disease in her body.

A year and a half later, I was sad to learn that Karen had a liver riddled with metastatic disease. It was at that juncture she wanted every chemotherapy agent known to mankind to take away her disease. I often wonder what her fate might have been had she chosen the mastectomy and chemotherapy from the start. Still, had she followed my advice, it would not have been her own choice and she would have followed a path that did not honor her spirit. Karen made these decisions for herself, and I had to honor them regardless of my personal beliefs. This was her journey and she may have chosen these lessons in this lifetime for some

229

undisclosed reason. The truth is, even if she had followed my medical recommendations, she may have
been in the same situation. There is no way to know for
certain. I have learned to always render my opinion, yet
also know that the final decisions need to be made by
the individual who will live with the consequences.

And so, here I was in the oncology unit with two
women who had taken very divergent paths in their
treatment of cancer and they were transitioning together.
I spent time with both families knowing that both of
these beautiful souls would not be able to abide in their
worn and tired physical bodies much longer. I spent private time with Karen and Ro, helping them to look at the
transition as a shedding of their old clothes. I reminded
them that they would be free, surrounded by magnificent love and light and that the denseness of their physical bodies would be gone. When they reached that state,
they would remember the peace and love that is at the
core of our essence. They were both in a very safe place
and were prepared for what was to come.

I was planning to leave for Omega the next day. I
went to the hospital one final time to give my love to
the families and to say farewell. It was Friday afternoon
and the sun was shining when I first stopped in the hospital day care center to say goodbye to my little Dean. I
would be gone for five days and needed to give my little
buddy lots of hugs and kisses. I then ran up to the
oncology unit to bid farewell to my friends. I was carrying my treasures from the House of the Virgin Mary—
two miraculous medals and the bottle of holy water I
had brought back from my voyage of enlightenment.
This visit to my friends was such a life affirming experience that just recounting it brings tears to my eyes.

I walked into Ro's room and her children and husband surrounded her bed. She was sleeping with her head elevated slightly to assist her breathing. She was covered in a blanket from home to keep her "safe and comforted." Beth, her youngest, was on one side of the bed with her husband and her brother, Chris. Barb, her older daughter, and Jules were at the foot of the bed. They were watching her sleep, listening to her labored breathing, and knowing that her physical existence was nearing an end. She had been unconscious for some time.

I talked to Ro and held her hand, knowing that on some level she would hear me. I asked the family if I could pin the miraculous medal onto her nightgown. They liked the idea and thanked me for what I had done for Ro and for them. I reminded them that Ro had given me far more than I could ever have given her. I pinned the medal on her gown beside her own medals. I blessed her with the holy water and she opened her eyes and knew we were all with her. I let her know that it was okay to go and that she would be safe. She was completely surrounded by love. She drifted back into unconsciousness. She had given us all a final farewell. I hugged and kissed the Vassalluzzo family and left the room.

Then I walked over to Karen's room, where her family was also sitting vigil at her bedside. I held her hand and told her that it was okay to go when she was ready. I also asked Karen's family to allow me to place a medal on her gown and bless her with the water that had traveled with me from Ephesus. They were just as receptive as the Vassalluzzo family had been, and just as Ro had done, Karen opened her eyes and knew we were present, and then drifted away again.

231

I left, deeply saddened at having to say goodbye to this family. They were hurting so profoundly. No mother should have to watch a child die. They were still having trouble coming to grips with the loss of this beautiful woman. They were trying to understand Karen's decisions to pursue alternative therapy first and were conflicted about why she had chosen that path. I explained to them that she may have had the same outcome and they had to let go of that judgment as it only caused pain. I advised them to just love Karen for the beautiful soul that she is, and believe that she will always be with them in spirit.

I was trembling as I walked out of the oncology unit to go to my car. The nurses knew that I was shaken and asked if I was going to be all right. Many physicians pull away from families during these times of transition because it is so emotionally draining, but I knew that this was when those who are left behind need a physician's healing most.

I reassured the nurses that I had just been given confirmation from Ro and Karen. They let me know they were safe. I extracted a promise from the staff to take care of these special families that I had to leave. I knew these compassionate and caring nurses would keep their promise.

As I drove away from the hospital, my heart broken, a fine mist of rain began to cover my windshield. I looked out of my rear view mirror and immediately knew that I was in the presence of a state of grace. A magnificent double rainbow was covering the hospital, starting from the cancer floor and arching over the entire building. I called up to the nurse's station and told them to tell Karen and Ro's families to look out of the window. These two wonderful souls had given us a final gift; a double rainbow in the midst of a beautiful sunny fall day. Neither woman regained consciousness. Both transitioned into spirit on September 30, 2001, twenty-three years to the day, after my brother passed over into spirit. I would not be present for the funerals, but I knew the time I had spent with the families during those few days before Karen and Ro died was more important than being at a formal service.

I cannot go to a funeral without being catapulted back to my brother's memorial service. I feel the pain of the loss and at times forget all the vital life lessons that Bart's premature passing has taught me. What I know to be true about relationships is that it is far more important to make your feelings known to the ones you love while they are alive. If you wait to pay your respects until they have passed, then you miss the opportunity to feel the cords of energy that attach your heart chakra to theirs.

By no coincidence, Dean's teacher from the day care center had seen the rainbows and had snapped photos. The pictures show the rainbows over the daycare center that Ro had been instrumental in starting at St. Mary. She felt that the nurses would be able to render a higher quality of care for their patients if they had excellent, loving care for their children when they were at work.

Mary Ellen, Dean's teacher, was obviously unaware of the significance of the rainbows when she photographed them. She had just appreciated their beauty and took the pictures as a reminder of a beautiful moment in time. When she learned what they meant to me, she gave me the negatives and I put them in a safe place with a plan to make copies for the families. I put them in such a safe place that I didn't find them until nearly a year later, but the timing of their return was divine as I will relate later.

The gifts from these spiritual events at the hospital had given me back some of the hope that September 11 had stolen from my heart. I was again reminded that although the physical body can at times be taken away prematurely, the spirit will continue to live on. We are often blind to the gifts of spirit, being as bound to our earthly existence as we are. Our physicality can at times become so dense and overwhelming that we forget it is just a small part of who we truly are. Our essence becomes lost in the daily routine of life on earth and this is not as it should be. As we grow and evolve, there comes a point when we are unable to separate the day-to-day functions of living from the spiritual realm that empowers and uplifts us. I know now that we must live the talk, and walk the walk, recognizing our essence, our true being. When we are able to do that, we are listening to inner knowledge and wisdom.

We must ask ourselves: *Does this action make my heart sing or sink?* The things that make the heart sink do not honor who it is that we are. Those things that make our heart sing are to be followed and pursued, as they help us to be who we truly are. At that time, I was listening to my inner voice and I was moving into a place of knowledge. I was a healer and I had the ability to help others to awaken to the healing potential that resides within them.

# Chapter 20
## *Soul's Reunion*

Travel had become a major project after 9/11 but
Penny arrived in Philadelphia from Houston without incident. After a brief stay in Bucks County, we departed for
Rhinebeck; both of us excited and ready to learn. It was
a gorgeous, sunny, autumn day in the Northeast. It was
unseasonably warm and we drove the entire way with
the convertible top down, enjoying the changing fall
foliage. Penny and I did not stop talking for the entire
five-hour trip. We had so much to catch up on since the

cruise, which had been just four weeks earlier. The world had changed drastically in that short time, and we discussed the possibility that the work we felt we were being called to do was even more important than we had initially believed. An opportunity for growth had just been given to the world and particularly to our country. What greater adversity did we as a nation need to grow and evolve spiritually?

Penny and I talked about the things that had brought us together, the coincidences and the synchronicities, and we came to believe that perhaps we had been positioned by the universe to move into a new consciousness and to set the stage for an awakening. We wanted to believe—in fact, did believe—that our paths had converged toward a greater purpose for this leg of our trip in this lifetime.

We arrived in Rhinebeck just after nightfall and checked into a bed and breakfast. After we unpacked, Penny and I headed for Omega to make sure we had our directions straight so we would not be late in the morning. We also wanted to explore the bookstore. The store was loaded with all sorts of spiritual paraphernalia and New Age books. As we browsed the shelves, I was telling Penny about how many patients I had to juggle and rearrange in order to be able to come for the course. A head popped around from the next aisle and into my life walked Alan, a surgeon from the Northeast, who had heard what I'd just said. Because so many times a chance meeting like this revealed something exceptional for me later on, I had a feeling that this meeting with Alan would hold a special lesson or meaning on my journey. Penny and I left the store with a pile of books along with a chakra scepter for Penny and a goddess drum for me.

(I guess I was feeling very drawn to the goddess energy within me, and Penny was feeling the draw of royalty within her.)

We arrived at the course to find our dear friends, Brian and Carole, as beautiful as when we had left them. We found it comforting to be back in their company. They had a gift for making people feel embraced by the strength of their inner light. We planned to have dinner with them during the week so we could catch up and share pictures from Greece.

The course began with Brian telling his story of spiritual awakening. We then quickly moved into exercises of remote viewing, meditation, and relaxation. During remote viewing, an object is placed out of site and the participants attempt to intuitively identify and describe the hidden object. During the remote viewing exercise, we were asked to quiet our minds and visualize the object Brian had placed in a box. Several people saw a red object. Some saw a stuffed animal. Alan saw a furry red lobster and he was right. I knew at that moment he was either terribly spiritually gifted or a plant in the audience! Brian guided us in a step-like progression to hypnosis and regression. We had two very powerful sessions watching both Brian and then Carole demonstrate different hypnosis and regression techniques.

Brian was the first to regress a volunteer from the group, a woman named Jamie who regressed easily. She was lead first into pleasant childhood memories, then to a birth memory, and finally into several past lives. She recalled two very distinct past lives. In the first she was dishonored and murdered by her partner who, it turned out, was her boyfriend in her current life. Then she remembered being married to a wonderful potato farmer in Ireland. They had no money, but were rich with love. When asked if she knew him in her present life, she giggled and said that he was a neighbor with whom she had a very deep and special friendship but no romantic ties. I was mesmerized by how touching this regression was to watch and experience. The expression on this woman's face when she was reliving her childhood memories and certain moments in her past lives was deep and poignant. She was such a gentle soul and she opened her heart to the class that day. It was easy to see her genuine nature shining through, and dare I say it, there was a familiarity.

I walked up to her after the class and introduced myself. I told her how moved I was by the session. I also told her that I could swear I knew her from somewhere, a rather weird thing to say at a regression training course. (The joke goes, "Do you know me from this life or a previous one?") I have a tremendous memory for faces and even though I meet innumerable people in my life, I can almost always remember a face I've seen. I asked her where she lived and she said Atlanta, Georgia. I told her that the only time I'd been in Atlanta was during the Avon 3-Day in September of 2000. We looked at each other again and screamed. Here, right before my eyes, was the Lone Wolf! The energy we had shared on the walk was clearly evident. We were destined to unite and serendipity placed us together once again so we could continue the relationship that had started over a year before in another city. The universe had done it to me again! We were obviously destined to connect in this lifetime. Jamie introduced Penny and me to her friend Tina.

That afternoon Carole regressed Penny to a lifetime when she was a member of royalty. Watching the change in her personality as she regressed into a lifetime of entitlement was amazing. The way she held her head and the intonation of her words reeked of sovereignty. I couldn't help but note that some of the more subtle regal traits are evident in her current personality

After that session, we were told to create a group and start practicing the techniques we were being taught. Our group solidified very quickly. Penny, Jamie, Tina, and I joined with my new buddy, Alan and his friend, Gail, who was a psychiatrist from Miami. We practiced together, ate together, laughed together, and cried together. We were a diverse group of individuals who had been brought together to grow and expand our individual and collective consciousness.

Alan had not been able to regress before this seminar, and I believe he may have been able to let go at this point knowing that another like-minded surgeon was leading him there safely. It was a gift to be so trusted. I was honored that he was able to share with me his innermost childhood memories and past life experiences, which had been locked away even to him. As a result, our friendship would grow beyond the limits of this physical world. There was an unspoken spiritual bond between us, and a level of love and understanding that came from a very different source than what we were used to—one that emanated from a spiritual light. It was a connection not unlike that which I felt with Yianni.

All of us had amazing moments as facilitators of healing. We would carry these experiences back to our daily lives and expand upon them. Alan became a Reiki Master and began to facilitate healing using hypnosis and Reiki techniques. He continues to practice surgery and has been successful at integrating his two worlds.

239

Jamie would actually leave the boyfriend who so dishonored her and would marry her soul mate, Rui, her current neighbor. She would continue her healing as a clairvoyant and "light worker." Gail, a prominent Miami-based psychiatrist, would make career changes which had been accurately predicted that week. Penny would go on to become a Reiki practitioner, helping those souls who are transitioning to spirit while in hospice care. Tina would find the wonders of motherhood, and her calling as a certified facilitator of Creative Journal Expressive Art. I returned to my surgical practice knowing that I had my work cut out for me in my ongoing quest to make a difference in the way we, as a society, choose to think about medicine and healing.

Alan, who is a wise and very spiritual being, had given me some simple yet valuable advice that week. He reminded me to follow my heart. He said that I was the "wielder of the sword" and that I have the ability to create great change. I needed to carefully choose my battles while spreading love and light along the way. He told me that I would meet obstacles, which at times would appear insurmountable, but I had the depth of spirit and courage to persevere. Alan reminded me to stay grounded and not get lost in the light since I was so new to it. Most importantly he reminded me to be patient, as things do not always occur as fast as I would like.

Jamie wrote simple yet profound messages in my journal:

* Love and light shine throughout you and your life.
* May your peace engulf your heart and your mind.
* All knowledge lies in silence.

- What you believe in is your own truth.
- If you want to remain constant, always change.
- Change is the only thing that is constant.
- Live in the moment—it is all we have.
- Thank you for being who you are and spreading light everywhere you step.
- It is amazing to think we have come around twice to meet—we must stay in touch.

As the week came to a close, we were so much richer for having shared this experience. I was anxious to go home and practice all that we had learned. There was a wonderful and moving ceremony at the conclusion of our course to remember and honor those who had perished in the events of September 11. During this ceremony I stood next to a woman who reminded me a little of Whoopie Goldberg. This amazing person was Terry Tipton and although our encounter was brief at Omega, our friendship and spiritual connection was profound. When we touched hands in the closing circle, we both burst into tears. We felt as though we had been reunited in this lifetime. She is a medical intuitive and our worlds had, in that moment, become intertwined again.

I returned from Omega, and jumped right back into the fire of being a general surgeon and running a medical practice. I wanted desperately to integrate spirituality and healing into my practice on a daily basis. Now I was supercharged and needed direction. I found it.

While sitting at a meeting of the hospital Foundation Board of which I was a member, we were discussing new opportunities for fundraising. I mentioned that it would be great to support the healing needs of our community by organizing a fundraiser specifically for breast cancer patients. St. Mary Medical Center

Foundation, which is a non-profit organization, helps to sustain the hospital by soliciting philanthropic support from the community. I thought a fashion show would be an ideal fundraiser. We needed funds to support the healing modalities for breast cancer patients and a fashion show would tap into female energy because it would fall under the fundraising arm of the Women's Guild. Some members of the Guild were negative at first, since a previous fashion show had been unsuccessful and the work to produce it was overwhelming. Before I knew it, I was volunteering to be the chairperson of the event. What was I thinking? I knew I didn't have the time to do it. Yet it felt right, and I had learned at this point to listen to my inner voice.

At the first fashion show meeting, we decided to make the evening a tribute to Rosemarie Vassalluzzo since she had been such an inspiration during her battle with cancer and had been an integral member of the Women's Guild for many years. I was blessed to have a team of hard working, passionate, and appropriately pushy women to bring this event to fruition. We began our mission with strategic planning in October, and then, after a break for the holidays, we manifested unbelievable support in the form of huge amounts of money and donations for the favors and items for the Chinese auction.

My dream to create a way to promote healing for women with cancer in our community was coming true. I had thought it would take years to develop a program like this. We were truly on a healing mission through the Foundation, and I was continuing on in my personal healing mission as well.

When I returned from Omega, Dean and Tom were interested in my new-found skills in hypnosis and regression. Tom wanted desperately to be regressed, but I explained to him that it isn't a game and I was not comfortable with him being a "regression tourist" until he was older. Dean accepted the whole concept and would be my teacher every night for the next month. It is our ritual to say *The Words* with Dean before bed. Joe and I go to his room separately and recite our special words as his sendoff to sleep. During this particular time, Dean also imparted words of wisdom to me that were well beyond his earthly age.

The first message I received from Dean was on my first night back from Omega. When I was tucking him into bed, he reminded me, at the ripe old age of barely five, that "life is good." I asked him where that came from and he responded that he had lots to teach me. Two nights later, while getting comfortable in his bed, he looked at me and said, "I am here this time to teach you about honor and peace. It is not an easy lesson, Mom." He looked at me and said, "That's it! Good night." I really didn't know what to think, but I was curious to know what the next day's lesson would be. During the next few weeks, I would get many lessons before bed from this little towhead.

October 8: "I'm here to teach you forgiveness and love. You need to teach this to your patients, Mom."
October 9: "Share with people who are hurting."
October 15: "Pray for people who are almost dying."
November 8: "Mom, touch each patient by helping them find their spirit. Tomorrow, Mom, help each patient completely."
November 23: "Remind people to share their manners."

243

I was receiving such beautiful messages from my five-year-old teacher. He obviously remembered who he is and had decided to remind me who I am. Had I not been awakened at that point, I would not have recorded these beautiful messages and they would have been lost as idle chatter from a child. Instead I recorded them in my gratitude journal. The last entry from Dean was directly below one of my own entries that read: I am grateful for the health and wellness of my husband and children. I am grateful for the patients who have trusted me with their care. I am grateful for every moment of every day.

My spiritual growth continued with my Master Level Reiki training in December of 2001, which was the most profound experience I had had with Reiki. After having spent so many years training to attain mastery over the physical body as a surgeon, my focus had now shifted and I continued focusing on mastery of the spiritual in my quest to facilitate healing through Reiki. Spiritual growth and development required that I trust the intangible and unseen, and I needed to learn to surrender and trust more. My Master Level training was perfectly timed because I was ready to move forward in this way on my spiritual path.

As fast as I was evolving spiritually, I was continuing to grow as a surgeon as well, specifically as a breast care specialist. I was learning new minimally invasive techniques to speed up the diagnostic process for my patients. I was open to new technologies and truly felt I was being drawn to bring together the technologies of the West with the healing modalities of the East.

The connections and friendships I had maintained over the years in the world of breast care would prove

to be an important influence in my evolution as a minimally invasive breast surgeon. My eventual transition
into teaching these techniques to other colleagues would
place me in the appropriate place and time to meet my
future business partners who would help me to actual-
ize my dream of developing a comprehensive breast care
center.

My non-physician breast care colleagues taught me
valuable lessons. They empowered me to embrace new
techniques in order to provide improved patient care.
They were passionate about what they did and that kind
of passion is contagious. Adopting these new technologies would save precious time in obtaining a diagnosis
while at the same time being much less invasive for my
patients.  ·

It is sometimes difficult to let go of ego. I was taught
in residency to take patients into the operating room to
make the diagnosis of cancer. I had to be open in order
to rethink that process. It would be hard to break old
habits, particularly when that meant I had to step out of
my comfort zone. I was used to having my patients
under anesthesia during their biopsies. Now I had to be
prepared to have them watch me perform the procedure. I had to be present in the moment with them. I
recalled the wisdom of my spiritual buddies: "Change is
the only thing that is constant." You are the "wielder of
the sword and have the ability to create change." If I can
be open and change the way I treat my patients, then I
may be able to open the eyes of my colleagues as well.
In this case less was truly more. I was now able, through
the new techniques, to make diagnoses that enabled my
patients to make decisions about their future treatments
in an expedient and less invasive manner.

Although saving time does not change a prognosis, waiting and wondering feels like an eternity to a person waiting to find out if he or she has cancer. Adopting minimally invasive biopsy techniques allowed me to stay connected and present with my patients throughout the biopsy procedure, and allowed for a much more rapid diagnostic return from the pathologist. This process created deeper relationships between the patients and myself and allowed them to be even more active participants in their disease process. Anything, from diagnosis through every phase of treatment, that empowers a patient to maintain control, accelerates their ability to heal. Additionally, with patients awake for their biopsies, I could use my Reiki training to facilitate the healing process.

I had been seeing the effects of Reiki healing on so many patients. When I am about to perform a biopsy procedure on a patient, I take time to be completely present with them before the procedure begins. This eliminates outside distractions and lets them know that they are the focus of my intention. This may be as simple as holding their hand for reassurance, placing my hand on their arm or in some cases, when a patient has tremendous fear coming into a biopsy, I may have another Reiki practitioner present. The progression to a less invasive and more expedient diagnosis made for a natural marriage of my Eastern and Western worlds.

I was expanding our ability to render state-of-the-art breast care in our office. I added breast ultrasound to our practice, acting from a position of knowing what was right for our patients and not from a place of fear that we wouldn't be reimbursed for the scans. I sent Stacy for advanced training in mammography and ultrasound to help her feel more comfortable with her development as a breast care specialist as well.

I was following my heart, and making decisions based upon knowledge, experience, technology, and intuition. I felt compelled to stay on the leading edge of breast surgery while I continued to find keys to further empower healing in my patients. I was beginning to feel more balance between my medical and spiritual worlds. There were fewer obstacles and more synchronicities in my everyday life. I truly felt I was on the correct path.

## Chapter 21
## A Stylish Celebration of Life

My committee worked very hard to make the fundraiser, which we were calling, "A Stylish Celebration of Life," a huge success. Tina McCaffrey oversaw the room layout and decorations. She came through with everything and anything we needed. Tina was the last to leave a planning meeting in the summer of 2002, which had been held in my back yard. We were sitting alone when she told me how important this fundraiser had become to her. She wanted me to know that in working on this event, she herself was being healed. Tina shared that she was thrilled that I cared so much about patients' overall wellbeing and was not content to end where modern medicine finishes. It meant a great deal to her to help facilitate my desire to make a difference in my patients' lives.

She proceeded to tell me things about herself that I had not known before. Tina had been diagnosed with cancer of the uterus twenty years earlier, just after her son, Kevin, was born. I mean literally after his birth, while still in the postpartum state, she had received the devastating diagnosis. I can't even image the feelings she must have had, being dealt that hand with a newborn and three older children at home.

I had no idea that Tina had been through such an ordeal and was surprised to find out that because of her surgery and chemotherapy, she felt she had not had a chance to be present with her newborn son and three older children in the year that followed her diagnosis. It was a devastating blow that I felt still haunted her.

Tina told me that her surgeon had not understood the concept of "healing," nor had he shown her any compassion during her ordeal. She used some rather colorful language to describe him and said that he did nothing to promote healing within his patients. His treatment of Tina had been so callous that even twenty years later, it evoked strong negative emotions in her. When she shared with me his name, I was speechless. Her surgeon was the physician who had conducted my interview at Hahnemann University some twenty years earlier, exactly one year after Tina's ordeal. He was the individual responsible for my acceptance into medical school. At the time of my interview, I had totally connected with this man. He had completed his training in my hometown and was still

250

friends with several physicians I knew from York. So the synchronicities continued. The man who had found something worthy in me had treated my friend and saved her life. Unfortunately he was unaware that she had never healed. We were both amazed at this coincidence. Tina said, "Well, he couldn't be all bad if he was in any way responsible for your becoming a physician."

We bonded that evening as we continued to discuss what she had been through, and our conversation made it even clearer to me how much a physician can influence the healing of a patient not only in the present, but for the many years that follow. Although I had known Tina for years, I had never known her intimately. Having shared the emotional pain from having had cancer, our friendship deepened. Once again, the journey was as spectacular as the destination.

September 30, 2002, seemed to come upon us almost without warning. The fashion show committee was excited to see how the event was coming together. We sold all 350 tickets well in advance and there was a demand for more; a problem that everyone who runs a fundraiser wishes would be their worst problem. The energy level surrounding the evening promised it would be an affair to remember, and throughout the event we laughed, cried, and celebrated life. Our beautiful models were either survivors of breast cancer or loved ones of survivors (and it must be said that loved ones are also survivors). They walked the runway like real pros, and the clothing, hair, makeup, and passion from both the stage and the audience was electrifying.

"A Stylish Celebration of Life" was a huge tribute to Rosemarie Vassalluzzo. I shared with the audience everything I found special about Ro and how she had taught

251

me about the importance of healing. Ro's spirit will continue to guide me on my quest to always include healing as part of the process of treating a disease. We raised more than $55,000 that evening and were well on our way to making the Breast Cancer Healing Ministries at St. Mary a reality.

In the days that followed, I looked forward to slowing down a little for the holidays and spending time with my family. I continued to feel the presence of the divine in my everyday life. I tried to integrate these experiences in the moment but when I didn't have time to process things as they occurred, I saw opportunities for acceptance. I was beginning to understand that some of the things occurring in my life were beyond explanation in the physical linear sense. I was still learning about surrender.

On Halloween night, I was paged by a doctor in the Emergency Room about a man with abdominal pain. The doctor thought the man had acute appendicitis. Although this gentleman had been having pain for only a few days, he required emergency surgery for appendicitis. After his surgery, I went into the waiting room to talk to his family, letting them know the surgery went well. I was anxious to get home to take Dean Trick or Treating. I changed into my street clothes and went through the recovery room to make a final check on the status of my patient. The nurses told me there was going to be a delay in sending him to his room, although he was doing just fine. I asked if I could bring his family member into recovery to just say goodnight. They agreed and I went back to the surgical waiting room.

When I entered, I found the McCaffrey family sitting in a state of shock. Jim walked up to me and told me he had arrived home that night to find Tina slumped over in a chair with a bag of candy in her hand. She had not regained consciousness even when the paramedics had resuscitated her. He informed me that she was being taken to surgery for evacuation of a bleed from a ruptured cerebral aneurysm. How could this be? Just hours before my friend had been completely healthy and now she was barely alive.

I went back to the OR to see what was happening with her and I could see that the neurosurgeon was clearly distressed by what he was finding. I returned to the McCaffrey's to give them an update and then went home to see my husband and children. I needed hugs and kisses from those who are so important to me. It is difficult at times to find balance between family and career. It was moments like these that reminded me of just how special hugs from Tommy and Dean are to my existence.

My friend was holding on to life by an invisible thread, and it made me feel very vulnerable. I waited until my children were tucked safely into bed and returned to the hospital. Tina's prognosis was very poor and I was trying to prepare the family for the possibility that she was not going to recover. I had been in this situation so many times as a physician. I knew she would not wake up, let alone recover. I knew this both medically and intuitively. It was so heart wrenching to see her family suffer. Knowing Tina would not regain consciousness, I knew I had to reach out and offer spiritual support and prepare her family for the inevitable—her passing. Her body was no longer able to sustain life with her severe brain injury and it was time for her spirit to transition to another place.

The next couple of days were very difficult and the hospital rallied around the McCaffrey family in every way we could. I was with my colleague, a neurologist who is a very close friend of the McCaffreys, when he performed the first set of brain-death criteria on Tina. The tests have to be repeated again twenty-four hours later to fulfill the state's requirement before mechanical ventilation is removed. I had decided to be present the next day as well to support Tina's family.

That night I was called in to operate on an elderly woman who had a perforated ulcer (a hole in the lining of her stomach). It was another life threatening situation that required emergency surgery that evening. After surgery I stopped in to the Intensive Care Unit to visit with Tina. I expected her to be alone but found her entire family sitting by her bedside. They were spending time together, preparing for the inevitable. It was a special and sacred time for them. They were able to laugh while remembering and celebrating this fabulous woman, wife, mother, daughter, grandmother, and friend. I heard many stories that night about Tina. I sat back and listened, appreciating the strength of this special group of people.

I left her room close to one thirty in the morning, and a few hours later I planned to return to be with the neurologist while he performed the brain-death criteria test again. My intuition and the family's worst fears were realized. Tina would never wake up. I would not have to endure the pain of removing the ventilator from Tina, her heart stopped spontaneously and she departed this physical plane. I received the call from Maria, another dear friend and committee member from the fashion show. She informed me that Tina had passed over without intervention. She wanted to let me know that the family would be at the hospital for a short while and that I should call her when I arrived there.

I left my house for the hospital to see the McCaffreys and make rounds on my patients. I went to Tina's room and she looked very beautiful. Her body was at peace now that all the tubes and monitors were removed. I had recently read accounts about the experience of passing over into spirit. Many people who have experienced near death describe floating above the physical body left on earth during the time of physical death. I sat at the bedside alone holding Tina's hand. Her skin was still warm and dry. I cried for the first time since she had been brought to the hospital. Before this I had maintained my composure for the sake of her family. Now I needed to grieve the loss of my friend. I spoke aloud to Tina, just as if she was awake and listening to me. I told her I loved her and promised to take care of the things that we had discussed in my back yard during the fashion show meeting the summer before. I told her that no matter how she chose to contact me, I would be listening and I needed to know that she was okay. I was expecting a message like Ro's rainbow or some subtle sign like that to tell she was fine.

I left the room and thanked the nurses for their superb care of Tina and her family. I walked down the hall and headed for the staircase. I still needed to make rounds and felt the need to walk up four flights of stairs rather than take the elevator to the surgical floor. I emerged from the stairwell slightly winded and headed down the corridor toward my patients' rooms.

A man was walking toward me, staring intently. His stare seemed to look right through me and he made me feel uncomfortable. I attempted to look away, but was drawn back to his gaze. He said, "Hello, Beth." I answered, "Hello . . . I'm sorry, but I don't know how I know you." At St. Mary it is not uncommon for people to know me or know of me, but they usually call me Dr. DuPree unless they are personal friends. As he reached over to touch my forearm, he said, "When you know how you know me, you will remember me." I was still shaken and in a state of high emotions after just having left Tina's room and I felt strange vibes coming from this man. I told him I needed to go and see my patients, but he held onto my arm. "I have a message for you," he said. "From whom?" I asked him, curious now. "Your friend loves you very much and she wants you to know that she is okay. She thanks you for being there with her family last night. She will always be with you." I was blown away to say the least. I asked him again, "How do you know me and who are you talking about?" He just calmly said again, "When you know how you know me, you will remember me. The message is from your friend Tina." I was in a state of shock. He then continued, "Only love is real and the gifts you will leave are your sons. Your children are so important. You need to be with them today. When you remember who I am you will find me."

With that he let me go and walked away. I stood there in the hall in a state of disbelief. I had asked for a sign from Tina, but this was beyond what even I could imagine. I walked to the nurse's station and asked if they had seen the man I had been talking to in the hall. I was afraid that they would tell me he really was not up on the floor and had just appeared to me. They said that he was a family member of a patient in one of the other rooms. Some things in the purely physical realm are beyond understanding. I composed myself before entering my patient's room.

I walked into the room of a woman who had been admitted the day before with abdominal pain. She had refused to have her gallbladder removed because she was afraid to undergo anesthesia for the surgery. She told me she was feeling better. I explained that I was glad she felt better and that she still needed to have her gallbladder removed at a later date. She would continue to have pain unless it was removed. We had discussed the options for surgery the day before and it had been obvious to me that she was very fearful of surgery. I tried to reassure her that she had every reason to think the operation would go well since she was otherwise healthy.

Now when I entered her room she told me she had changed her mind and had decided during the night to have the surgery after all. I asked her what had changed her mind, and she replied that I would think she was crazy if she told me the truth. I asked her to try me—I was having a rather strange day myself. She answered that her sister, who had passed over into spirit a year earlier, came to her in a dream the night before and told her to trust me, that she would be fine, and that she was in very capable hands. I assured her that I did not think she was crazy. I hugged her and thanked her for trusting me.

I went back to the nurse's station and sat down with the patient's chart in my hands, and needless to say, tried to process all that had happened that morning. I understood that I needed to surrender because all the mental shifting and manipulation of these events would not make sense no matter how I tried to figure them out. I just had to accept them. To quote my friend, James Van

Praagh, "And so it is!" I had to accept that some events are beyond my explanation.

The mortal side of me wanted more information about the messenger that Tina had chosen. I looked at the patient charts and found out that my messenger was a retired postman. Only Tina would be clever enough to choose a United States postal worker to get a message to me. Although the message from Tina was a gift for me, being the bearer of this type of message isn't always a gift to the messenger.

Having the ability to communicate with those who have passed over into spirit is not always a gift. Over the next few days and weeks I had some very interesting and sometimes disturbing conversations with this messenger. He truly had been blessed—and cursed—by his ability to see and hear things most of us in the physical plane can only imagine. His knowledge of the world beyond this realm haunts his daily existence. I will be forever thankful for the message and for the messenger. I wish him peace, love, and light.

It had become obvious that my life and consciousness were opening and awakening in ways conferences and books could not totally prepare me for. I was reading less about spirituality and experiencing more of the divine. My personal relationships with souls I had past connections with were teaching me lessons about love, faith, and trust.

My practice was shifting to a point where surgery, as crucial as it is to treating cancer, was the least of the things I could do to help my patients. I would never stop performing state-of-the-art breast surgery, but the actual operation is just the start of a shift in consciousness that takes place when healing begins. It may be the disease that brings patients to my office, but it is the opportunity for growth and healing that keeps them there for treatment. I knew I would be able to facilitate the healing process much more effectively with the Breast Cancer Healing Ministries in place. My patients now had the resources they needed to release fear and follow their path of healing.

Chapter 22

# Change is the Only Constant in Life

In December of 2002, Astra Zeneca, the pharmaceutical company that manufactures multiple breast cancer drugs, honored several individuals for making a difference in breast cancer care within their communities; I was fortunate to be one. We were selected by the makers of the drug, Tamoxifen, to receive the Horizon of Hope Award. As the only surgeon honored for this event, I was proud to be recognized alongside so many talented and amazing cancer survivors and advocates. It was refreshing to know that others felt compelled to support healing in their communities, and it was even more wonderful to see a drug company applauding the work so many of us do as our passion. They acknowledged the impact going the extra mile, beyond what is standard medical care, had on patients. The effects of healing have a far greater reach than can be seen by the naked eye. I was pleasantly surprised to find so many other physicians at the San Antonio meeting who were also awakening to this knowledge.

The New Year brought to the forefront my goals and desires for the future. Stacy and I had been actively looking for another associate or two to join our practice. We were determined to not settle for a warm body, and great surgeons were few and far between. We were outrageously busy. Too many surgeons were leaving Pennsylvania as a result of the malpractice crisis. Our geographic area has very high malpractice premiums and this has kept many young physicians from coming to the state. Without additional help in our practice, I would be unable to devote time to the aspects of surgery that were calling to me. I knew I needed to start backing out of general surgery and dedicate my time to breast care, which was clearly my passion. It was important that the person who shared our practice was of the same mind as Stacy and me. Health care was changing, but not fast enough to keep up with the shift in consciousness that was occurring within me.

Our current health care model has mortally wounded the doctor-patient relationship. Doctors have less time to spend listening to our patients and connecting with them because we have to keep our practices financially viable. I was keenly aware of the importance of connecting with the heart chakra energy in my patients. That aspect of medicine takes time to develop. Insurance companies have decreased reimbursement yet they've increased demands on our time. In many cases they've placed restrictions on where we can send our patients for tests, where we can perform procedures, and what tests we can order. They have, at times, placed the physician and the patient in an adversarial relationship, which is not conducive to healing. As a result, physicians are frustrated and dissatisfied.

That is not to say that we, as health care providers, are not also responsible for this breakdown. As physicians, it has been virtually impossible to unite as a group to help direct health care policy, which has, in some cases, been modeled as a business relationship. Therefore, the connection between a patient in the healing process and the physician, a facilitator in that healing process, has been lost in the business of medicine. We are not businessmen or politicians at heart; we are practitioners of medicine and healers. Most importantly, we are not omniscient. We cannot cure every disease or ailment.

If we partner with our patients and work together to promote the best possible outcomes, we are in it together. Patients and families need to have open channels of communication with their health care providers to allow a healing bond to grow. If complications or unexpected outcomes occur, doctors must remain committed, following through and supporting patients and their families through adversity. By remaining committed and providing the best care possible, we will know we have done all that we humanly can to make a difference.

There is nothing more meaningful and satisfying than having a patient extend a heartfelt thank you for

263

having a positive impact on his or her life. I love what I do because I am given the opportunity to make a difference in someone's life every single day. I am in medicine because I love being a healer. It took me years in this profession to figure it out, and I can imagine that it may take some physicians several lifetimes.

How I do what I do is as important as what I do. I believe this is why so many physicians have burned out in our current medical model. Many are working tirelessly in the business of medicine, and are missing the opportunity to connect with the human spirit and truly make a difference—not just for their patients but also for themselves. They are missing out on the wonderful gifts their patients have to give them. Healing works both ways. Physicians don't have to buy into Reiki, or energy healing, or becoming enlightened spiritually, to learn this lesson and change the way they treat their patients. We just need to remember why we chose medicine as a career path: to help patients heal.

Stacy and I tried to find new associates but to no avail. In January of 2003, I made a gigantic step in my career anyway. I chose to limit my elective surgical practice to surgery involving diseases of the breast, thyroid and parathyroid. Leaving general surgery was not simply a personal decision. It turned out to be a political decision that created some controversy within the hospital.

I felt compelled to do that which made my heart sing. It was the lesson I had been teaching my patients for years. I told them it was important to follow their passions and make the changes in their lives that honor them. How could I preach something I was unwilling to practice? I am fortunate to have the opportunity to follow my passion.

Having nights and weekends to spend with my family would be something new for me to experience. I wanted and needed to spend more time with those beings that chose to be with me in this lifetime as my children. They were growing up so fast. Because of the demands of my practice as a general surgeon, my time with them was shorter by the minute. I needed to realize how fortunate I was that I had the opportunity to focus more intently on my passions, my family, and breast care. It was a gift and all I needed to do was make it happen.

Stacy was committed to general surgery because that was what resonated within her soul. She was young and her journey as a surgeon was just beginning. I knew that she would some day be married and would want a family as well. I wanted desperately to find other general surgeons who would fit into our practice. This would allow Stacy to follow her passions and have some quality of life as well. My leaving general surgery would translate into every night on call for her. I had to deal with my guilt for that and surrender my need to take care of her.

I learned along the way that she is responsible for her journey and that the decisions that she makes for herself—good or bad—are her decisions. For some reason I felt the need to protect her. I wanted her to have a smooth course in her development as a surgeon. I never had a little sister (that was my role in the family) and I suppose she was my surrogate little sister-surgeon. I felt compelled to protect her from some of the hurt and pain I had experienced along the way.

As I reflected on that pain, I realized that it often gave me the opportunity for growth and made me tougher and stronger. I needed to let go and allow Stacy to feel her own anguish and develop the strength to deal with some of the struggles in the political arena of surgery. Together we were trying to figure out how to make this transition smooth and seamless.

I wanted and needed to start writing this book and I made a promise to myself to get started. I had to make time, which required another lesson in time management. I was continuously awakening in the wee hours of the morning—at 4:44 A.M.—with ideas and stories that needed to be included in this book. I would see the time flash clearly on the clock in my bedroom. I shared with friends that I was always waking up at this time, and they informed me that they were also waking up at the exact time. Someone suggested that maybe that was when our angels and messengers choose to communicate with us. I had to get started writing if I ever expected to sleep though the night again!

I began writing the manuscript in my journal during a flight to Miami in February of 2003. I was headed for a breast cancer conference and hoped I would have the opportunity to spend some quiet time reflecting and writing. I was aboard an empty US Air flight out of Philadelphia direct to Miami and my creative juices were flowing. Before I knew it, I had arrived at my destination and my pen ran out of ink as we touched down on the tarmac. My hand was cramped from writing for two and a half hours straight, and my head was spinning. As we began to disembark, a friendly smile caught my eye from the row across and behind my seat. An attractive African American woman commented on my nonstop writing during the flight. She said she was impressed with my determination and ability to focus. I shared with her that I was writing a book about my spiritual awakening and the lessons I have learned as a breast cancer surgeon about healing. She stood up and I could see that she was wearing a US Air uniform and a lymph edema sleeve (garments worn to help prevent swelling in the arm after lymph-nodes are removed). I knew instantly that she was a survivor of breast cancer. As we departed the plane together, Michelle Lowery shared with me her experience with breast cancer and the book she wrote about the journey titled, *The Unexpected Traveler*. Our meeting was brief but the connection was strong. I have since read her book and loved her story. I am often reminded about the need for each of us to tell our story and be heard. Michelle found healing in her writing and I applaud her for her strength and the insight she had into her breast cancer process. She was an unexpected gift on this particular leg of my journey.

In the past, being able to combine my spiritual life and my professional life had been an effort, but these were becoming increasingly, and more seamlessly, intertwined. My trip to Miami to learn the latest and greatest in breast care had become a journey of spiritual evolution as well. The year before, I was able to connect with Carole, Donna, her friend whom I had met in Greece, and Gail, the psychiatrist from my regression course. This year I would be with Carole, Brian, Alan, Gail, and my old and new spiritual buddies from Ethicon Breast Care. My worlds were no longer separate and I realized that as I allowed them to come together, they fit quite nicely.

Many people keep their spirituality safely tucked away within their hearts. Once they see someone who is open with their spirituality, they often feel safe enough to open up and share their own beliefs. I am quite vocal about my journey, no throat chakra issues here, and this creates a safe place in which others can share their beliefs and thoughts.

Dinner with Carole and Brian Weiss was wonderful, as usual. Carole and Brian were busy traveling around the world, educating those who were opening to the spiritual realm, and I was lucky enough to find them in Miami. My surgical resident at the time, Christine McGinn, who was doing an elective rotation at St. Mary, wanted desperately to meet Brian. She scheduled the conference in hopes that we would be able to have dinner with them. A nurse from Miami had given her Brian's books years before when she was in the midst of a very difficult time. They made all the difference to her in her quest to find answers to some very difficult questions in her personal life. She wanted the opportunity to let him know how much his work had helped her and to personally thank him.

Christine McGinn had been born Christopher McGinn, and as Christopher, had been educated as a flight surgeon and helicopter pilot in the United States Navy. She was now officially, having undergone trans-gender surgery, reassigned as Christine McGinn, D.O., a female surgical resident.

Christine had been our resident for the few months preceding this trip, and both Stacy and I were impressed with her surgical skills and her work ethic. She was a great person who had endured the torment of being trapped within a body that didn't fit with her internal wiring. She had gone public about her trans-gender surgery on a CNBC special as part of her healing process. Being able to connect Christine with a man she felt had, in so many ways, helped to save her life, was a small way to let her know that she was loved. Because Brian's work was instrumental in Christine's healing, hearing her heartfelt story gave Brian the essence of what it is that heals a healer.

I didn't get to talk to Brian much that evening as Christine was engaged in conversation with him the entire time. Their connection was clearly our reason for being together that day. I did have a lovely conversation with Carole and Rob, my old friend, who was newly awakened as I call it. He knew there was more to the world than merely the physical realm, he just needed to remember where he put the batteries to his spiritual flashlight. Corporate America has a way of making us forget that we are spiritual beings just having an earthly experience. He was starting to remember, though, and the three of us had a great time with Brian.

I returned from Miami more resolved than ever to shift my practice to total breast care. I loved it, was good at it, and needed to be doing it full time. I had to figure out why I was even resisting the shift, since it made so much sense. When I really allowed myself to look at it objectively, I was able to see where the resistance was located. I was feeling responsible for bringing Stacy to St. Mary and knew that she was years away from limiting her practice to breast care—if she would even want to choose that someday.

I felt badly that we were unable to find more individuals who wanted to practice surgery in Bucks County. I felt guilty about the lifestyle that breast care would afford my family, knowing that Stacy would be taking call nights and weekends. As my resistance grew, so did my temper. I did not like the person I saw myself becoming.

I had become resentful of being called out to the ER during office hours to see a patient in Emergency when I had women in my office that needed me to treat their breast cancer. Yet, who was I to judge which person needed me more? I resented being awakened at night because of patients who needed surgery at 2:00 A.M. I was burning out and I was only forty-one years old. I never wanted to become one of those physicians who began to resent their patients for interfering with their lives.

Before, I always found I was able to be centered and find the compassionate person within me who loves surgery, the person who knows that how I do what I do makes a difference. But as time pressed on, I was less and less able to tolerate the schedule I was maintaining. My husband and staff were becoming less tolerant of my behavior. My temper was hot and my fuse dangerously short. I knew only I could make the changes necessary to find the person I truly needed to be.

In May, Stacy and I decided to ask another surgeon if he wanted to share patient care responsibilities. We would cross cover call in an attempt to bridge the gap in call coverage for Stacy. I was completely honest from the outset that this was a temporary change until after Stacy's wedding and honeymoon. I set October 1 as my definitive date to stop all general surgery. That would give Stacy two weeks after her return from her honeymoon to get settled back in.

I felt much more centered once I made a plan. I was able to get to this point only after an awakening weekend spent at Far Cry Farm. I received a call from Terry L. Tipton, medical intuitive and founder of the Terry L. Tipton Foundation. She and I had met briefly at Omega yet the bond between us was undeniable. I had not heard from Terry for some time when she called to invite me to a "soul sister" retreat to bless her sacred ground at Far Cry Farm. Here was a woman who I had spent all of ten minutes with in Rhinebeck, New York a year and a half earlier, yet I knew that I needed to be there. It was a last minute decision to attend but the timing was perfect. Joe knew that I was really on edge and something needed to give. He didn't know how else to help, so he helped by telling me to go with his blessings. He sent me off to Maryland with his GPS in hand.

Far Cry Farm was located down a long unpaved road and as I drove to the house, I could see the shoreline, complete with sun shining over the water, and the unmistakable sound of seagulls welcoming me to their home. I arrived at the retreat on Friday afternoon with a rose in hand as an offering of friendship to Terry. I spent the first evening getting to know Terry and her adorable husband Mark before all the other guests arrived.

I had a room in the guesthouse, which had been set up for visitors to the retreat. That evening I wrote a very difficult letter to a friend, which allowed me to release and free emotions I had been holding onto very tightly. I cried as I wrote it, and again as I read it. It didn't matter if I sent it or not. I just needed to release those emotions that were holding me in a place that was not healthy. I came to Far Cry to get away from distraction and allow myself to spend some time healing.

I went to sleep around midnight and was sleeping soundly until the light outside of my room came on. I looked at the clock and it was 4:44 A.M. I got out of bed and turned the light off. I figured there was a motion detector that had tripped the light. The next morning I found out from Mark that there was no motion detector

271

outside my room. I chalked it up to another reminder that I needed to get cracking on my book.

The other guests arrived in the morning and we began a weekend filled with yoga, meditation, healing circles, drumming, dancing, singing, chanting, journaling, crystal healings, and intuitive readings. We ate whole foods and drank pure water. There was no cellular reception on the farm and no need for news from the outside world. It was what I needed to find my way into my future. I set my goals on the first morning, an assignment Terry had given us. I wanted to release negative energy surrounding relationships I continued to hold on to in my life. I needed to forgive myself for actions both done and undone. I wanted to reconnect, awaken to my higher consciousness, and be able to communicate with my guides, something I had never quite been able to do. I also wanted to go forth on my journey of writing *The Healing Consciousness*. I was able to identify my obstacles, as I perceived them, and discovered ways to make them dissipate. My list of obstacles was only five items long:

1. Time
2. Focus
3. Modern Medicine/thinking
4. Financial responsibility for my family
5. Responsibility to my staff and partner, Stacy

I was fortunate that my list was short, and in the end none of the items on it seemed insurmountable. My time could be managed more effectively by better balance in my surgical practice. By limiting my care to diseases of the breast, I would have more time for my patients and family. Taking more time with fewer patients would make a greater impact on those beings.

As for the direction of modern medicine, I wanted to have *The Healing Consciousness* finished and published sooner rather than later; I thought I had an important message to share. I wasn't quite sure who would benefit from reading the book but my job was to put the information out there.

Financial things would just have to work themselves out and I was willing to surrender this perceived limitation. My staff might choose to grow and develop with me, or they might decide another path was right for them. Money cannot be the motivation for staying in a practice where healing is the primary goal. It seemed so clear, yet to reach these conclusions, I needed to make the time for my mind to be quiet enough to hear the answers.

The women I met that weekend all had very special gifts. Terry has been a constant source of amazement for me. She will forever be one of my angels on earth. My roommate, Robin, gave me something I will always treasure. When we retired for the night, I shared with her the story of the light from the night before. When I told her about the light going on outside the door at 4:44 A.M. her face lit up. She told me to read the book, *The Messengers*, if I hadn't already. A few weeks later a copy of *The Messengers*, by Julia Ingram and G.W. Hardin, arrived in the mail. I read it in a day. It was fantastic and the timing was perfect. It is one of my all time favorite reads. I can honestly say that it came into my life exactly when I needed to read it to help me continue on my path.

It is the story of a man who was going through his life in a conventional way. His journey became quite interesting when he had angelic interventions and then several amazing regression experiences. For him, four forty-four

273

in the morning was the time when he received angelic messages. The spiritual realm is very active when our subconscious is alert and our bodies are asleep. That number sequence continues to be very special in my life.

My sister, Susan, and her husband Bruce were visiting from Australia. Tom and Dean were going to my parent's house during their last week before school started, to visit with their aunt and uncle. We wanted to spend as much time with Susie and Bruce as we could before they left. We hadn't spent time with them since our trip to Wyoming a few years before when I had just started this whole spiritual process. Susan, my "soul mate" sister, visited me at the beginning of my spiritual awakening and here she was again as I journeyed into an authentically awakened life. How coincidental.

We were so connected we couldn't be closer if she lived next door to me in Pennsylvania. We had reached the same point in our lives through completely different paths. She was an accountant and was very analytical about life when she left the U.S. After she moved to Australia, she had her own spiritual awakening and had grown both personally and professionally. She was no longer fixated on numbers in a book. She was trained as a social psychologist, yoga master and energy healer. We started on opposite ends of the work spectrum yet came together where it mattered most, focused on healing.

While Susie was visiting, I wanted to share some of my experiences with her. She had heard about the channeling sessions I'd been participating in. I wanted her to be able to have a firsthand experience and perhaps find some guidance in the messages she might receive. As it turned out, Gretty—my friend from the Greek island cruise—and her sister, Babbs were in town and wanted to get together. We made arrangements to go to a channeling session together. Once again, it was a profound experience, with messages being given to us that were life-enriching.

In the text that follows, I paraphrase the messages we received from Raphael that day. She began by sharing that our planet is in a time of enormous transformation, and as this occurs, there is an awakening of the heart. We are being called as a collective consciousness to awaken to our essence and develop a stronger connection to source, whatever we as individuals consider that source to be. To some it is the Christ-energy, but to others it could be thought of as love energy or love consciousness.

She said we must not fear the future, and we must move into a place of grace and ease as we journey with the flow of life into what is to come. Being connected to the source of life, and being a beacon of knowledge and peace for the world, will help bring an overpowering energy of love to those around us; and even more ambitiously, through a network of like-minded people, to the world. First though, we must disengage from fear and judgment. Relying on the feminine within us—whether we are male or female—may help to lead the way to the source of light and love.

In one of the most moving messages we, as women, were asked to connect with the energy that could be identified with a being such as the Mother of Jesus. For those of us who were not Catholic, this was a novel concept, but as women and mothers, we were able to identify. We were asked to place a statue of the Virgin Mother in a central place in our homes, a place where we receive the most joy, as a reminder to stay connected to

275

a sacred heart. We were also told to create a grid with symbols of struggle (for instance, a cross or something that symbolizes strength and divinity) around the outside perimeter of our homes. This would become a portal of love and light through which female energy could connect to the universe. It was intended to work as part of a greater grid system, connecting other people to source. Although I admit it sounds *out there*, it wasn't threatening. It was gentle and comforting. There was nothing to lose by creating a sacred space in my home.

On the evening of the full moon, I received a call with a prayer of intention from a friend who had just activated her energy grid. Joe, Tommy, Dean, and I placed our handmade crosses in a triangular pattern around our property and said a prayer of intention to activate our energy grid. Afterward, I called my sister Sue who followed through in Australia with the placement of her crosses. She called Barbara Schlager and so on. We were all connected in an energetic sense and there was a feeling of peace that came from our ritual. This was not about being Catholic or belonging to an organized religion. It was all about connecting to Love energy (or Christ energy) and being one with the universe, the source of all that is good. Balance must be returned to our planet, and each of us has a very different, yet special, role to play in the process.

This grand plan to restore the planet is very ambitious, but there is always a first step in every grand plan. We must begin with ourselves; balance our own lives before we can begin to balance our planet. As I experienced Raphael's channeling, I realized I was into the fourth week of laryngitis. I wasn't really sick; I had just lost my ability to talk. It became clear to me that it was

my body telling me I needed to act on my intentions
and not just speak of them any longer. I felt this was
referring to my leaving general surgery once and for all
and embracing my desire to focus on breast care. When
October 1 arrived, I followed through with my plan, and
my voice returned from its six-week hiatus.

After that channeling session, I began to see and
hear more of Mary and the cross. It seemed as though
all of my patients had a cross or a miraculous medal
when they came to see me. Perhaps that had always
been the case, but I never noticed it before. Or perhaps
this divine female energy was becoming stronger. There
was even an old Jewish woman who came to see me,
who had in her possession a rosary that a friend had
given her to bring to the appointment—just because it
couldn't hurt. She did not have cancer but she clearly
had faith.

When I was in Manhattan in September, I was walking down Broadway after purchasing tickets to the show
Aida for my son Tom's thirteenth birthday present. I
turned down a street thinking if I walked a block to the
next cross street, I could catch a cab south. As I walked
down the street, I felt a wave of energy overcome me. I
looked up to find myself standing before the Free
Church of the Virgin Mary. I walked inside and immediately felt embraced. Again, here was Mary, and I could
just accept that she had become a part of my life. I
remained within the walls of this magnificent house of
worship and prayed for divine guidance on my path. I
had never prayed to Mary before. I had already placed
the crosses around my house and put a statue of Mary
in my bedroom. I was open and listening. I truly had a
sense of calm as I departed the church. Nothing in my

life was surprising me. I had adopted James Van Praagh's attitude of "and so it is," as wonderful experiences continued to define my life.

## Chapter 23
# A Mother's Message

In October, I met with Kelly again for a personal channeling. My spirituality had taken a deeper track at this point, and I was developing a stronger loving connection to Mary and what she represented to me as a woman, mother, and healer. I had brought rosary beads with me and a Miraculous Medal that had been given to me by Marie Duess, a friend and former patient.

Marie was about to embark on a medical mission in Bosnia, and would be staying in a little village called

Medugorje, where the Mother of God had reportedly been appearing to several villagers over the last twenty years. I asked her to bring something back for me. Marie gave me her mother's rosaries and her own Miraculous Medal for safe keeping while she was away. She wanted me to have them *just in case*, or until she was able to purchase these items for me and bring them back.

It didn't surprise me that on this day of channeling, the mother-like energy that flowed from Kelly was different from what I had become familiar with. This energy didn't need a name or a strict identity. It was just an all-embracing, all-loving, powerful and compassionate force that took my heart in her hand and empowered me as I have never been empowered before to love and feel loved.

The messages were so sweet, motherly, nourishing, inspiring and awakening. I was told to: Pray prior to my work; get on my knees, embrace children—my own and others; return to the elements of the earth—drink pure water, eat pure food; sing; put out fires with prayer; understand that it is the heart that is of the greatest importance.

She was speaking gently and without haste, "And your job is to nurture the mothers. But before you can nurture them you must nurture your own children and give them the essence of who you are, as you do to the other mothers . . . And know that as you serve and bless and nurture the mothers, you are nurturing their families and their children, and in turn the mother earth . . . And how you can heal your mothers, is by finding your ability to love yourself and your own mother unconditionally. . . ." I interpreted this last message to mean the mother within me.

Other things about my future were revealed at this channeling such as the path my work would take and the people I should become involved with. These things have in fact come true. But that was not the most important lesson that day. Immediately following this mother-like energy, a more familiar energy replaced it to interpret much of what had been said. To paraphrase:

We as a race are beginning to see things from the inside out rather than from the outside in. There is a difference between male energy, which views the world from what it sees on the outside and then looks inward, and female energy, which views what is inward and sees how it relates to the world outside. The male gives the seed from the outside in and the woman brings and bears the child from the inside out. And that is what women are bringing to the world now—the aspect, the philosophy, and the understanding of working from inside out, and seeing the picture as a whole. When we see the whole picture, and not just a fragment of it, we create balance. How do we find balance and begin to heal our planet? The answer is that the Love Energy (the Christ Energy—that is, the *savior* energy) resides within all of us. The love is within all of us, and the divine feminine energy must be used to remind our world that the answers we are looking for are within.

When I left this session, I felt so humbled and honored to be entrusted with such important messages. I drove directly to the hospital. I felt compelled to share this amazing experience with my dear friend, Marie, who I believed, would understand. As I began to relate what had just happened to me, I could see Marie's face light up. Marie explained to me that she had been praying for me, praying that something like this would happen. For

Marie, who is a devout Catholic, it was the Blessed Mother who she prayed to on my behalf. She had asked Mary to pull me closer to her heart even though Marie knew I wasn't raised in the Catholic faith. Because I worked so closely with women, Marie told me she believed I had a special role to play in doing Mary's work, though she didn't know what it was. She was so pleased that I had had such a beautiful revelation from a female/mother source.

My messages from this source were affirmation of the power of prayer for Marie, who was about to leave on a life-changing trip of her own. She was deeply moved and joyful for me. This series of events was the final confirmation she needed before embarking on what her husband and friends felt was a dangerous medical mission. She knew in her heart that she was on the correct path. She was acting from a place of love not fear.

I was so full I felt as though I would explode. I knew that Marie and I were on a journey together—taking parallel pathways in the same direction. It was wonderful to share this with a friend who understood. We were feeling tremendously blessed.

*Chapter 24*

# *It's a Wonderful Life*

The second annual fashion show to raise money for Cancer Healing Ministries at St. Mary was fast approaching. We were down to the wire. This year's event would be larger—attended by more than 500 people. A small private school in the area, Grey Nun Academy, offered to let us hold the event there since they had a large auditorium in a separate building. I was the Chairperson of the event again, and I was fortunate to have an amazing group of volunteers to help. This autumn was the "Season of Trying" for me. I was trying to do too much at one time, but being a queen of multitasking, I was determined to do it all.

My partner was on her honeymoon for two weeks in September, which meant running the practice solo. I needed to spend time with my sister who was visiting from Australia. At the same time, I was studying for my ten-year board re-certification for surgery, which was to be held on October 17. I had chosen to limit my practice to breast care as of October 1, and was dealing with the controversy my decision had created at the hospital because now there was one less surgeon performing all aspects of general surgery. I was taking everyone in my practice to the Pennsylvania Breast Cancer Coalition Conference on October 8 in Harrisburg. I had committed myself to giving the keynote address at a conference for women, which I called "Creating Balance in a Chaotic World" (as I was hoping to create balance in my own world.) I was also committed to a radio show, a television show, and four other speaking engagements all in the month of October because it was breast cancer awareness month. Concurrently, I was working with my web designer to create our office website. On top of it all, I was writing this manuscript, which I had hoped to finish before the close of 2003. And then there were my maternal responsibilities to my sons. If I had any further obligations, I would have to be committed to some sort of institution for hopeless multitaskers. Just when I thought I had enough on my plate and enough change to deal with in my life, I came upon Fallen Willow Farm.

I was scheduled to perform surgery on a friend from out of town. My practice and hospital were both out of her insurance network, but she chose to come to St. Mary for her procedure anyway. She wanted to have more than a surgical procedure, she wanted healing, and so we planned to have an energy healer present in the operating room during surgery. She found comfort in having her surgery performed from a place of love and light. I had assembled the team to do more than just surgery; we were committed to helping her heal.

I had contacted my Ethicon Breast Care representative, Suzanne, and asked her to obtain some equipment I would need for the surgery. She had connections and said that she would be glad to pitch in. We had become friends, so we decided to meet in Newtown at a little sandwich shop to arrange for transfer of the equipment. I had cleared my schedule that week to study for my boards and we planned to meet on October 14. She called that morning to tell me she couldn't make lunch and asked if we could meet for breakfast the next day instead. We made a date for breakfast at 8:30 A.M.

Suzanne was delayed in traffic, so it turned into a nine thirty meeting. I dropped Dean off at school, and before I could get to the restaurant, I got a message from Joe to call the office. When I called to speak with Joe, Donna informed me that there was some sort of problem in the delivery of new equipment that was being brought in to the radiology department. I had to reach Rob, my enlightened Ethicon friend to sort things out. He was our old rep and the girls from the hospital called him when they didn't receive an answer from Suzanne to rectify the problem. Ironically, I was meeting Suzanne for breakfast and could have had a solution to the problem in minutes. I called Rob's cell phone to let him know I would be seeing Suzanne and that I would have her take care of things at the hospital. I am used to getting his voice mail, but as luck would have it, he had missed a flight and was sitting in an airport with time to talk to me. Rob, who flies weekly, swears that this was only the second flight he had ever missed. The conversation delayed me for my appointment with Suzanne. (*Suffice it to say all of my distractions caused me to arrive a full twenty minutes late for my breakfast meeting. Had I been on time who knows where my path would have taken me?*)

Because of my tardiness, Suzanne had been drawn into a conversation with two women sitting at a table next to ours. When I arrived, she introduced me to Lois and Denise, her new acquaintances, and they brought me up to snuff on what they had been discussing. Apparently, the day before, Denise's dog had been euthanized, and they were discussing how hard it was to lose a beloved pet. Lois was still grieving the loss of her horse from some time before. By the time the breakfast was over, Suzanne had promised to find Lois a new horse, and then spontaneously we were off on a road trip to see the farm where this horse was going to live.

I must admit that I wasn't thrilled about this little field trip as I really needed to study, but Suzanne had done me a big favor by bringing the equipment that I needed for my friend's surgery, and it was only a short drive to the farm. Lois was thrilled to have us come see her farm. It had been on the real estate market for eight months and no one had even come to see the place. Joe and I had just completed a rather large addition to our home and absolutely were not in the market for a new home.

As we followed Lois to the farm, I was trying to figure out where a sixteen-acre property that I hadn't seen before could be hidden in Newtown. When we turned down the lane to the farm, the quarter mile, tree-lined drive embraced every fiber of my being. It was a beautiful fall day and the hue of the leaves was breathtaking. The vivid oranges, reds, and yellows called out to me. I felt energy in my solar plexus that was so welcoming. It was as if I was coming home for the first time in my life. The place resonated energy that I was deeply familiar with. As we rounded a bend and the front of the 1740 fieldstone farmhouse came into view, my heart leaped with familiarity again.

We pulled up next to the barn and when I got out of the car, I told Suzanne that Joe would never forgive her for bringing me here as I never wanted to leave. While we walked around the property and explored the grounds, I was drawn into a sense of calm and into a sense that I was surrounded by pure water, pure fire, pure earth, and pure food. The overall sense of authenticity was intoxicating. I was hearing the messages clearly again: return to the elements of the earth in your food, your clothing, your home, your water, and in your work. I couldn't help but see myself living and thriving on this property. I was consumed as I had never been consumed by any place in my life. It felt so right, and I was once again overcome with a sense of calm and familiarity.

Lois gave us a guided tour of the house, and as I walked through it for the first time, I was already deciding where my paintings and personal belongings were going to be placed. How silly it was! All I could think of when I walked into the library was who I could give our sixty-five-inch TV to; it just didn't belong in my new homestead. It was all I could do to contain myself and finish the tour. I wanted to run to my office, grab Joe, and bring him back and show him our new home.

The events and synchronicities that happened to place us in the right place at the right time were uncanny. A few minutes difference in either direction would have resulted in a completely different outcome that day.

The farm was the crowning glory of my fall, and it consumed my every waking moment as I tried to think of a
way to make it become my reality. There were also times
when I tried to walk away from it, thinking that I was
being irrational in my desire to move my family from a
place that had always been home to them. We lived in a
beautiful neighborhood in a new home with great neigh-
bors and a backyard that I had worked so hard to create.
Had I lost my mind, wanting to live in an antique house
that needed years of work and lots of love? Was I being
selfish in my desire or was I acting from a place of inner
knowledge about what my family and I needed to flourish? I wrestled with this in my head, but with every trip I
made to the farm I became more resolute in my goal to
move there.

One evening when I was placing the final coat of
urethane on Joe's bar in the room he had just completed, I asked him if he was really okay with the move. He
said, "I want to be where you want to be and if this farm
is calling to you and it feels right, then I am going to be
there with you." I think he must have gotten that line
from one of the old movies he is always watching, but it
was what I needed to hear from him.

I spent the evening with my guys unwinding from
the stress of the day. Finally, around 9:00 P.M., I started
working on my keynote address for the morning,
"Creating Balance in a Chaotic World." Dean was helping
me to organize my notes at the kitchen counter. I am
always best when I speak from my heart and this talk
would truly be from my heart. When I was trying to
come up with a way to visually connect with the audience, I remembered some crystals that were sitting in
Dean's bedroom. Dean is a very old soul and resonates

with the energy that crystals emanate. He surrounds his room with every crystal he can get his hands on. The week before I had purchased a beautiful pink rose quartz heart from Chris, my crystal-connection, at the local flea market. He had given me a bag of polished rose quartz pieces to give to my patients some weeks earlier, and I had them sitting on the desk in my bedroom. The concept was suddenly crystal clear (forgive the pun) and the teaching props were at my fingertips. I would use them to show how rose quartz crystal pieces in a disorganized state can represent chaotic energy lacking balance. Although each piece of quartz was beautiful in and of itself, without being placed in an organized form they had no meaning. When the equivalent amount of crystal is in the form of a heart, it represents balanced energy and control of chaos. If the heart remains in a stable and nurtured state, in which it is honored and respected, then balance can be maintained. If on the other hand, the heart is not properly cared for, it can be broken and fall into a state of chaos once again.

It was an epiphany—the rose quartz that energetically represents self-love was what I needed to use for my patients to promote balance and self-love. After my talk at the college, I called Chris and asked him to cut 100 rose quartz hearts to give to my patients when they are diagnosed with cancer. He loved the idea and told me that he would sell them to me at cost since he understood how important they would be for the healing process. He even found small pouches to place them in to keep them safe and protected. Helping others to heal would facilitate Chris's own healing.

The four talks I had been asked to give in the next week went very smoothly and I found that the less formal preparation I did the better the talk went. It was confirmation for me that it is the heart that matters most and the words, when spoken from the heart, are words that resonate within the soul.

I used this approach when working on my comments and sequence of events for our fashion show, which this year would honor Tina McCaffrey. "It's a Wonderful Life" fashion show was intended not only to raise funds for Cancer Healing Ministries, but also to raise the spirits of the people who participated. We could feel Tina's presence throughout the event.

"It's a Wonderful Life" was Tina's favorite movie and so it was a perfect theme for the show. I had never seen it, but after renting and watching this movie, I understood why. What a fantastic story and life lesson. How profound for us to be coming together to honor a woman whose life touched so many beings and will continue to impact so many lives through the Healing Ministries initiative at St. Mary.

As we approached the night of the fashion show, Joe and I were coming to terms with the reality that the farm was going to be ours. We were under agreement of sale by the date of the fashion show—November 8. Now we had to face the difficult part of getting through the process of realtors, inspectors, engineers, and builders. We even had to deal with the negativity of a local newspaper writer trying to find an angle for her column. What an educational process this was. I had faith that if it was meant to be we would end up owning the farm.

We were in the process of making a huge life change, while I was running a major fundraiser and completing the other tasks that I had placed on my list. I continued *doing* as Joe continued *being*. That is why we are so good for each other. At times like these, he keeps me grounded and helps me see reality since I often get caught up in the vision. Remember, he is the one who is holding on to my kite string. I never see anything as an obstacle, I see challenges and I love a good challenge. Once again, it is the balance of our relationship that maintains our commitment to each other.

I had no idea when we chose the date for the fashion show that it coincided with the convergence of the planets to create the energy surge of the Harmonic Concordance. I never even heard of this energy event until a week before it occurred. I would love to take credit for being clever in choosing the date, but I must give the credit to the divine source that chose to work through me to make it happen. The week before the event, I began to receive emails and calls from friends telling me of this amazing energy convergence coinciding with the fashion show.

Marie Duess had just returned from her medical mission in Bosnia with not much more than the clothes on her back. She'd given everything—from boots to pajamas—away to the refugees in Bosnia. The mission was so much more than she could have ever imagined. It was a life changing event and everything she returned with held special memories. She did bring three gifts for me from Medugorje, a place that she calls the Gates of Heaven.

She carried back a statue of Mary, which I have sitting across from my desk and in full view every day as I do my work. The second gift, which I also treasure and keep with me at all times, is my first chain of rosary beads. The beads are made of soft pink hearts—the symbol that had become so powerful for me during the two

291

~

weeks Marie had been away. The beads were one of a kind—Marie had not seen any others like them in her travels there. She knew they were meant for me, but she had no way of knowing that pink hearts had become important in my life while she was away. It was divine intervention at its finest. Marie told me that the priest who had seen apparitions of Mary blessed these things for me. The third and most important gift was her safe return home so that I could return her mother's rosary and miraculous medal to her.

Marie was one of the fashion show committee members, and as we immersed ourselves knee deep in making it a perfect night, I felt that because of what had happened to her in Bosnia, the divine energy of Mary was prominent at the fundraiser that night.

The evening went almost without incident. The actual program began with the angelic voice of Shea Roache singing Ave Maria at 8:13 P.M., the exact moment the Harmonic Concordance began on the east coast. Shea's song was followed by a slide presentation prepared by Marie. It highlighted the difference the Healing Ministries had already made in the lives of cancer patients that past year, and ended with a heartfelt tribute to Tina McCaffrey that brought the audience to its feet.

The models and the fashions were spectacular, and this year all the models—men and women—had survived cancer. All of the female models had at least one of their breasts removed and reconstructed, and that didn't stop them from wearing plunging necklines and tight fitting, sexy dresses. They were radiant and glowing both inside and out. One of our models was still devoid of hair from chemotherapy and another had just had her second mastectomy and reconstruction a few weeks earlier. Each of these men and women had a sense of wellness and empowerment as they strutted and danced down the runway. With each outfit they donned, they gained confidence, and by the end of the evening they were dancing with the audience. For some of them, the evening was the culmination of the healing they had been working toward and for others it was just the beginning.

We had a surprise model at the end of the show. A waiter who worked for the caterer (which was owned by McCaffreys) came up and asked if he could take a stroll down the runway. He felt he needed to be a part of this wonderful energy. "Why not?" I answered. And so he danced his way down the catwalk, and the audience went wild. As this gorgeous young man danced with Mary, my lead mammography technologist, on the runway, I found out from his friend that his name was Rafe—short for Raphael, the name of my favorite archangel. I knew we had angelic presence there that night.

The evening was a tremendous success because Tina and Jim McCaffrey have had such a strong presence in our community. They have touched so many lives, and in turn those who have been touched felt compelled to honor Tina. "It's a Wonderful Life" was phenomenal—we raised more than $120,000. The total was more than double what we raised the year before. Tina was so large in life that she continues to be ever-present in our community in spirit.

My commitment to empower the healing process in every patient continues to be paramount in my life. The more I am open, the more I see. The more I realize what is possible, the more I know what can be.

## Chapter 25
## *And So It Is!*

My clinical approach to cancer surgery remains based in western medicine. That means the treatment of the disease called cancer begins with surgery, chemotherapy, and/or radiation to treat the physical body. In my short medical career, we have made great strides in Western medicine. Our diagnosis and treatment of cancer has become less invasive, more precise and targeted. We have not yet figured out how to prevent cancer; our main focus is still on treatment. Technology is the backbone of cancer treatment, but it cannot stand alone if we aim to treat the whole patient.

Treating a lack of balance in the individual, the dis-*ease*, begins after or in conjunction with the treatment of the physical body. Some patients need to finish with their standard medical treatment before they can tackle the task of looking within themselves to find what it is they will need to create healing on a spiritual level. After treating the cancer that is the symptom manifested by the body, the complex process of healing may require lifetimes to be completed. It is necessary to identify what caused that particular part of the body to stop vibrating at the same frequency as the rest of the healthy body, causing the tumor to form and become clinically evident.

What lessons have I learned from my experience treating patients with cancer? First and foremost, each individual needs to find healing in whatever form is necessary to create inner peace and wellbeing. Self-love must be real and unconditional, which requires detachment from blame. Saying you love yourself is different than showing you love yourself. I demonstrated self-love when I followed my heart and created my practice in a way that honors who I am. The process wasn't easy but through the adversity I grew.

I loved myself enough to make a difference in my own life and I am teaching my patients by example. I know that every day I make a difference in someone's life by caring for those who have breast disease. Though I know I cannot cure every person who walks into my office, I do possess the tools and the love to empower that person to find the healing that every human being deserves. My ability to facilitate healing has been augmented by the spirits of Ro and Tina, who gave of themselves to make a difference for so many others still here on earth.

Our medicine, as well as our planet, is in a great state of lack. Practicing medicine for the most part has become fear-based and is devoid of love. Releasing this fear is of utmost importance. We cannot practice medicine with the constant fear of legal action at the root of our system. We must look deeply within ourselves and find the healers that reside within us.

A partnership is required for healing, and in the process, energy is exchanged from doctor to patient and from patient to doctor. It is the heart chakra connection that represents the energy transfer between the two. It works both ways, as the patient heals, the physician, and medicine in general, heals as well. As we begin to heal medicine, we can also heal our bodies; then we can begin to heal our souls. As our souls heal, we will see our planet shift into a place of love and light where there will no longer be manifestations of dis-*ease* and war. The shift that must occur is great, but if we work at awakening the consciousness of one being at a time, we can see the ripple effect as the light and love spread, expanding throughout the planet. Although it may be that medicine treats the symptom, it is love that heals. I believe that finding the love and light within each person will ultimately heal Mother Earth.

So often we fail to realize how profoundly each and every one of us affects those with whom we come in contact. If you think just about the things in your own small corner of the world that would be different without your presence, it is almost incomprehensible. What would your family be like? What would your workplace be like? What would your community be like? If you think that you have no impact, ask yourself what you can do to become more connected. If you know you have an effect on these areas, think about how you can have an even more positive impact on them. Realize that the connection and energy between two beings is what truly matters in life.

When I began my career in medicine, I thought the surgery I performed was the most important aspect of my relationship with my patient. "Nothing heals like cold steel," they used to say to us during my residency training. Money, power, and ego were very present in medicine during those years, and had I not had such a close look at them, I may not have the insights I now possess. It is this method of surgical training, which has been present for years, that produces physicians who think the actual operation is the most important aspect of healing the patient. Every aspect of medicine has been tainted by the system we follow, focusing on treatment of symptoms and overlooking the human being with the disease. Hopefully, we will see a shift in consciousness within the medical profession to again incorporate healing as an integral component in the training of our health care providers.

I did receive excellent surgical training and I will be forever thankful to those surgeons who spent their time and energy teaching me. Yet now I know that cold steel is not what heals, but the love and warmth that emanates sincerely from my heart. This awareness required a shift in my consciousness and a greater awareness of the human being whom I am treating.

I am simply a facilitator in the process of curing disease and healing dis-*ease*. When I began the journey of writing this manuscript, I thought it was just the field of

medicine that needed to make a shift in its consciousness, but I have come to realize that a global shift in
consciousness is required for our planet to heal. We, as a
human race must be able to find healing within ourselves if we are going to be able to heal our planet.

As I reflect on my journey, I am reminded of the gifts
my friends and patients have so lovingly shared with
me. By adopting and living an authentic life, Lauren and
John built their dream house and started a successful
business raising alpacas. They taught me to look within
my heart to find my passion. It was Lauren's threatened
mortality—an adversity to anyone else—which created
the opportunity for her to grow and awaken to her higher self. She gave me the opportunity to awaken to my
essence by sharing her journey.

My soul's mission had been trying to surface, yet it
was being held captive by the constraints of modern
medicine and my surgical practice. Lauren chose to think
outside the box since her future was uncertain. The
word prognosis took on a very different meaning for me
after her experience. She chose to take risks based upon
what she had to gain, not what she was afraid of losing.
Every day became a gift; she learned quickly to seize the
moment. When faced with mortality it becomes a matter
of living dreams and manifesting that part of destiny
that she could control.

Lauren and John created their own reality. They
embraced parenthood and chose to be present with
Francesca as she grew. Through the process, they were not
afraid to share their fears and beliefs. They introduced
many physicians to Reiki energy healing, past life regression, and hypnosis. I admit that at first I participated, not
out of belief in Reiki, but out of love and respect for

them. I would have done anything to facilitate healing in Lauren. But as it turns out, my belief in Reiki healing has occurred in its own perfect time. My love for Lauren and John is eternal, as they have given me the opportunity to grow and expand beyond my physical self. They have helped me to become the healer, parent and loving being that I am.

As Lauren continues on her path of self-discovery and healing, many changes have occurred in her personal and professional life. Although some have been incredibly painful, she has grown from the adversity. When I ask her if she would trade the experiences of the past nine years, she responds. "I would not trade a minute as I have loved every moment that I have been raising Francesca. If I hadn't had cancer, I would have been working all the time and someone else would know my child instead of me." We too easily forget the small blessings of each day. She reminds me that she is on a journey and the destination is not nearly as important as the experiences!

My idea of what it means to heal has also been guided by my relationship with Christine S. O'Donnell, who has grown light years spiritually in the past five years. As her body deteriorated quickly in its ability to function independently, her spirit grew well beyond the physical realm and her reach is immeasurable. She is a being composed of more love and light than I may ever know. Through her dis-*ease*, she was strong, gracious, and loving with a magnitude not of this world. She never felt sorry for herself or held pity parties. The only parties we held were to honor her, and my favorite was a private pink pajama party to honor our feminine energy. When she asked the Archangel Raphael why she got this disease, the answer was clear: she chose this dis-*ease* to teach the rest of us about the importance of healing. She needed to teach the physicians who loved her to be healers again, as our souls had forgotten our true essence.

Chris was here to remind us of our birth vision as healers. If we remain so focused on curing our patients, we may miss the opportunity to connect with their spirit and truly facilitate healing on many levels. I am unable to go back to the pure Western medical model that trained me, as I would dishonor all that Chris has given so many others and me through her sacrifice in this lifetime.

As I know with every fiber of my being that the soul is eternal, Chris will be ever present in my life. She is no longer in physical form, yet I hear her, I feel her presence, and welcome her guidance. She has taught me to be a better mother, a better wife, and has completely awakened the healer within me. The priorities in my life are now so much clearer because of her existence. Chris passed over into spirit on November 2, 2005, two years to the day after Tina passed away. She survived years longer than we ever thought she could.

Her death was peaceful and she does let me know that she is with me in spirit as she was with me in life. The evening that she went to sleep for the last time, a tiny ladybug held vigil perched on the ceiling above her bed. Both Amy Harvey and I have been continually blessed with the presence of ladybugs since that early morning when Chris's body went to sleep for the last time. It is the dead of winter as I edit this manuscript and yet ladybugs still find their way to me, allowing me to feel the presence of her spirit.

Through the journeys I have shared with my

patients, I have become a better surgeon, healer and person. Dawn's cancer threw fuel onto the flame that was smoldering in my heart. She ignited the fire that started my transition from general surgeon to breast care specialist. Then Lee Ellen, my childhood friend, gave me such insight into what it is like to be on the other side of the breast cancer diagnosis. She helped me realize that I can't force the process for anyone—healing must come in its own time and in its own form.

It is my sincerest hope that readers from all professions who deal with those who are vulnerable, or who are in a vulnerable state of mind themselves—that means patients, lawyers, therapists, as well as physicians in every specialty—use my narrative as a springboard for their own awakening and grasp how safe I was while these synchronicities were happening. I was in no danger of losing anything by opening up and accepting possibilities. On the contrary I am richer for it, and I am aware that I must continue to search, to learn, and to accept even that which may appear unbelievable.

Although I have reached the end of this book, I have truly just begun to live my own authentic life. I am not afraid of anything that life has to offer me because each adversity I have experienced has opened doors of understanding and opportunities for the growth of my soul.

When I was seventeen, I remember being angry with God for taking my brother from me when we were both so young. I can still feel the pain of that loss, yet now I know I wouldn't have the level of understanding I do about reincarnation if I didn't feel Bart's presence back here with my family. I knew the minute I saw Robert's eyes, but it took time to fully realize the connection; it was the energy Bart and I shared during our seventeen years together that was so familiar. The familiarity was unmistakable, and many members of my family could also feel this connection to Robert.

Robert has played an integral role in our family, helping some to realize the patterns in their lives that were unhealthy and needed to change. His presence has brought comfort in my parents' lives that none of us as daughters could. He in no way replaces Bart, but is a reminder to each and every one of us that our souls are eternal and that we do this dance over and over again, lifetime after lifetime.

After college, Robert had a calling to a life flying jets in the military. It was no surprise that he was a natural in the skies. He has recently completed flight training school in the Navy and in this way he is following his soul's true passion. It makes my heart sing to know that he—Bart's essence—is flying again.

As I move forward on my path of self-discovery, I remain open to the experiences the universe has to teach me. I am a willing and able student of any healing modalities that come my way. I continue to practice mainstream surgery in the treatment of cancer, as I believe that we have been given the technological advances to fight this disease. I have been seeing amazing healings and outcomes with my patients. I am a work in progress. I am a student of energy therapy and I am willing to explore any avenues that produce healing. Change is the only thing in life that is constant and I am always open to change.

The messages I have received are clear: when the planet begins to shift in its consciousness, there will be no need for the cancer energy to be present to teach us

303

these lessons, for we will have collectively learned them. As we are able to create the vibrational level within our bodies to eradicate the cancer energy, hopefully we will no longer need the wisdom of Western medicine to treat the disease called cancer.

We are just beginning to enter a period of discovery about our body's innate ability to heal and be cured of disease. We must remember that not all cancer is to be cured. It may be a soul's path to experience disease and to teach others–just as Chris's disease taught so many. We must never lose sight of what is truly important— healing is of the utmost priority and must occur at all costs.

We can all be healed, although some may not be cured. But this, in itself, is perfect. Until we are able, as a collective consciousness, to evolve beyond our physical existence, where material possessions, mechanistic advancements, and final destinations are the focus, dis-ease will remain our opportunity for growth. When we finally *get it* there will be no need for dis-*ease*. Every day of our lives is a gift if we choose to honor the present.

I have learned to thank the universe for the gifts it has provided for me. I am grateful for the health and well-being of my family. Joe trusts what I feel in my heart and he is willing to act on my intuitions simply because I tell him that I have a *knowing* about something. That is his most precious gift to me. He has honored me along my path, where many other male egos may have been less able to do so. I am so fortunate to have awakened in time to truly enjoy my two beautiful sons who are my light in every way. I look toward our future and wonder what else my children will teach me and remind me about my essence. I am so fortunate to have the opportunity to

304

move to Fallen Willow Farm and bring light and love to it as it, in turn, restores me.

I have embarked on a visionary project to create the first comprehensive breast care center that will focus on state of the art breast cancer care for patients while, at the same time, incorporating healing into the process, every step of the way. I knew that my 444 would resurface again and on 04/04/04, I had breakfast with the man who would be yet another angel on earth to bring this vision to fruition. I was introduced by a fellow surgeon to a physician entrepreneur who was in the early stages of creating a model for centers of excellence in breast care. I wasn't even on the list of forty physicians he was to meet with that weekend, yet we were destined to work together. He doesn't even know how powerful that sign (444) was for me that day, but suffice it to say, it was a life changing day for myself and the many others this vision will affect. This center will be a model for others to learn from and emulate. I have always chosen to lead by example and this project is no different.

As we finalized the plans for our breast center, the Susan G. Komen Breast Cancer 3-Day came to town. I had the honor of recruiting and organizing the medical crew. Beth and I were true to our promise to give back to the event that had given us so much. I believe that it was participation in this event as a medical crew-member that solidified Stacy's decision to shift her practice.

Stacy has now, four years into her practice, chosen to follow what has become her passion as well. She was brought in to my practice at the right time, and in her own time, through her own journey, has decided to focus her practice on the treatment of women and men with breast disease. We are all where we are meant to be at this moment in time.

Living on the farm, we have had, and will continue to have, the opportunity to grow together as we work toward a common goal. Bringing life back to a beautiful homestead is a fantastic objective. I needed to reconnect to who I am as a mother by getting back to the pure earth, pure water, pure food, and pure fire. My angels remind me of my need to reconnect to the mother within, in order to heal the mothers I treat and subsequently help heal the Mother Earth.

Joe's creative passion for building has been refueled with our plans to restore the farm and our sons are blossoming into men right before my eyes. Don't ever overlook a chance meeting at breakfast that could change your life. Some things are just meant to be.

. . . *and so it is!*

## *The Lessons*

~

Be Present in the Moment

The Only Constant in Life is Change

Fear Paralyzes / Knowledge Empowers

Life is About Your Journey not the Destination

Although it may be that Medicine Treats the Symptom,

it is the Physician's Love that Heals.

Lead by Example

# Resources

Andrews, Ted. *Animal Speak: The Spiritual & Magical Powers of Creatures Great & Small*. St. Paul, Minnesota: Llewellyn Publishers, 2001.

Apollon, Susan Barbara. *Touched by the Extraordinary*. Yardley, Pennsylvania: Matters of the Soul, 2005.

Brennan, Barbara Ann. *Healing Hands of Light: A Guide to Healing Through the Human Energy Field*. New York: Bantam, 1987.

Chopra, Deepak. *The Seven Laws of Spiritual Success: A Practical Guide to the Fulfillment of Your Dreams*. New Delhi: Excel Books, 1994.

Coelho, Paulo. *The Alchemist*. New York: Harper Collins, 1994.

Ingram, Julia and G. W. Hardin. *The Messengers: A True Story of Angelic Presence and the Return to the Age of Miracles*. New York: Pocket Books, 1997.

Lowery, Michelle. *The Unexpected Traveler*. Brawley, California: Wind Canyon Books Incorporated, 2003.

Morse, Melvin and Paul Perry. *Closer to the Light*. New York: Ivy Books, 1990.

Myss, Caroline. *Anatomy of the Spirit: The Seven Stages of Power and Healing*. New York: Three Rivers Press, 1996.

Northup, Christiane. *Women's Bodies, Women's Wisdom*. New York: Bantam, 1994.

Redfield, James. *The Celestine Prophecy: An Adventure*. New York: Warner Books, 1997.

Ruiz, Don Miguel. *The Four Agreements: A Practical Guide to Personal Freedom*. San Raphael, California: Amber-Allen Publishing Co., 1997.

Schulz, Mona Lisa. *Awakening Intuition*. New York: Three Rivers Press, 1998.

Siegel, Bernie. *Love, Medicine, & Miracles*. New York: Harper and Row, 1986.

Sogyal Rinpoche. *The Tibetan Book of Living and Dying*. New York: Harper San Francisco, 1994.

Weiss, Brian. *Many Lives Many Masters*. New York: Simon and Shuster, 1988

Weiss, Brian. *Only Love is Real*. New York: Simon and Shuster, 1997.

Weiss, Brian. *Through Time into Healing*. New York: Simon and Shuster, 1992.

Van Praagh, James. *Talking to Heaven: A Medium's Message of Life after Death*. New York: Penguin Putnam, 1997.

Chapter 12 p10 Albert Einstein quotes
www.brainyquote.com

Chapter 16 p1. TBLD, p10, p. 11

* Signifies the person's name has been changed

# About the Artist

At the age of 59, Frank Champine, a retired secondary school teacher, found a mass in his breast that brought him to my practice. During our first encounter as doctor and patient, he was drawn to a spiritual painting behind my desk. He shared with me his interest, and recent enrollment, in a class on Chinese brush painting and sitting meditation. Just four weeks before we met, Frank had enrolled in the course with the Medical Mission Sisters in Fox Chase, PA. That day, I loaned him a book I had purchased from Dr. Pak Lee, the artist who had created my painting. Subsequently, Frank was diagnosed with breast cancer. At a time in his life when he wanted to focus on his spiritual education and development, he was waylaid. He endured surgery, chemotherapy and several complications from his treatment.

It was through the adversity of breast cancer that his passion for spiritual painting developed. Frank sees his work as an expression of prayer and a source of healing. I am honored to possess his first composition, which adorns the x-ray view box in my office. He paints from his heart, as is evidenced in his work.

For 5000 years, every student of Brush painting has initiated the work with seven strokes. The presentation below is of orchid leaves and is symbolic of spring. The orchid is the first of Four Gentleman, or the "Four Persons," as his instructor Sr. Mary Gavin calls them. Within the Confucian scheme of things, the seven strokes represent the order of society. Frank used this painting to quiet his inner being.

The painting symbolizes the relationship between myself, my partner, and our staff. Frank's painting is so powerful yet simple in it's message. I felt it was the appropriate painting to adorn the cover of this book. As his work evolved, he added the orchid. His first orchid composition was created for his wife and soul-mate, Christine. The dragonflies he added for me. His other works are featured throughout this book.

310

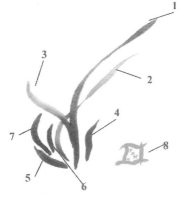

In the Chinese style each brush stroke represents a person:
1. Beth DuPree—leader of the "family" office . . . forceful and
   confident. Points the way to the heaven and God. . . .
   The energy stroke.
2. A close associate or friend—partner; one who supports
   the leader but does not overpower her.
3. The friend who is closely linked but forces you to look
   at things from a different perspective. Keeps you
   grounded and "honest."
4. Supporter of your plan or ideal (4-6—your staff)
5. Supporter rooted in your philosophy
6. Supporter helpful in carrying out our mission
7. The God line—the one who always refocuses the office
   back to the leader and the quest for God and heaven.

As a follower of St. Francis of Assisi, the patron saint of
the environment, Frank shares my belief that the disruption of
the earth opens the door to an increase in cancer and disease.
Frank is concerned that women are suffering because of the
outrages we have imposed on our mother earth.

Frank now facilitates workshops through Authentic
Education on various educational topics. He uses those opportunities to educate both men and women about breast cancer.

He is an award winning schoolteacher who was named
Pennsylvania Teacher of the Year in 1984. He lives with his wife,
Christine in Langhorne, Pennsylvania.

# About the Author

For nearly twenty years Dr. Beth DuPree has performed surgery on thousands of patients. The personal and energetic connection she shares with her patients is as important to their healing process as the surgery she performs. Dr.DuPree has come to realize that the surgery is but a small part of what patients need to truly heal. Her focus as a physician has shifted from one based solely in Western medicine to one that combines the wisdom of Eastern Medicine with state of the art Western medical technology.

Beth was born and raised in York, Pennsylvania and is the youngest of seven children. She is a graduate of the University of Pittsburgh, and Hahnemann University School of Medicine. She completed her surgical residency at Albert Einstein Medical Center in Philadelphia. Dr. DuPree has practiced surgery in Bucks County, Pennsylvania since 1992. She specializes in the diagnosis and treatment of diseases of the breast. Beth lives with her husband Joe and their sons, Tom and Dean.

# Spiritual Messages

## July 1, 2000
### The First Channeling

Kelly positioned herself cross-legged on the couch covering her legs with a blanket. She explained to us when she channeled Raphael, she would say "Hello" and that we needed to say "Hello" in return. She said Raphael would sing and our true messages are in the vibration of the singing, but the words are the translation. Kelly breathed in deeply as though she was breathing in the energy of Raphael. She sang and intoned in a soft voice, making hand gestures toward each one of us. We were all sitting on the edges of our seats filled with wonder and to be honest with some doubt. (Some of us more doubtful than others.)

[Raphael singing, chanting, and laughing]

R: *Hello.*

Us: [Beth, Emily, Lee, Amy] Hello.

R: [Very hearty laughter] *Hello.*

Us: Hello.

R: [Singing and more chanting] *I am so happy to see all of you. For you are very beautiful and I am so happy that you are here with me, and that we can be together and that you come in your physical body at this particular time in physical form as female, and I am so happy to see all of these females, for you are quite beautiful and it is that as a unit you comprise a beautiful, beautiful light being that it comes from a very early source; and a place in which one is at the essence of their origin, and it is that, when one passes through this place in which you would also speak of as the place prior to incarnating here into your physical body, you come forth with an original understanding and your essence is so open and so clear, and there is such great clarity in your origin and who it is that you are and why it is that you are here, and where it is that you are going. And when you bring your energies together you are able on a cellular level to return to a place of great lightness and joyfulness and playfulness, and also it brings one closer to a remembering as to who they are. And so all of you are coming together at this time is so, so very important and I am so happy to see you and I encourage you to be together more often, for this is so beautiful and it is very much like opening a corridor that brings you into a place in which you become closer to your origin and to your essence and to your light and to your truth and to love and so HELLO!*

Us: Hello.

R: [Singing] *It is so special for me to speak to beings who will find themselves at this time in a female body, for it is that there is a great transition at this particular time not only on your planet but in that place in which you find yourself which is this country that you are residing in at this time. In which there is going to be a greater and greater shift from the dominance of male energy to female energy and if you listen there has been a word that has come about which is "Goddesses."*

*It is that you are moving from seeing the figure of enlightenment and love from a male standpoint as God, to Goddess, and that the balance now is coming to a place in which there will be a great shift, in which the female energy will become stronger and stronger and become very dominant at this particular time in your evolution. For you are moving into a time of enlightenment, a time of remembering, and a time of awakening and moving into a place in which you can begin to understand who it is that you are and remembering that. And it is that because of the mind of the male and the ego which is so strong and has been so very present for so long and very positive for it* has created many good things for all of you. But it is time now for the presence of knowing, and the presence of being, and the presence of being particularly in the present, in the now, in which the female origin is able to do this because it is the creator of life and it is also the being that takes away life, for it is the womb that is so precious, and all of you have brought and are life.

It is that in this process you can remember and become closer to the miraculous origin of your being and it is that part of yourself that has an easier time moving into a place of understanding and compassion and enlightenment and is able to remove ego at this time, in order to move forward into a place of greater love and the godliness of yourself. For as you are very much aware you are God and God is within you. For it is that you have the opportunity to shine forth that light and that love in every word that you speak and every action that is taken. And it is the female energy at this particular time on your planet that will be bringing such great change forward and raising the consciousness to a level in which you all will be able to create an easier flow, and resistance and fear will begin to be eliminated as well as war.

I am so very happy when beings such as yourselves are remembering who they are and open enough to be able to remember me, for I am you, and you are I, for we are the same and we are one and we have always been together; for I am simply a part of yourself. A reflection of who it is that you are and that what you have chosen to do at this particular time is to come to me in order to remember a part of yourself. For I am part of you, and you are looking at me and as you look at me it brings an awakening and as the awakening occurs it begins to allow your cells in your body to sing and open and to remember love. And in that process, through daily action, you can create change that will bring the consciousness to a level in which we will be able to eliminate together all of those things of the material: ego, mind, fear, and greed. And I am so very happy to see you.

Perhaps I am speaking too fast and this is not helpful. For

315

*maybe, perhaps I should speak slower, for often I forget that I am talking in a language that is not my own in many ways, and I have difficulty relaxing, should we say.* [Laughter ensues from Raphael.]

*And it is that I am so happy to see you because it is that when I see you I see a part of myself and when you see me you see a part of yourself, for I am simply a reflection and a reminder of who you are, of your origin and I am here tonight to be here for you in any way that can help to allow you to remember your essence and yourself, and so perhaps it is time for me to be quiet and for you to go inside of your beings and to ask yourself what it is that you need to know or to understand in order for your true self and essence and light and love to come forward and be able to create change within your body and then in those in which you touch as well. And so think about this for a moment and take some time to hold your heart and tell me what it is that you need from me this evening and I will be very obliged to help you anyway that I can.* [Raphael begins to sing again.]

*What is it?*

B: The question that I have, Raphael, is for some reason I have been brought into your presence through my practice and I think there is a direction that should be happening or something that is coming and I don't know exactly what it is, but I feel there is a reason why I am here and that we were meant to be able to connect.

R: *Of course, of course you are here, and it is so interesting that the being that you have met that has brought us to connect is the mother of all of you, for she is the mother of the female energy and of the womb. And has brought one, two, three, four girls into her life as well.* [Helen has four daughters.] *And it is that this connection here, is to remind yourself that what it is that you are doing at this particular time is so quite beautiful and that you are a very, very beautiful being that is very, very enlightened and moving into a place in which you will be able to transform and change consciousness and thought within human bodies simply by your presence as you already know and do. For you are beginning to understand that the act in which you do in particular situations is very much minor compared to the connection that is made between you and other human beings. And it is that you are able now to remove the idea of what is at this particular time thought of or labeled as illness, and remove that label for it does not exist. In holding or labeling a particular thing it creates and holds that pattern through resistance where it is and you will be able to see the being in the present moment as where they are moving toward a place of enlightenment and realizing that where it is that they are so so perfect and you have come very much forward into this process of understanding. The reasoning of moving into a place in which we are becoming communicating together is because I am very anxious to communicate with you regularly to help you to help each other to become more acquainted with the idea of creating physical healing through pure light and love. In which you will be able to do the physical things necessary in order to do it but yet at the same time through your presence of your mind and the ability in which you find yourself and you will be able to create simply by the touch and it is such a very beautiful thing, for you will be in the process a trail blazer, you will be cutting down a pathway that will allow others to be able to follow behind with greater ease. And sometimes when one is cutting down such a great pathway, and it is full of so much and it is overwhelming and there are so many things to do and so many people and it is that sometimes one needs someone to stand in front, far ahead and say, "Here I am," this is where it is that you are going and it is so worth it. And they help you to find your way.*

317

*And it is that you have the ability to move into a state of consciousness that will allow transformation through the physical body to occur miraculously and move into a state in which not only will you be doing and combining the work of, should we say, mechanical, and mechanistic view, but also the work of being able to focus and create a hologram of all. And it is that in that process you will be able, through touch and creating the love consciousness in your body, to be able to create change in the molecular structure of this being, so that the vibrational frequency can come to a place in which at the time of shift during illness into present moment and understanding and letting go of resistance, for all illness comes in a state of resistance and helping to allow others to surrender. It is in that the surrendering, whether it appears that there is healing or not, for it is all healing whether it moves itself into a place for transformation or into another world.* [As in death of the physical body, the spirit of the individual has healed and moved on.] *Or it moves itself into a place of transformation in the physical body, which it resides in. It is the understanding and opening to surrender that can allow the being to change and grow and move into a new molecular structure that will allow more light into that being which will then be transformed to all, and so I am so delighted to be able to help you in this process of touch that will create this miraculous opening of surrender at a very quickening pace, rather than one in the past with mechanistic views that had been quite slow. Do you understand?*

318

~

B: I understand. I don't know if you guys understand, but the Reiki Therapy that I started doing over a year and a half ago is the beginning of energy therapy and energy healing, and it's made a big difference as far as with my patients. I see it already and part of it is, am I seeing it already in my mind that it made a difference or was it something that was truy happening and the patients are truly doing better? [That was my answer on that particular day, but I had no idea how this process was going to unfold! It wasn't until I began to reread these events in my life while writing this manuscript that I truly understood. I then asked Raphael about the experiences that I had had with regard to the Reiki Energy that I had been sharing with my patients. I had found that my patients required less postoperative pain medicine and were having a more profound experience through the surgical procedure than they had in the past. I asked her if this was all in my head or if there had been a shift in "the process?"]

*R: It is whatever you see it as, you create the reality in which you see. If you see them well, then they are well. If you see it happening and healing. It is healing. For it is in your understanding of truth, your understanding of knowing, and in your belief that you allow healing to occur. And so of course it is helping and it is perfect and of course it is beautiful and it will expand into something much greater than you can begin to imagine at this time, for it has the possibility to transform so, so many lives at such a great pace and you are such an enlightened and loved and blessed being with an opportunity to create such wonderful change and I am so honored to be able to help to accelerate that process in any way that I can and it is that it is such a very beautiful thing and that you should be so, so very proud, for it is that your work that you do is of great honor and great compassion and it is so, so beautiful. And it is important for you to know that each being that you touch, when it is touched with love, creates change in that being that changes their structure and their life forever. Whether it is that the physical healing occurs or not, it is not for you to judge. For that is which must be surrendered to something that is a part of your self, that is a higher part of you and them, for judging what is best is something we cannot do at this time. But giving as much love and as much light in the process in helping to remove resistance is something in which you can do and it is so very needed at this particular time here on your planet and I am so very honored to be around your presence arount this particular work.*

*What is it?* [She began to laugh very heartily.] *I always find it so funny for to have an opportunity to ask an angel a question and*

319

*you could ask anything you want and no one has a question and you sit there and say, "I do not know, I have no question" and then when you leave you say, "oh I could have asked this and I could have asked that."*

B to L: Don't you want to know how you can heal . . . yourself?

L: [Chuckling] I don't know. Why don't you put it into words for me Beth, go ahead.

B: Haven't you ever thought, "How can I heal myself?" Have you thought that at all?

L: No, I guess not, no. I am a firm believer in modern medicine.

B: I'm just asking because that is something I always have patients say to me, "What can I do to accelerate or help my healing process?"

{I then butted in and asked Raphael what Lee could do to find healing? Lee quickly corrected me by letting me know she wanted the best modern medicine had to offer to treat her cancer and the healing was less important. Clearly my friend was here to teach me that I couldn't choose her path for her. Our channeling continued with a question from Lee.]

*R: Talk to me, do not allow this other being talk for you.* [Group laughs]

L: Ah, that's just a part of our Beth.

*R: What is it you want to ask me, for you are feeling a resistance around what to do with what you are hearing and that is a beautiful thing and I am happy to see that for that allows you to go deeper within your own being to come to your own truth to find what it is you need from me at this particular time.*

[Pause]

*R: I can wait, I have all the time in the universe.*

L: Okay, when you have those feelings of déjà vu, does that really mean you've been here and done this before?

*R: Déjà vu! This is a very interesting word. DEJA-VU. Give me an example. For do you mean that you are feeling as though you have done something before and you are wondering if that is a reality in which you have already experienced?*

L: Yes, and does that mean you're on the right path this time? Like it feels like you do it over and over again until you get it right?

*R: Yes, you do. And it is that one of the laws of the universe that has been so very much forgotten by the human race as they have fallen into such a great deep sleep is that they are the creator of their reality and their particular life in which they find themselves in at this time. And it is that when you have this feeling as though you have done something before, it is that you are living in many different realities at once for the reality in which you find yourself in is simply an illusion. It is as though there is a play and you are an actor in this play and you are playing out whatever it is that is necessary in order for you to create change within your body in order to experience love. For so many beings say to me what is it that I am here to do, for what is my purpose? And it is not that your purpose is to be a chef or a doctor or a nurse or a computer analyst or a mother or a father, or whatever it is, but it is that you are to love and to feel love in your heart and to move into a place of gratefulness and light and love and non-judgment, and that is where it is that is your purpose and when you are able reach this, you have reached a state in which you will not have a feeling or a need to reincarnate again. For you will be able to move into the light, and allow that sense of ego and self to release itself, that sense of identity for you will*

321

*be at peace with all that is. And so when you see parts of something and you feel as though you have done them before, you have. For you have done them so many times for you have done them over and over and over and over again. And so it is that if one can remove the "chaptering in the mind" and "the skepticism in the mind" and the fear and ask themselves in every moment, "what is it that love would do here?" and act from a place of love and see the light and see the God, and see the love in each being for each being that is sitting here and each being on your planet and all beings are a part of who you are. They are part you, for you are all one being which has chosen to separate into a state of ego and identity in order to interact and relate in order to find a place in which you can change and to grow and when you move into a state of non-judging them for who they are, and what they are saying or what they are doing or what they are wearing and simply loving each being and feeling peace within your heart, you will have no need to be in this illusion and to create it over and over for you just will be. Do you understand?*

L: I do, but isn't that part of the fun of being? Being able to be in this illusion?

*R: Yes, for it is to be fun and it is to be joyful and you are to run in the rain naked and you are to make fun and you are to eat ice cream sundaes and you are to do all the things that are joyful, for joyful-ness brings you to the center and the idea and the feeling of love and so the illusion is a beautiful thing and it is not to be judged either, for being in the illusion is perfect as well, but you are asking if the illusion comes to an end or if is done over and over and over and the answer is yes, but there is a time in which you may choose to sim-ply remove yourself from the illusion and to just be.*

*What is it?*

Group member: And is that the state you are in?

*R: [With laughter] I am in that state for I am everywhere all at once and I enjoy being here with you so, and I enjoy your rain and your snow and your ocean and all the things you have created here for they are so beautiful. And no wonder you want to stay for they are very inviting, and I would want to stay too, but it is that my job is to help you to come through in whatever way that I can and to remind you of your essence and your origin and to remind you that you are love and light. And you are here to create joy and laughter and light and fun inside of yourself, and to then to transfer all that to as many beings as you can until all beings are in the state of abundance and love and flow and you can then just be together in peace. What is it?*

A: I need a new career? What career should I have?

R: *How do I know?* [Laughter] *What career do you want to have?*

A: I don't know.

R: *Well, then how can I know? It is that one must go inside and take away all parameters around fear and go deep and ask themselves what it is that they do that brings them a sense of joyfulness and what is it in their heart they are wanting to do. And remove all ideas of "I can't, and I don't, and I won't and I couldn't, and it's too hard and I have to travel there and I will not get paid enough and they do not have benefits and it does not work for me," and all the barriers that are created around it and just allow all that to melt away and to go deep in your heart. Ask yourself, "if you could do anything in this lifetime that you would desire to do, what would that be?" And ask yourself to give you that answer and listen to your heart and your body and listen and listen and listen until you hear it, for it is inside of you, that knowing of who you are and what it is that you are wanting to do and to create. And when you begin to hear it and when it surfaces for you, then create it and make it happen and remove from your mind any obstacles there, for they are all an illusion as well and are created in one's mind and can be easily eliminated. And you can move into a state of enjoyment and light and*

323

*love and abundance all at once through your consciousness of your thought. And so I have an exercise for you in particular, at this very moment, and that is to remove any words that are of no or can't or won't or don't or wouldn't or couldn't from your vocabulary for one week, and to remove any ideas of complaining [Raphael laughing]. Oh there is a lot of complaining, and when it is removed and you listen to what it is you are saying, you realize that you, through your thought and your mind, are creating that from which you are saying, and you are so beautiful and have so much to give and it is alright for you to allow yourself to be free and to allow the pain that you feel in your heart.*

[Tape stopped to be turned over: missing information]

*R: Whatever it is they see, and what they do is fight against the mirror, and do you know what the mirror does? It fights back. And so if you are to be able to remove that pain, you must look at yourself in that mirror and become friends with and love it and treat it well and do things for yourself that will create indulgence and life and love, and then that mirror reflects back onto that which you are giving to it and it does good things onto you, for you are in great need of love and in great need of experiencing warmth and being held and loving yourself and knowing and remembering you are beautiful, so beautiful, and that you can do whatever it is you want. Deep in your heart you will find those answers. For I ask all of you as you are together today to create a place in which you have fun in an idea in which you can only speak to each other in words that are positive, and that any words such as no, don't, can't or wouldn't or shouldn't, or any words such as this can be removed for several hours that you can communicate with each other and it will be a very fun game and it will create an awareness of what it is you are saying, what it is you are doing and what it is that you are creating. Let the pain go, by loving your pain. Do you understand?*

Group member: Yes

*R: You are such a beautiful being and I am so happy you came for this is not something that you were really wanting to do. And you were kind of dragged along and now that you are here, your heart is opening and that it is okay and I love you so much. It's okay, you just need lots and lots and lots and lots of hugs. And so, it is your job tonight to give her so many hugs that she cannot stand it anymore for she does not want you to hug her. Make her say, "stop hugging me."*

Group member: How can I keep from taking my husband for granted?

Group member: She's only been married a year, come on now. [Group laughing]

*R: All of those things that you are grateful for you must recite to yourself and to him. And it will simply move you into a state of gratefulness, and in gratefulness you cannot take for granted anything, for you are in the state of gratefulness. So speak aloud of those things you are grateful for everyday to him and to yourself, and you are not taken for granted—you are sometimes in awe for all your blessings, and so let that be known for there is no such thing as taken granted really for anything unless you are feeling as though you are unable to give in the same way, and the way in which you can give the most is to just acknowledge your gratefulness for what is. It is alright and you do more than you realize and you are very much loved. And it is also important to move into a state of appreciation for yourself and to love yourself and to know what it is that you do is so beautiful and that you also are contributing to all that is and when you find the greater appreciation for yourself you will automatically find that for him. So gratefulness is the word I give you today, so think about this.*
    *What is it?*

B: Raphael, is it possible for you to know whether my

brother has been reincarnated back into my life at this point in time?

R: *Yes* [with laughter], *do you know that your brother has been reincarnated back into your life at this time?*

B: I think he has.

R: *Yes, so why are you asking me?* [Laughter from the group] *Well, you must trust what you know. For if you cannot trust your own knowing then how can you heal the sick? For of course he is here with you. And so who is he?*

B: Richard, my brother's best friend from this lifetime, his son.

R: *Yes, so just love him up as you do. It is alright. It was a gift given to you to inspire you to remember what your work was and it was a beautiful gift, although it appeared painful and wrong and although you feel as though you owe something that you are in indebted in some way, you are not. You are not indebted to anything. You are only in debted to yourself and to give what is good to you to remember that the most important place to give first is to yourself, and to your family and to your husband, who is so much fun and often very relaxed, but sometimes feels as though there is time for things but not always as much time for what he would like and so you must care for yourself first and not feel as though you are indebted to take care of the world because of the sacrifice of another. For that sacrifice was not a sacrifice at all but an agreement that occurred in order to allow that being to go to where it was needed to go, and for you to do the same, for shift to change on many levels within the framework of family.*

*And it is alright and you must love yourself and love him, and forgive yourself and him, for whatever you are holding and resisting around that and let it be, and know that you must, as you do, understand to care for yourself and your family first and create any healing*

*that must be needed there. And then your healing and your mission-*
*ary work which I see it as so much for you is very much second*
*place. For often one feels as though they have a calling and they are*
*doing something more important and it is. And you do have a call-*
*ing and a very, very special gift and will create, and have already cre-*
*ated, enormous change in many beings and on this planet. But in order*
*to create the greatest change you must love yourself deeply and know*
*that the sacrifice was perfect and that it was not a sacrifice, it was like a*
*fire cracker going off and lit under your butt.* [Much laughter from
Raphael and my friends.] *And "I'm sorry" and it is perfect and he is*
*perfect and love him where he is. And love those beings, those little*
*beings that are in your home for they are very special.*

L: We always tell our kids that their grandparents are
watching them from heaven. Is that true? Can I tell them
that?

R: *You can tell them whatever you want for you create whatever you*
*want to. Of course this creates great comfort for these beings to feel as*
*though they are watched over by another. They are your children. Your*
*children are your grandparents and your grandparents are your chil-*
*dren and so of course someone is watching them. It is all one you*
*see. It is not as though there is this man with a white beard sitting*
*in the sky and angels with wings sitting next to him and the grand-*
*parents and all the people sitting next to the gate and they are pray-*
*ing over the children as that is so funny and we get great amusement*
*of this idea you have created but if it gives you comfort you may*
*think what you wish.*

*It is alright to cry if you feel like you need to cry and your heart*
*is feeling open for that is my job.  I love to make people cry.  It is*
*perfect and for it reminds you of who you are.*

*What is it?*

Group member: How can I help my sister make a transition to a better place in her life?

327

R: *Talk to me about this being.*

Group member: She doesn't love herself.

R: *What is it that you love about her?*

Group member: She's caring sometimes.

R: *I ask of you to be strong for this is trying on you. And I ask of you to see all the things in her that you love and I ask of you to tell her about those things you love about her. And I ask you to see her in the way you say she can be sometimes. See her that way now in your mind and tell her about all those things that she is when she is that person that you feel that you can love, and love her and encourage her and see her well and see her capable and see her strong and see her able and see her independent and see her moving forward and opening that door and stepping out and allow her to step out of that door because she is moving toward something rather than away from something for she has always moved away from something but never towards something. Help her to look forward as to where it is she is needing and wanting to go. Help her to remove her past and to allow it to dissipate for she is so in the past that she cannot be in the moment let alone to move forward to where she wants to be. Help her to write down and create on paper where it is she wants to go,*

*what would be the best place and do it not because you are wanting it to move away but because you are helping her to move forward and in that process see her well, see her in all the things in which you are wanting for her because you are wanting for her to be all it is that you do love and find all of those things about her that are special. Tell her them, and this maybe very hard for you, but there is some anger and some resentment but it is important at this time for you to be a bigger person here and to be strong and to help her find her way so that when she opens the door and moves forward she will be able to move ahead, walk ahead to a place in which she will be able to stay rather than feeling as though she has to turn around and come back in the door and this is her path and it is because she*

has always left before because she was moving away from something
that she was fearful of and it is time now for her to move forward
towards something in which she is loving to move forward to. So I
ask of you to compliment her, to give her love, to hold her and to find
all the things you love about her and to tell her those things and she
will become strong much faster than you can understand the human
body has great ability to change and shift when given the proper
nutrients. She needs love from you. Is this helpful?

Group member: Thank you.

R: You are welcome. Is there anything else that you girls need from
me?

R: [Signing with her hands and singing] I want you to play
these games together for me which will be much fun for you. You are
not allowed (see I cannot say "not, can't, don't, not") [laughter], you
are going to speak in a way that comes only from words of love and
positivness and remove any words that are different from that and
let's see how long you can last. And I will be listening and watching
and I give it a few minutes. It is alright to make a mistake and continue doing it all night long and it will be great fun for all of you.
Love each other and remember that when you come together, you
reignite that joyfulness and playfulness of youth and it brings forth
opening and remembering your origin which is quite wonderful.
And give lots of hugs to this one [referencing Amy]. I will be seeing this one again soon. [Referencing Beth] Much love and much
light to all of you for I love you dearly and remember that whatever
it is you are needing and wanting it's there for you that you are loved
and you are cared for and you are protected and that God and Love
and Light is with you and within you and that all that you need is
within you and you can pull that strength forward whenever it is
needed and be there for one another and bring light into this world
for that is your work and that is your job. So God Bless and good
night. Goodbye.

*July 13, 2001*

*The Second Channeling*

R: *Hello.*

B: *Hello.*

R: *Hello.*

B: *Hello.*

R: *There is much happening here around your heart, and there is a great opening, and it is pounding back and forth. You are beginning to reach a vibrational frequency in which you have opened your heart to the point in which you are able to take in more energies and more information than you have in the past.*

 *Your capabilities of absorbing more information and many different energies are very vast, and consume and are easily taken in. And your ability to receive all of this input is something which you are very good at, and yet often you feel as though you are not receiving enough information, input, and that there is more energy that you could be bringing into your sphere of influence. And it is important for you to know that there is no end to your tank shall we say. For many beings have a tank, and they can allow other energies and input to come in and it comes to a point where it is very full and when it is full, that being needs to step back and in many ways empty this tank and then fill it with other things and nurturing.*

 *You have a very unusual tank, in the sense that you have an opening at the bottom. And so it is that you can receive many energies, without attaching them to your tank, so that an opening can happen and there is a cycling of all this energy, moving out and this is something you have learned and adapted to over the years. And sometimes there is a feeling of being overwhelmed, but in general there is great ability and an overall capability of passing through this, and that is why there will be no limitations to the amount or number of beings or energies in which you can participate in the process of healing with.*

*Do you understand?*

B: Yes

*R: Hello. What is it?*

B: I felt very drawn to come back to see you again.

*R: Yes, for I am so very happy to see you and we have many things to do together. It is very important for you to recognize that you have great talent and an opportunity in this lifetime to be a trailblazer and to allow great shift in consciousness around the human body to take place. But because of your ability of integrating and allowing much information to come in it is also very important for you to integrate all aspects of your life. As we have been speaking of perhaps in our last meeting. And you can bring about a place in which you can have as much enthusiasm and energy for other areas in your personal life and family as you do in your work. And it is that you see all of these beings as a part of your extended family in which they are.*

*But there are particular beings that have come into your life in a controlled or contained way, and these beings need attention from you as well. And it is important for you to know or to remove the thought that because there is so much giving and energy putting out, that the tank is empty when it returns. And yet if you can begin to remember that the tank is a cycle and a circle, that it is passing through and reentering and that this is just simply more energy coming in, and that you can just absorb it without returning great energy to it. Do you understand?*

B: Yes. Why in our time, on this planet, is cancer becoming such a plague? What have we done?

*R: It is that you as a being or a person or as an organism or as a group of individuals, who from my perspective sees you as a whole of a great large bowl, should we say. And you are of a certain consciousness and it*

331

*is that there is a place in which you are residing in; it is a planet in which you are speaking at this time of Earth. And on this you reflect back to one another all of the things, because you are a mirror of each other. And your planet is very unhealthy, and in great need. There is a sense of shift in its harmonious way of particularly functioning. For it was that in the past it was said that if you were to observe Mother Nature, and go into a place to see the miraculous things which it does and how it operates that it is something so amazing that often cannot be comprehended by the human mind. And yet the physical body, the vehicle that your spirit is in, in this incarnation, is just as miraculous and spectacular and functions on so many incredible levels on its own and does so many things without guidance, for it is a miracle.*

*And it comes from one very tiny seed, such as the same in your forest, so both of the microcosms, the reflection of your human body and that of your universe, are the same. For they are, when looked at very closely, they are the very same thing. And when separated apart from the way in which individuals of this time are looking at them, they appear to be very different and yet they are simply a reflection of each other. And as the forest or the earth, or the place in which you think of as your home, that you are living on, creates such CHAOS, for there is such destruction and disregard and many of the elements which are necessary for all aspects of the earth to run in a way in which it needs to do, have been disconnected or destroyed or eliminated and it creates great chaos. In which it becomes out of control and cannot function in a way that it was meant to.*

*So the body is simply reflecting in its human self that which it is observing on your planet. There has always been disease [dis-ease] in the body, throughout your history, of different kinds and different names and so on, and it is often a way of balancing and taking out the weak and creating sense of strength for your planet. But at this particular time, it is simply a reflection of what is happening to your earth and it is a very, very sad sight and so the body is in great* chaos and it is unable to do it's job in the way in which it knows. And it becomes as if it is fighting itself and in that there is a fight against all things, a fight against your cancer, a fight against disease or a fight against drugs or a fight against something. For there is always a war being waged upon something, and as long as a war is being waged upon something, it can only create fighting back and it just becomes larger and larger until there is so much fighting that there is nothing left, and it is dissipated and so it is important here to recognize that one of the ways to begin to heal is to do this through as much love and respect not only for the human body, and the beings, but for the planet, and the consciousness and all of these beings that are experiencing this particular dis-ease that you are speaking of, are giving you and other beings a wonderful gift. For they have created an opportunity in which they have elected themselves to come here at this time to experience this particular disease in order to show its fastness and in order to show its reflection that there is something very wrong happening here at this time in your food and in your planet and in your mental state and in your consciousness and in your words and in your press and on your television and in all the information that is bombarded upon all of you at this time.

And although it appears to be very devastating and sad that these beings are experiencing such great pain and difficulty, they are a mirror and they are a beautiful gift. And they have been brought to you and to all other beings as an opportunity for one to awaken and open their eyes to see and to create change, and so it is perfection in what it is. And the perfection is there but often difficult to find perfection in such great suffering. But it is a process in which you as an organism as a being, as a consciousness, as a human, must reverse and move back into a place of great [more] simplicity and acknowledging those things that are of great importance. And part of the ways in which this can happen is eliminating the ideas of such great fear and moving into a state of love. And so when you do your work and you do it with great love and seeing the wellness in the beings in

333

*which you are placing one's hands on, you are creating a spread of consciousness that creates change that is far reaching, much further reaching that you could possibly understand. And that is why your work at this time is so very important, because not only is it creating change among the person in which you are touching, but it creates change in all of the people that they touch and all of the people that those people touch and it is exponential. And it grows very, very quickly and in the process, as long as you are healing with complete love, without any sense of fear, and you are seeing great wellness and love and joy and perfection and even perfection in great disease, then you can begin to create perfection and release war above the body, which will allow then a shift, to change the consciousness of that being.*

*And when that being returns to one's family or small nucleus of beings, that* [shift in consciousness] *radiates about them, and it spreads to others they see and creates a chain effect which creates a shift in the molecular structure of the physical body, which is a reflection as to that same structure which you find within your planet, and it begins to reflect back on to one another more love. And it is extremely important that you realize that your work is so very important, you see and can perceive perfection and love toward all of these beings, and as you touch them realize that when it is touch with light and love it is a rippling effect that is extremely profound and very significant and is making greater change in the consciousness of your planet than is possibly understood.*

*What is it?*

B: That was a lot!!

R: *Sometimes I forget that I am speaking in your language. I am bound by the vehicle that I come through. I do not need words in my universe. You appreciate words. What I say is not important, it is the vibrational energy which is of greater importance.*

B: Will we be able through treating in pure love and light to create a shift to eradicate the disease process as we know it?

R: Yes, for there is no need for disease. And as you very well know this disease comes into the body from some type of other dis-ease in their life or in their make up. So it is when love is the source of all things, the need for disease will be eliminated completely. For when one is in a state of love at all times, there are no problems shall we say? And so it is that there will be no need for this. So as you spread the word and the light and the love to all of these beings, you are creating a shift that can begin to be spread to the very young, and as the young begin to understand this concept, they will have much less need to create disease in their life for they will be healthier beings at all levels.

Yet there is such a great diverse group of beings coming at this time for your planet. For there are many light beings who will be able to spread this word of much love and be able to move very easily into the new consciousness, yet there is a polarity of other beings who find themselves in a great state of lack. That they are in such a great state of fear because of the circumstances in which they find themselves, in that they can perpetuate more disease should we say, for there is such great disease within their beings. So it is of great importance for those beings who are in a state of joy and love and abundance to take time to create as much shift as they can into the young lives of these beings who would find themselves otherwise.

B: Are my children going to be part of this process? It is as though their presence of touch creates a change in those they meet.

R: Those beings are very special and it is that beings that come to another, come in matched vibrational frequencies of that in which they are with. And so that your vibrational frequency is at the conscious level that is very significant at this particular time and so it is that you have attracted other beings of great consciousness as well. However, they will not need to do the practical day in and day out work that you do in order to create the same amount of shift and

335

*change. For their mindset is very different and they are able to do this with greater ease. For it is that your mindset has been, through programming, that one must work very hard in order to achieve great gain. And yet they are seeing and learning and understanding that they can create great change, through their thought and through simply being. And so they will very much more be in the state of the moment and of the now, as they see you very busy moving around. For you are very much like a butterfly and they are like a flower. And they sit and you come and visit and sit on them and then you fly away and they are very busy being, while you are busy fluttering away. They are busy being and enjoying and experiencing where it is that they are. By just being, they create great joy in others. For simply another observing the flower in itself, creates great joy. For they will have a very different mission than you, for they will come about it and approach it in a different way and you are the catalyst and the very important being in their life for you have created an understanding and opening which has allowed them to have great strength and so this is part of your agreement that you came together to do in this lifetime. And so if you are asking if they are very special and have great work to do, for of course this is so true for them.*

    *What is it?*

B: Is it possible for you to bring through my brother?

*R: Your brother is long gone, for he has reentered here on the physical plane and he is not accessible to you in that way at this time. You will see this being again and as you do your work, you are bringing with you, him; for he is in your hands. The essence of who he is is with you as you create shift and change in other beings. But he has chosen to reincarnate here on your planet at this time and he is not in a place in which he is willing to be contacted or create discussion with you at this time. And yet, there is much love for you. And yet this being has done what it is that he felt was needed to do at this time. It was part of a much greater plan and although it may have not appeared that way at this time, he is very happy to see that you have taken the ball and shall we say run with it when it was necessary to do so. But he has already very quickly seen that that was occurring and there was no need to stay in a spirit state for he was anxious to return to your planet and has done so.*

*I know that you would like for me to bring him here so that you could talk and I wish that I had the ability to do so today. However, he is just not here now. He is with you in your heart and in your spirit and in your hands, his essence is always with you and so who he is has chosen to relive again.*

B: Will he recognize me in this incarnation, that he has been a part, a member of our family, the Baughmans?

*R: His subconscious is very aware of this and at this particular moment his consciousness cannot absorb this, nor is that the best thing for him at this time. He needs to play and be joyful; this is what is important at this time. As this being ages, you will be able to relay this information and his essence will understand it as truth, and it is of no importance to him right now and is unnecessary. For you know in your heart, all that you can do is the work that you have started to do because of the transition that has occurred. And all that it is, that this being can do right now, is experience joyfulness and allow his own soul to move into greater light so that he can pass through this time as a more aged being and not have the need to recreate this scenario.*

337

B: How can I help a patient transition to their next level? How can I help them to accept the death of their physical body?

*R: It may be helpful for you to go to the place where babies are born and to see this transition and to remember that it is simply a transition back—that it can be very difficult entering as it can be very difficult leaving. and that they are returning to their origin that they have come from. And that it is truly a transition into a beautiful place,*

*which is exactly as they have chosen. And sometimes it is so hard to
see and remember and understand that it is their choice for they have
created their own reality. You can speak to them about the light that
you see around them. Speak of the beauty that is in them and the
gift that they are giving to others, to come close to them in this
process and to see all of the great light and the beautiness that is in
them, and that they are so much bigger than the physical body that
they find themselves in at this time. That they are filled with love and
light, and that it is just like one is in a home, and it is different to
move and pack things up and that when one goes to a new place it
is a small adjustment and they find great joy in this new place. It is
as though they are disregarding their clothes and are putting on a
new set. That the old clothes were worn and tired and old and it is
okay to take those old clothes off and to shed them and it is okay to
be exposed and go naked into the light and to absorb as much of it
as they can and to remember who it is that they are and when they
are in that nakedness they are so free. And that they cannot be free in
their decayed and old clothes and they have to feel as though they are
locked inside something and they will fly away.*

*And when they are in that sense of freedom and openness, the
joy that they will experience is so profound and they must remember
that they are moving into a place where all things are all knowing
and the peace is indescribable. And in that state, they may choose at
some time to put on a new pair of clothes, and that is alright too.
And sometimes they are leaving behind, as they move into that freedom, other beings who are still captured in their physical body and
they have more great sadness for leaving them, than they do for
going themselves. And we must remember that it is okay and that
these beings that they are leaving behind, need to experience this, for
whatever reason, and that they will be safe and cared for and protected. And that where it is that they are going, they will be able if they
chose to be, created or contacted that they can do this. So it is not
something that you can translate to them, it is hard in that moment*

*to remember that. But remind them that it is a shell, it is a piece of clothing, that they are in, but it is not them. They are much bigger than the physical body that they leave behind. And that the body will be easily disregarded and sent away as an old pair of clothes would be. But it does not mean that the being is not there. And they are so beautiful, that it is so perfect, that it is okay, and simply comfort them and remind them, because all beings know somewhere that this is true in their heart, and they remember and understand that it is simply a birth to a new world.*

*What is it?*

B: You had said before that you are to guide me on the "fast track," yet I can't imagine being faster than my current state of fastness. I am asking for guidance.

R: *It is not a speed that I am speaking of, for you are already fluttering about. It is about creating more change in the time that you are allowed or allotted or are in. And that can happen when you create an ability to be exactly where it is that you are and to be fully present where you are. For that will allow your work to be encompassing and to create change much faster than presently. Because you have so much and you are often thinking about who is coming, or what will be or how many more there is to do, or to see. That sometimes there is a loss of the now and it is that if you create an opportunity to simply be exactly where you are at a given time, completely present in that particular moment, without thought anywhere else. You will be able to teach those you are in contact with to be completely in the moment in which they are, because even if you ask them if there is pain and there is moving very quickly to the light, if you ask them if where it is that they are at this particular moment, in this very second where they are, if it is okay. Their answer is always "yes" it is okay in this second. That they can be there in that moment and as you become more present in each and every moment you begin to share with these other beings the ability to be in this moment as well. And*

339

*when they begin to eliminate their projection of what will happen and what fear it is that they are having, and simply be right in that particular second that they are experiencing, that without projecting fear into the future, they often are able to create healing within their physical body at a much faster rate and may not have a need to necessarily exit the physical body in which they find themselves.*

*Because it is often a projection of what could or would be in the future that creates such fear in their physical body, basically create that as an opportunity to exit [their physical body]. So when I speak of faster it is in many ways slowing you, for you will just "be"more, but things will move at a faster pace because there will be less gaps in which your mind will be moving about very quickly. For to be all present, will allow time to consolidate. As if there is a glass of water and all the ice cubes that are in the glass, are all of the thoughts that you are having in between the water, or in between what is happening in the present moment. And as you begin to remove or eliminate the ice cubes [the distracting thoughts] you have the same amount of time should we say, but the glass will have more water and the water represents the people which you are presently seeing and so it will create more purity and less distraction in the communication that will be taking place.*

B: So, I am teaching by example. When a patient can't release the fear of death, how can I get them to learn that every day is a gift to them and that all that we are guaranteed is this exact moment? No one knows when the exact moment of their exit from this planet will be.

*R: So maybe giving them a book of paper, acknowledge and write down what they enjoy each day, and seeing what is perfect and beautiful that they are experiencing. So that these days can begin to expand and become greater and more filled with love and in the process they will begin focusing on of course that which they are enjoying rather than that which they are afraid of. And asking them*

340
~

*to do this and bring it back to you when you visit again is very powerful, for it is something that will create great shift in their opportunity to be present.*

B: The Gratitude Journal

*R: It is very important, for a being can live many years, hundreds of years, and yet they can pass through into the light and be reborn very quickly into the same state in which they left with very little growth. And another being can live ten years and have learned lifetimes and lifetimes and lifetimes in their ability to observe, and be in the moment and appreciate. To see the beauty and to see the love and to see how beautiful it is here and to see all the wonderful things that you have to enjoy and to experience and to hear and to see and to smell, and they can move lifetimes, leaps and bounds faster than a being who has been here for many years. For it is not the amount of time, but what occurs during that time, so they will return, and it is their opportunity in those very last moments, they can move forward past lifetimes and not have a need to recreate something again and again. So you can help them to move at a faster pace into enlightenment, into a state where their consciousness is filled with more love simply by being able to sense and appreciate what "is"rather than to fear "that which can be."*

B: Lee can't seem to understand the concept of healing.

*R: For there is a box which she likes to live in and it is very safe in this box because everything is black and white. And when you open this box and she looks out she says, "no thank you." She comes back in very much like a turtle does. What you can do is open the box, she may come out and stay out for a bit. She needs to be free. She is in such a great state of resistance that she has forgotten how to play, how to fly, and how to let go. It is important for her to take off her clothes and run into the ocean and do things that are unexpected. She needs to play.*

341

B: Is Stacy the right person for this practice?

R: *She is meant to be here. It is that she will be able to move into this state at a rate faster than you could realize. Simply see her in that place and see her doing the work in which you are wanting and see her in all the things you are wishing for, it is very important. For she needs great praise and this is something that you are very good at and it is important to praise her as much as possible in that process. It will allow her to open more and more and she will be able to integrate into her thought process what it is that she sees. And an opening for beginning to understand all the things which you are and so it will be alright with this being. And praising her is very important!*

B: Chris's ALS, what can I do? Communication is very difficult.

R: *She is trapped. She is here for you and you feel that you want to be there for her. But she is here for you now, for she is teaching you the ability of what you are speaking about, which is to be fully present in the now. For she can only be present in the now, for she is trapped in that moment. She cannot move forward or backward. She can only be where she is, so bring her things that she can smell and taste and experience or see or hear. And being with her and experiencing it fully without allowing the mind to go anywhere but right there, is an opportunity to create joy for her and an understanding of being present yourself.*

*I am very anxious to continue our work. And I want you to remember as you begin to open your heart, more and more, and your hands work with great love, as they do, you will have much greater impact. And when you are there doing that work, and you can only be focused in that moment, bring that, and integrate that into all aspects of your work and you will create greater change at a greater pace. I send you much love and light. I ask of you to take some time to do some "in the moment" things with these little beings, for they have so much to teach you.*

342

# September 13, 2003

## The Third Channeling

R: *Hello.*

Group: Hello.

R: *I am so glad you are all here, for we have much to do and much to talk of, for it is of no coincidence that I find all of you here today to speak with me for I am in great gratitude that you were able to hear your essence and to know your way and to find your way here with ease and to be able to hear my calling that it was important for you to be here at this particular moment in time. For as all of you very well know, your planet is moving into an enormous time of transformation and as this transformation occurs, the awakening of the heart is beginning to occur and the sacred heart is finding its way into a place in which the knowing of the design and the knowing of all that is, is beginning to awaken within your essence and your soul is knocking on your door. And as this soul begins to find its way many of you will experience enormous changes in your lives, and sometimes they will come in a form of separation from those in which you love and other times they will come and many others will choose to leave physical form at this time to move to another place to do their work there. And at the same time many of you will begin to be in a place in which enormous ease, coincidence and flow of life will come your way and you will move much more with grace and ease into what is to come ahead.*

*It is very important that there is no fear of the future, for there is nothing to fear, for it is quite beautiful and it is very much a place in which you will feel at home with yourselves and your being and your heart and your essence. However it is beings such as yourselves who are very connected to source are being asked at this time not only to bring forth the message of light and love to as many beings as possible, but are also being called forth to follow your hearts and* to allow the light within you to shine. For it is at this particular time as you can hold the light and begin to see it in all beings, even those who perhaps are in a lot less light, however not necessarily darkness, to find any speck of light that is within them and to imagine it growing and expanding and beginning to see the love in all beings. For you are in a particular time in history in which your souls are awakening and being asked and called upon to bring forth the divine light of love into the planet at this time. And so you are being asked now by the angels and by the source of all light to bring forth your best side of yourself. To shine forth the love in your heart, to disengage from fear and from judgment. And to move into a place in which you can bring forth that of peace, understanding, and light to your planet.

There is a grid, should we say, being formed by many of the light workers at this time. And it is something which I will share with you. However, it is very important that as I share this to disengage from any religious beliefs or ideas or any resistance that may come forward in this process in which I will speak of. Also it is very important at this time to know that the energy of the woman is coming very strongly to your planet. For it has been the energy of the male, for a very long, long time and it has brought a lot of anguish and fear and war. And as you see the escalation of war occurring at this time on your planet at the same time you will begin to see the escalation of love, prayer and moving toward that of divine love. And so we are asking that all beings in this state of mind bring forth all that they know to bring about this change into the light. It is of great importance that women such as yourselves who are very strong and connected to the sacred heart and to the spirit, bring forth at this time portals in which you can invite only that of divine light, so as the polarization begins to occur it can become much stronger in the places of love. Do you understand?

Group: Yes

R: Uh ha! And so at this time, it is important to know that you are part of a group of women that is coming together around the world and around the planet at this time in creating what is called a grid of light and this grid begins to take place in many different places in your planet and in many different cultures and through many different religions and in many different ways of going about it. For there is no correct or incorrect way to do this and however for you at this time and the beings that you are, you will begin to connect with the energy of Mary. Do you understand?

Group: Yes

R: Mary is becoming extremely strong at this time on your planet for those such as yourselves, and is bringing the message of the sacred heart and of the cross. You may have recently been connected to that of something of your past and to that of the cross and to that of the light of Mary and of Jesus and although this has been sometimes disconnected for you, you are now beginning to awaken into a place in which it will help to create the portal of light for you.

You are each being asked at this time to have a statue of Mary and to put this statue in the sacred heart of your house. The sacred heart is the place in your house in which you have and do receive the most joy. In this place, please place her and then go outside such as the woman in which I am channeling through and many of her friends and many of her loved ones have also done and you will create a triangle around your house of three crosses. This will protect you and keep you very safe and connect you also with the energy of Mary and will begin to help you to stay in the light and also to be very strong to bring forth more love to more beings. People around your planet will be doing this in many different ways in which they connect with divine spirit. It will not be for them of crosses or Mary, for that is not necessary. It is only for those at this time who can connect with that to return them to their source. Do you understand?

Group: Yes

*R: In Africa and many many other nations around your planet, in Israel and the Middle East and in Europe and South America and in Asia, people and women especially will be doing this ritual in different ways and it will connect all of you together. You as women will be connected in this grid—it will be a portal of love and light and it will bring the female energy back into the planet and create some balance that is needed at this time. For your Mother Earth is very much very sad and crying very deeply out to all of you and asking you at this time to return to your sacred heart. Hello!*

Group: Hello!

*R: What is it that I may answer for you at this time?*

Susan: Raphael, did you hear me this morning when I tried to reach you?

*R: Yes, you are very connected to Mary and it is the rosary that is helpful for you at this time. [Singing/Chanting] What is it?*

B: Hello, Raphael.

*R: Hello.*

B: How are you?

*R: I am good*

B: I wanted to first make sure I have your permission . . . to use . . .

*R: YES! YES! You may use my information and you may spread it, however I am asking something of you. You are to bring as many beings to me as possible in all avenues. And so one avenue you are choosing is writing and you will bring forth that information and then you will read it. Also, this one is a vehicle for me to speak and you need to bring people to her to your place of work to bring forth light and love, that is very important and that is being asked of you if you are wanting to use my information.*

B: You will have that.

R: *What else is it?*

Group member: Recently in a meeting, it was brought to my attention that I was to do other work of a spiritual nature. Can you help me with direction or give me information that will help me?

R: *Put your hand on your heart and I am going to ask your question and you are going to answer from your heart and not your head. What is your calling?*

Group member: It's children, I guess.

R: *Yes, now say "children," don't say "I guess."*

Group member: Children

R: *And how can you help the children?*

Group member: I have a school for children.

R: *Yes, and what is your work there?*

Group member: I direct and teach them.

R: *And how can you help the children to remember who they are?*

Group member: Through art, music and writing.

R: *Yes! Yes! Creativity. You are very creative. It is important to eliminate anything in the curriculum in which the children do work or creativity in a mechanical way. And it is important to put large pieces of paper on the wall and then to have lots of paint lined up open with different colors. And to bring them together in a circle and then to ask them to take a paint brush and put it into what ever color they love and to take the paint over to the paper and begin to move the brush in a way that feels good to them and then to bring another piece and another. And what you will see come forth onto the paper from the children is the source of their soul and this will allow them*

347

*to reconnect with who they are. Often, many of these children come from a very mechanistic viewpoint in their home in which that of who they are in their life is being shut down, and by bringing them into a place in which they can open their creativity in this way, you are giving them the gift of their own light and something that they can then carry with them throughout their whole life as a place to reconnect to their soul. This work is very powerful and important and should not in any way be thought of or disregarded as silly or not of great importance, because what you do is very significant, for they are receivers that need love and nurturing to grow. Do you understand?*

Group member: Yes

*R: So begin to do this and then many doorways will open in your own creativity as well, and it will become clearer and clearer as to what your work is.*

Group member: Do children see an aura around me? I go places and children look at me and people say this all the time.

*R: Yes, Yes. When you are in the grocery store, they look toward you and that is because they sense that you are connected to them and you can awaken their soul and that is why it is so important that you do this work and you do not negate your gifts. This is them giving you permission to do your work and know that that is your calling.*

Group member: Thank you.

*R: You're welcome. What is it?*

Group member: One of my biggest challenging teachers in my life is my youngest child, and he unbalances me. And I work so hard to keep balance in my life, and our relationship puts me in a place where I say things, I do things, that are just not me. And I just don't know where my control is or what the problem is and I'm struggling with it.

*R: Yes, there is enormous struggle here. First, very important for you to know is is that he does not unbalance you. You allow unbalance to occur. Secondly, it is important to know that he is in a struggle within his own right and his own soul, searching for who he is. There are four quadrants that you are aware of: the mental, the spiritual, the emotional, and the physical, he is very much in his physical/mental and you are often in your emotional and mental as well. And the two mental aspects very much collide and so in order for this change to occur, you must move into spiritual and emotional. When you awake, meditate or pray each day to see only that within him that you love, only that within him that is perfect, and only that within him that shines the greatest light. Find that in him, show it and reflect it back to him. As you become more balanced in your own right, his ability to push you off balance will become less and less and he will become balanced as well. He appears to be your greatest challenge and at the same time, he is closer to you than anyone in many ways. It is very important for you at this time to do prayer and meditation for at least twenty minutes each morning and to look at him very closely and to see in him something each and every day that you love and to recognize that to share it or to give it or to say it to him. He is wanting to escape and he does this in ways that you disapprove of. And he escapes into music and sometimes into, I guess your word is drugs, and you cannot judge him for this. And know that he is very sad in his heart, and what you can do is to unconditionally love him and accept that he is choosing this and almost give permission for it. For it is in the permission of it that its charge will disengage and it will go away, but in fighting it, resisting it, focusing on it; it gets larger. He is very brave and very bright and very strong and has a lot of self-will and self-determination that within you rises, and you see it within him. And then you have fusion. And so you must disengage out of your mind and into your heart and to love*

349

*and adore him and see what in him that you will love, and it will begin to disengage.*

Group member: Will he be okay if he goes to work in Georgia?

*R: I do not know of this Georgia. It's not as though he goes because his heart is calling. Talk to him. Try to help him to hear his heart, to open his heart and to release his anger.*

Group member: Where do you think the anger is coming from?

*R: Ridicule by others, difficulty at school, ridicule from other children. Not meeting expectations of the world around him, feeling very angry.*

Group member: Will he find his way? Will he be okay? I want to fix him, but I know I can't.

*R: Oh, yes he'll be alright. No, you can only love him, love him, love him, and love him and see him in the light, and see him fixed. There's no fixing, but see him well, see him at peace, see him prosperous, see him open, see him connected, see him in this light only. That is your job.*
*What else is it?*

Group member: Raphael, you mentioned to me about the three crosses. Could you tell us more about them?

*R: You are each to go to get three crosses they are to be about this size or you can make them out of the earth. You are to take them and place them in a triangle around the sacred heart of your house to hammer them into the ground. Put them so they are out of the way and will not disturbed. You will put the point in first, then the second, then the third. You will do this with two other women who are aligned in light and love. You can do it today if you want, you will go and place them, put Mary or that of sacred female energy for you in the sacred heart of your house. Place the three crosses and send love. Then add the three of you and go to the next home and do the same and you will pass the prayer and then we will call you when there are eight more people and when you have twelve we will acti-vate it for you. Twelve have already occurred and you are in the sec-ond phase of the next twelve. It will occur soon and you do not have to do it in the rain. It will happen soon for you and you will feel enormous shifts in your homes and in your energies and for you [Beth] perhaps to be first and for the energy to mostly be focused to this being. What is it?*

Group member: LIGHT? For each and every one of us how can we each be more open to the *light*?

*R: It becomes so quietly with meditation and prayer and asking to find your way and to do the will of spirit each and every day, for it is only within that, and in each moment ask to return to your center and be guided by the light in all of your actions. And when you are moving forward doing something that is incongruent with that, ask yourself, "is this what spirit would want for me today at this time at this moment?" And you will easily move into a place of knowing where you should be going and what you should be doing and how you should be acting and what you should be speaking and thinking and feeling. However, do not judge yourself too harshly and remem-ber that this is a process and does not occur in one minute or one day or one hour or so on. What is it?*

351

Group member: We have a sister who right now is very much in a state of lack, and despite all of our reaching out to her, she is very resistant to awakening and open-ing her eyes.

*R: She cannot hear this from you, there is enormous jealousy here. And you are too overpowering to talk to her too much…you give too much advice. And so the best thing for you to say to her is "you are so capable and able and I know that you will find your way." And only you can tell her this. Do not give her any advice for it just makes her resistance much bigger.*

*As far as your writing goes, when you write, if you wish to bring forth my information, which I am in grate gratitude for, to spread to many, it is important to also acknowledge the vehicle which I am using and to acknowledge this. What else can I bring to you at this time?*

Group member: As a light being, I absorb negative from some people sometimes. How do you use it to protect you or is it better when you feel this that it is a warning from spirit. Do you understand why I ask?

*R: Yes, It is important to create the ideal so that you are not necessarily engaging in that energy, for there is no need to engage in it at anytime, anymore—it is over. It is important to know that you do not need to have a warning from spirit, for you will not be engaging in any energy that is not of the greatest light so you will not need warnings, because you will only be in the places that are in enormous safety, protection, and love. If your intuition says to you, you are uneasy with where you are, immediately listen and move away. However, you are very protected and need to engage in projecting a shield of light around you that only allows that of divine energy to find its way. As you do this, you will only be attracted to places and to situations that are only of this light and you will not necessarily need the protection, for when protected fully do not even engage in such darkness.*

Group member: I often run into very unlovable lost little souls.

*R: Unlovable? Who could be unlovable?*

Group member: They don't love themselves, but they are takers, drug dealers, and they are people who lie, cheat, and steal and have lost their way. I know I have to give

352

my son love, but what else can I do for him?

*R: You can only see the speck of light left in there and focus on it and it can begin to grow. There is light and in your strength of finding that light, you can change them and the outcome of their behavior and their ability to find their way into their soul. And try to see it in the big perspective as you work with them and know that they are part of you and you of them, that they are you and that they are a soul connected to all just as you are. And that in the process throughout their life, they have forgotten their way and they have only been able to see the darkness and in seeing it and focusing on it, they have engaged in it and it has become larger for them. But that in darkness there is enormous pain, and to recognize and to acknowledge their pain, and to try to find the speck of light that is left, the glimmer of hope that is their being, and to share whatever light you see in them with them and to know that shift even the slightest bit can occur and if the slightest bit of shift can occur in their cellular being, in their vibrational frequency, then they will not be attracted to those difficult and terrible things in which they engage. And so you are asked to be strong here and not to find your way in despair and disbelief from all that you see and to remain in faith for you've lost a lot of your faith in looking at them and seeing the difficulties that there are and wondering in that, how this could be so. But, you must find the light in there for they are your sisters and brothers just as much as the ones sitting next to you.*

Group member: I've had a message about writing a book or doing a movie about children who committed suicide?

*R: As long as the message does not only focus on despair but brings forth ultimately the message of change and help, then the message can be kept, for not to indulge in all the darkness or impact to create more of it. It's important to educate and bring beings aware and at the same time to bring forth a sense of wellness; a sense of peace; a*

353

*sense of joy. And so if the energy can be directed in a way in which the message can be one of help then it will find its way.*

B: Thank you Raphael for our last physical meeting on earth. When I was stuck in the driveway, that was very sweet. Thank you, because I missed two accidents on the way home, and I didn't realize until I was getting home and I totally felt your presence, and it was a gift that you had given to my parents too, because I would have been in an accident when I drove home. And I also feel your presence very heavily in my book. Just the drive to get it completed for the message is so important.

*R: It is of great importance and it is very time sensitive, much more time sensitive than it has ever been before, for a sense of urgency is upon us all. It is time to what many of you have known for a long time and have been having spurts of energy and changes and moving, stopping and going. And now you are going to move into a state that is more continual and it is less spurts, it will be very large and big spurts and in that there is a sense of urgency in putting aside your stuff should we say, and stepping up to the plate and doing what you know rather than talking of it.*

Group member: May I ask one more thing?

*R: Yes*

Group member: When you asked me to put my hand on my heart, the sensations that I get in my heart area, is it of a spiritual nature when I feel pressure.

*R: It is not physical. See, there is the physical heart and there is the sacred heart. They are very different. The pressure you are feeling is the sacred heart wanting to open.*

Group member: Okay. It keeps me up at night, it wakes me all the time. I pray to the Virgin Mary. I always say a

Hail Mary before I go to sleep and then I wake in the night with the pressure.

*R: Yes, you're heart is opening literally. You're literally opening your sacred heart so that when it is time for you to move forward to transfer yourself, it can be of greater ease.*

Group member: Is this something that is going to happen soon or is it slow?

*R: It is unknown. It is collective consciousness moving forward and it is dependent upon the evolution.*

Group member: Do you receive messages with the opening?

*R: Yes*

Group member: Okay, so when I am woken up with messages or dreams and this pressure, is it something I need to act on, it's confusing me.

*R: Mmmm, try to release the confusion and feel and ask for the truth prior to sleeping and ask only that truth that is of great clarity to awaken you and if it is to awaken you that you are to write it down and to have a paper near your bed.*

Group member: I have these dreams about this real estate that was stolen from me and it just keeps coming back. Is there any significance to that or is it just . . . I find it nagging.

*R: I do think it's important for all of you know that all the money required, or anything that you require or are holding onto, will be of no importance  And it's quite funny to watch from above all the gathering, but know that all that is gathered is left behind and also know that you are safe only within and not from anything that is without and that your protection can only come from within you and*

355

when the time comes the consciousness of who you are is what will bring you most peace and the ability to shine, and that from which you have will simply dissipate and is only to be used for the love for others and to support your family and your friends.

It's time for me to go and I send you all a lot of love and light and ask of you to activate to this great gift if you feel connected to this and it feels right to you.

Thank you.

*October 3, 2003*

*The Fourth Channeling*
*Mary's Message*

I had made a date with Kelly to return to her home, to have the personal channeling that was placed on hold to accommodate the needs of my sister and my friends from out of town. I arrived on that rainy afternoon in October expecting my familiar friendly guardian angel Raphael to come through with her words of wisdom.

When I arrived at Kelly's door, she greeted me with her sheepish smile and her characteristic giggle and said, "Beth, I have a question? Would you be open to having a channeling with Virgin Mary Mother of Christ?" Well I was taken aback, not expecting to hear this question from Kelly's mouth. As I was processing the information in front of me, the front door of her home flew open from the wind. I took this as a sign from the universe that this was to be. As I had driven to Kelly's that day, I had felt the same Mary energy that I had felt in Manhattan in September when I happened upon the free church of the Virgin Mary. I saw crosses in all of the street signs coming up Old York Road, and thought that it was all in my head.

I went to my car and retrieved the rosary beads and miraculous medal that Marie Duess had given me to keep until her return from Medugorje. When I came in the living room, Kelly was sitting on the couch and placed a blue scarf over her head. She had a bowl of water beside her and her rosary beads in her hands. This channeling was completely different than the ones with Raphael. I was initially worried about what to ask Mary. What do you ask the spirit of the woman who gave birth

357

to Jesus? It became quite obvious that for once in my life I was to listen, and I was to listen very carefully and continue to listen daily to her messages as they are to guide me on my path and empower my essence to be who it is that I am.

Kelly had placed the blue scarf over her head, and wrapped it around her shoulders as well. She made the sign of the cross with the water three times over her forehead, mouth and heart. She held the rosary beads very tightly in her hands. The voice I heard and the sentence structure were completely different from those of Raphael or Kelly. This was completely new to both of us.

[Very soft and gentle chanting]

*Ah Maria*
*Ah Ne*
*Ah Maria*
*Oh say na Maria*

[Very long Pause]

*It is the Mother.*
*Tell her that she is loved.*
*Tell her that she is a mother and that her motherhood is of impor-*
*tance now.*
*Tell her that it must be first, that the mothers are awakening to their*
*motherhood.*
*And that the Mother Earth is asking the mothers to nurture their*
*children, as the Mother Earth needs to be nurtured.*

*The Mother Earth is crying and the children are crying, and there are*
*many children crying.*
*And you nurture other mothers, women who are mothers who use*
*their breasts to bring nourishment and to nourish.*
*The breast is given to the woman by God to nourish the child and to*

bring forth the love of the mother, the essence of the mother's love through the mother and into the child.

The breasts have been polluted, just as the earth has become polluted. And the earth's ability to nurture has been raped of its resources. And as a reflection the mother in human form, in the material world, is being raped of the nutrients needed for the breasts to be clear, to bring forth what needs to be nurtured.

And your job is to nurture the mothers.
But before you can nurture them, you must nurture your own children, and give them the love and the essence of who you are, as you do to the other mothers.
And know that it must be done in a state of grace and humbleness, and that as you serve and bless and nurture the mothers, you are nurturing their families and their children, and in turn the Mother Earth.

The Mother Earth is crying and is so sad, and many of your children are dying.
There is great famine and despair.

And as you nurture your own children, and love them and hold them, it is felt within all the children around the world.

The mothers are awakening to God.
And that of God is awakening within many of you now.
And it is just beginning to whisper, and those of you who have good hearing are hearing the whispering.
And the whispering will become louder and louder and there will be a very loud screaming, and when the screaming comes it is an awakening that was needed for those who could not hear the whispering.
And know that when others hear the screaming that you hold their hands and that you let them know that they are safe

You will see me and hear me everywhere you go.

359

*You will see that of the cross and Jesus because he is coming,*
*not in a form of physical form, that has been perhaps thought of*
*throughout your history, but in a form in all of you.*
*He is awakening within you and in all those who you see and touch*
*and heal.*
*YOU ARE TO PRAY PRIOR TO YOUR WORK AS YOU DO*
*TO BE HUMBLE*
*GET ON YOUR KNEES*
*[Long pause]*

*There are two boys and their hearts need to reopen.*
*[Long pause]*

*As the breasts bring forth the milk unto the child, it connects that*
*child to the earth.*
*And when it is not connected to the earth, it cannot heal the earth.*
*The earth is asking you to stop.*
*Her core is crying,*
*and when her core cries, her children cry, and when her children cry*
*the tears fall.*
*The droplets of milk that come from the breasts cannot pour, and*
*they become diseased as a reflection of that of the Mother.*
*And how you can heal your mothers, is by finding your ability to*
*love yourself, your own mother, unconditionally,*
*And to feel love . . .*
*Then to love these boys regardless of achievement, outcome or per-*
*formance.*
*And know that NONE OF THIS MATTERS.*
*But that the HEART is of the greatest importance.*
*So place your hands on their hearts and love them with all your*
*heart, and as a mother ask what it is that you must do to awaken*
*them so that they may hear the grace of God to avoid the screaming.*
*[Long pause]*

*Humbly recognize that you embrace and empower a very large group*
*of women.*

360

*Remind them of who they are,*
*and in doing so are very much angering the woman's ability to rise.*
*The woman, feminine, will be that who will be able to heal your*
*earth now, who will be able to love your Mother Earth and the chil-*
*dren and create peace.*
*Peace cannot come any longer through the male energy.*
*And so healing them* [the mothers], *helps to heal the earth and*
*the motherness that connects you and I and all things, for all things*
*come from the Mother.*

*You are to be quiet,*
*And to know that a Blessing on each and every being that you see,*
*who you are to heal, can be done very gently, humbly and even with-*
*out notice.*
*As simply as the laying of your hand upon the top of their head.*
*Whenever you see a child, put your hand on top of their head and*
*smile at them and they will understand.*

*It is time now to be the Mother that you have pushed aside and to*
*put it in your forefront as you cannot expand or heal that of the*
*MOTHER until your Mother is healed.*

*YOU ARE BLESSED.*

*SPEND TIME ON YOUR KNEES.*

[Long pause]
[Rosary bead movement]

*There will be a time of darkness.*

*Return to all elements that are part of the earth:*
*In your food*
*In your home*
*In your work*
*In your clothing*
*In all things*

*RETURN TO THE ELEMENTS OF THE EARTH.*

*Anyone in which you feel you have wronged, or feel as though you must apologize to, should be done now.*

*Drink much water, blessed water, holy water and sing.*

*Ask yourself in every action if this is the will of God, and remind yourself to connect to the elements of the earth, so that they are pure.*
*Pure water*
*Pure food*
*Pure dirt*
*Pure fire*
*There will be fires.*
*The only way to put out these fires will be through prayer.*

*And in the fires is the screaming, but know it is a good screaming, like when a baby is born, it takes its first breath and screams and all knows it is alive . . .*
*It is much like this.*

[Rosary bead movement]

After this amazing experience I was speechless. Kelly came out of her channeling state and was overcome with emotion. We both had just been given such an unbelievable gift and now we were just in a state of grace. After she composed herself she asked if I would still want to talk to Raphael. I was not given the opportunity to ask Mary any questions. I was actually speechless. (Difficult for anyone who knows me to think that I could ever be speechless!)

*October 3, 2003*

## The Fifth Channeling

Kelly proceeded to channel Raphael with the same sense of familiarity that I remembered.

R: *Hello.*

B: Hello.

R: *Hello.*

B: Hello.

R: *I am so happy to see you, for in our last visit there were many, and our opportunity to speak was limited for there was a being that was with you and a part of who it is that you are that was having a difficult time, and it was very important for her to receive some sense of reassurance as to who it is that she is and where it is she is going. For I am missing her and am happy that you are able to visit with her, for she was able to bring you messages that you were needing to hear and I see that you are listening.*
*What is it?*

B: I am so happy to be here with you today and I thank you because my sister Susan needed that to happen. She is back in Australia and I'm sure you know, and I will be talking to her tonight, so I will be seeing how she is doing.

363

~

R: *This is good. Say hello for she is very happy to be home and it is that her work will begin to expand and to move into a new arena and that you are beginning to, or energies are being able to, connect on a deeper level. It will become more and more (what is your word here?), but you will become much closer as the years go forward.*

B: I can feel that already. I have several different questions that I need to clarify. I guess the first one I will start with is, in my work with my patients and the healing process, I need to know if there is a healing modality or specific energy type work that I should be learning or focusing on to promote healing on a cellular level other than the radiation/chemotherapy, other than the standard modalities that we use at this time?

*R: Those beings that find themselves in your office come knowing that there is an opportunity for you to see them and an opportunity for them to be heard and you are very able to hear and to listen to their story and this is very much a part of the healing process, is you listening to their story. And the work that is being done in the sense in which you call traditional is of great importance of course. However the ability to connect in opening the heart that has been shut down is of great importance as well, and the modalities that can occur around this is something in which you can begin to facilitate through listening, speaking, and referring, for it is not in your work to open their hearts in this way but to guide them through your credibility of who you are to others who do work such as this.*

*There are many beings that will come into your life that will be able to facilitate in this process and many of them are already around you so begin to use those resources of those in which you already know to bring forth heart-opening as process and know that the beings who choose to come into your office for their healing are already awakened or want to ask to be awakened more, or are being guided by another to ask to be awakened, and through their disease they have the opportunity to create heart-opening shifts and connection into that which is of importance in this particular time in history.*

*It is fortunate and unfortunate at the same time that you will be seeing more and more beings and that it will continue to expand. Of course, the unfortunate-ness is of the great disease that is expanding and continuing to grow unfortunately. Fortunately, it is that through this disease as of many others, there is an opportunity of a connecting and awakening of one's soul essence and remembering of who they are. And, a choice is often made to either leave the plane and remain in a sense of disease or to be able to heal, and of those beings on a greater scale percentage wise are finding themselves or coming to you because of the aspect that part of them is resonating with the vibrational frequency that is being held around the work that you do. And, in order for them to be attracted to this, they must already be holding a certain vibrational energy that is what often brings them to a place to where they are open, ready, and willing to bring about change. The question was, is there another modality, perhaps the answer has already been stated.*

B: I am feeling very drawn to—I don't want to say take control—but to become a guide or a leader in the hospital in which I work.

R: *Yes, you will be doing this. This is of great importance and then will be connected to other hospitals and you will eventually facilitate this for an association of hospitals in states. You will begin here with Mary. St. Mary's hospital and you will be doing/directing/organizing or orchestrating for others to come. Is this what you are speaking of?*

B: Yes

R: *And then it will catch like fire like a flame very quickly to other facilities and at one point there will be an overseeing of all of this and orchestrating of it, but not on an administrative level, but on an advisory connection.*

B: When we spoke last time about the energy grid that is awakening and starting throughout the world, we talked about the next twelve people in this grid. Are there other people whom I know that should be included in this grid? And if so . . .

R: *Yes there is a woman who was with your friend Chris.*

B: Barbara

R: *Yes, this being.*

B: I know that I have to contact Barbara because I think she is one of the physicians that is suppose to work with me in our holistic and wellness programs and actually bring the vision to fruition. I think she is one of the people.

R: *You need to speak with her and speak to her of the grid. The activation of the grid will take place when the moon is full. It is not time yet.*

B: I have another friend who is an anesthesiologist who is doing energy healing and I feel very strongly that she is supposed to be part of this process.

R: *Yes, it is in her work that there is a quiet of the mind and ability for the body to stop. What is your question of her?*

B: Right now she is trying (at her own personal detriment) to save a hospital's anesthesia program. I have seen the physical strain it has taken on her in the past year, and part of what I see is my role in—I don't want to say intervening, but helping her to see, to throw herself the life preserver, to allow herself to leave that environment that is not nurturing to her soul and her spirit and to make a geographical shift to a place such as St. Mary where she can be supported and bolstered and brought together in an environment that will help not just her but other people to experience the gifts that she has. And I know she is just really torn because she doesn't want to leave a hospital broken.

R: [Singing and chanting]

*There is a hole like a black hole in the hospital, however there is at*

*the same time blackness, a disconnection of the mind and ability to*
*sleep, and ability disconnect through her work of the patient, to not*
*be present, and it is important for her for she has been eliminated*
*through creating or seeing the right amount of something she has*
*been eliminating the engagement or connection to patients to the*
*process, and she must flip that into experiencing and connecting to*
*the patient in an awakened state.*

B: I understand.

R: *And that will take place for her and she will be forced to do this.*
*There is a lot of concern here about money and there not being*
*enough and that she will not be able to remain or to have that of*
*what she is needing or wanting and so there is great resistance here.*
*But no matter how much she resists or holds on, it is a sinking ship*
*and she may need to wait until it sinks before she gets on her*
*lifeboat. And it appears that is what she is doing…and when she*
*sinks, then you can throw her the life boat and then she'll be ready*
*but she is not ready yet.*

B: Although I can see wonderful changes in my life (at
least I can see them as wonderful) I am still concerned
with my partner Stacy and her ability to handle the new
stresses of her life since I am not doing general surgery
and I want to know if there is anything I can do to help
her without doing the work for her. Or maybe this is just
part of her path she is supposed to be on, but I want to
make sure I am not hurting someone else in order to
help myself.

R: *She is ruby red and capable and able and seriously wanting to*
*move forward, and taking it very seriously and will do fine. It is like*
*when a parent chooses to go somewhere that they know they need to*
*go. And the child is standing at the door having a tantrum crying.*
*The parent feels bad that they have left the child, but once they pull*
*out of the driveway the child stops crying. There may be a tantrum or*

*two, but once she is engaged in it, she will be embedded in what she is doing.*

B: What can I do to help my husband find his passion? He has been spending so much time helping me and enabling me to follow the path that I needed to follow, and I want to be able to help him truly find what resonates with in his heart.

*R: He is very easily satisfied with simpler things than you, and needs lots less and sometimes feels ambushed and overwhelmed and his mission is to just to be and to enjoy the simplicity. And there is no great need for him "to do." For it is not in his doing that his essence shines, it is in his being. And, for you, much of your essence shines in your doing and a lot of your doing and "doingness," brings him to wanting to be more in his "beingness." The more that he is "being," the more you are wanting to do; it is that you are together to create great balance. And he is much more satisfied than one realizes.*

B: My oldest child, I don't know what we did in a previous life, but we continue to lock horns everyday. I am trying to help him to understand time management and I want, obviously, to help him to succeed in the things that he wants to succeed in.

*R: You must let him fall and fail and then he has enormous strength and on his own accord and on his own time he will find his way and do very well. But you must show him that it is okay to fall down and so do not advise him, let him fail and it will be very difficult for you, but know that in the larger picture, he will gain much more knowledge than succeeding in the letter [I think that she meant grade] or succeeding in the way that one must perform.*

B: I am speaking to a very large group of women in a few weeks and I'm sure you gave me the topic because I didn't event think about it when it popped out of my head about *Creating Balance in a Chaotic World* at *A Day for All Women*, and I have multiple different areas in which I have already pulled quotes and pieces and books that have fallen off the shelves at me and things like that. Any divine words that you would like to impart upon me to help these 600 to 1000 women to understand the importance of balance and how they can achieve it.

[Singing prior to the answer.]

*R: It is important for them to know and to recognize their power. And that their power and their source of love and compassion finds its way in all walks of life. For as you well know, it comes as they mother and nurture and care for another, but it also comes in their work and in their efforts. And that the vibrational frequency of the feminine is finding its way to the core of all that is. And as it begins to do this it is bringing forth something that will allow enormous changes to take place on your earth and on your planet. And ask them to love themselves and their sisters and their mothers and their daughters and to know that they can be all that in which they are wanting to be simply by allowing themselves to be that in which they are; through loving and nurturing who they are and loving themselves first. That in being a better mother or caretaker or success-ful being in business, they can only do this through that of a nurtur-ing of themselves; and the caretaking upon who they are. And tell them that they are very loved and accepted and appreciated and that they are that which allows the world to move forward.* [I took this to mean that without the womb, the feminine, there can be no propagation of the species.] *And I have something in which I will give you to show to them and it is that in which you speak of which is BALANCE.* [Kelly gave me a rock that day that had BALANCE carved into it that she had gotten years ago in California.] *And it is that . . . they are to be com-mended for all of their hard work and love and compassion. And that they see the world as a whole and that they see the world as some-thing in which all things are encompassed. Where the male sees it very much in a sense of linear, step-by-step, moment-by-moment, logic-by-logic. They see the whole picture and as they do that in many of the professions, that of science becomes quantum physics, and that in medicine becomes holistic medicine, and that in food becomes whole food, and that in mothering becomes seeing the whole child, and that in all things around the globe through science, through computers, through philosophy and through all aspects of life, even the artwork. It comes from within now and rather than being something that is drawn or seen outward.*

*That you are moving as a race from appearing to witness all things from the outside in; from the inside out. And that is the dif-ference between the male and the female energy in that the male views the world from what it sees on the outside and then looks inward, compared to the female energy that views what is inward and sees how it relates to the world outside. The male gives the seed from the outside in and the woman brings and bares the child from the inside out. And that is what it is that women are bringing now to the world; the aspect, the philosophy and the understanding of working from the inside out, seeing the picture as a whole. And when we see the WHOLE PICTURE not one fragment of it, we of course we have and create "BALANCE."*

370

~

B : Thank you.

*R: You are welcome. Is there anything more you need at this time?*

B: That was my list. Thank you for the confirmation. And I will absolutely give Kelly credit in my book and plan to bring you and her to my hospital to do a group channel-ing with a group of women. To be able to reach out to a larger group of women.

*R: Yes. It is the female now that is of great importance. It is the birthing of the Christ energy that is why you will see and hear*

*Mary. She is birthing the Christ energy again, but this time not in a physical form. And it is for now that I say good day, good bye.*
[Singing]

~

My belief is that the Christ-energy resides within all of us, the love is within all of us and the female energy will be that which is able to remind our world that the answers that we are looking for are within our hearts.

~